PRACTICAL CLASSICS

50 REASONS TO
REREAD 50 BOOKS
YOU HAVEN'T TOUCHED
SINCE HIGH SCHOOL

Kevin Smokler

Prometheus Books

59 John Glenn Drive
Amherst, New York 14228–2119

Published 2013 by Prometheus Books

Cover image of desk © Ryan McVay/Media Bakery
Cover image of chair © Lawrence Manning/Media Bakery
Cover border of books © Lauren Burke/Media Bakery
Cover design by Jacqueline Nasso Cooke

Inquiries should be addressed to
Prometheus Books
59 John Glenn Drive
Amherst, New York 14228–2119
VOICE: 716–691–0133 • FAX: 716–691–0137
WWW.PROMETHEUSBOOKS.COM

17 16 15 14 13 • 5 4 3 2 1

Library of Congress Cataloging-in-Publication Data

Smokler, Kevin.
    Practical classics : 50 reasons to reread 50 books you haven't touched since high school / by Kevin Smokler.
        p. cm.
    Includes bibliographical references.
    ISBN 978-1-61614-656-6 (pbk. : alk. paper)
    ISBN 978-1-61614-657-3 (ebook)
    1. Best books. 2. Books and reading—United States. 3. Books and reading—Psychological aspects. 4. Literature and psychology. 5. Smokler, Kevin—Books and reading. I. Title.

Z1035.9.S63 2013
011'.73–dc23

5153 8329 3/13

2012036293

Printed in the United States of America on acid-free paper

For readers, books, and the joy they bring.

CONTENTS

PART 4. LOVE AND PAIN

PART 5. WORKING

PART 6. FAMILY

PART 7. IDEAS AND LEARNING

PART 8. VIOLENCE AND LOSS

PART 9. WE THE HERO

PART 10. THE FUTURE

ACKNOWLEDGMENTS

Deep breath—

Thank you to my wonderful agent, Amy Rennert, who placed a very long and uncertain bet on *Practical Classics* and its nattering author.

Thank you to Mark Hall, Meghan Quinn, Jill Maxick, Steven L. Mitchell, Melissa Shofner, Julia DeGraf, and the entire staff at Prometheus Books for being really good at all the parts of publishing at which I'm really terrible.

To my panel of experts: Rebecca Joines Schinsky, Jenn Northington, Stephanie Anderson, Josh Christie, Bethanne Patrick, Michele Filgate, Kit Steinkellner, Jenny Blake, C. C. Chapman, and Baratunde Thurston. They are all smart people. More important: they are all good friends.

An alliance of writers who have been doing this much longer than I have advised me and answered my questions. Without Holly Payne, Peter Orner, Katie Crouch, Dani Shapiro, A. J. Jacobs, Susan Orlean, Justine Musk, Wendy McClure, Jeremy Chamberlin, and Rodes Fishburne, *Practical Classics* and I would have been up six creeks without a boat.

A nice chunk of this book was written while I was an artist resident at the Ragdale Foundation. The staff and fellows I met there were something else. Big hugs and bigger gratitude.

To everyone I conversate with on Twitter® (@weegee), thank you for your attention and time.

To the kids at Philz Coffee Castro who kept me fed, alert, and let me squat.

My friends in San Francisco, New York, and Austin have heard more than enough about my year writing this book. I hope I've repaid their support by producing something fun to read.

My parents and brothers for believing and making me proud to be a Smokler.

And to my wife, Cariwyl Hebert, who believed, listened, read, and said yes. Our story is my greatest.

—Exhale.

INTRODUCTION

I must have been a nightmare in high school English class. English was my favorite subject, and I'd loved reading since before I could crawl. My friends and I talked about books with the same mania with which we hoarded quarters for the arcade and wolfed down mozzarella sticks at Denny's®. I even had English teachers I liked and keep in touch with today. But with the self-righteousness only an adolescent boy can invent, I saw these teachers as criminals who had stolen books I would have enjoyed beside a swimming pool or in a beanbag chair and turned them into something to be dissected, tested, essayed on, and graded. I didn't care what they did to calculus or chemistry or Spanish. Just leave my damn books alone and don't spoil them with . . . with . . . education!

The jerks.

Teaching me was their job. I saw it as a betrayal akin to spending a day at the amusement park then getting socked with a final exam on roller coaster physics. I was an imbecile. But I believed I stood for some literary justice only I was equipped to protect. Books are an essential part of my fun, and you dare make them obligatory? What's next, turncoats? An in-class essay on *The Legend of Zelda*™? So I spent the better part of my high school English career beating this drum filled with nonsense and generally making everyone else's experience a drag. I complained loudly that Homer was wasting valuable time by including Telemachus's story in parallel with Odysseus's; that of course Gregor Samsa was a cockroach, not just "an insect," so move along, please; and that Joe Christmas was a self-destructive moron, so why was Faulkner wasting my afternoon with five hundred pages of Joe Christmas acting moronically?

The moron was me. I was being a martyr for a cause no one else supported and I invented because being righter-than-thou felt good. But if that's true, why, until very recently, did I still feel the same pang of resentment and obligation upon revisiting books from high school as an adult? It certainly wasn't the books' fault, but somehow I was blaming them for sucking the fun out of reading. In my memory, I've conflated not only *The Scarlet Letter* and *O Pioneers!* with that killjoying but also bad complexion, awkward prom dates, and final-exam cramming. And if high school were the best years of your life, you probably weren't spending much of them reading anyway. We're perfectly aware that time has passed and that we've all changed and that we can all read whatever we want for whatever reason we want. But we still see a book from those days long ago and think "I remember that from high school." Then we sigh.

I'm a little wiser now. I know the canonical books of high school are called "classics" for a reason, and it's not because some scold on Sunday morning TV or a secret cabal of English teachers declared them so. But that doesn't shake the idea that "the classics" and readers get off on the wrong foot, an unbalanced relationship defined by their colossal standing and our adolescent feeling of not quite grasping them but being graded on how well we do. Coming back to them later, we find the classics imprisoned in amber. Either they're lost monuments from tenth grade or old sages we've kept on the shelf, thanks to our own literary obsessions. Either we can be the kind of reader that read *Invisible Man* in high school and never looked at it again, or we can be the kind of nut who reads it once a quarter and gets angry when someone doesn't appreciate it exactly as much as we do.

Those of us who love the simple act of reading, I suspect, are somewhere in between. *Practical Classics* is my attempt to find a place for this kind of reader, someone who loves to have worlds opened up by books but finds the act of reading as joyous as fainting into a chocolate cake. This same reader also has very real demands on their time—jobs, families, mortgages, and health. It's a whole lot of sound and fury signifying nothing to declare one should revisit the classics but include no guidance on how or when. Let us then redefine our relationship to classics with clear eyes, open minds, and the wisdom of our lives now. I have to believe that classics earn their stripes by containing something not just enlightening but sensual, not just provoking but practical. Can't the classics be "good for you" by also being helpful? What a shame it would be to reduce them to a letter grade and a dusty old obligation from long ago.

Practical Classics is premised on the idea that we should reread these great books not just because they are great works of art. By definition, if a great book has run the gauntlet of time, shouldn't it also point us toward how to lead a great life?

It's with that foolish optimism that I revisited the great books I was assigned in high school as well as those most typically assigned in high schools across America. I reread them from the point of view of a married thirty-eight-year-old man—a dedicated reader, sure, but also an omnivore of the twenty-first century, with all the competing demands of movies and television, of music, video games, and social media. And while I love all those things too, perhaps growing older and living in this over-clocked age has given me new appreciation for art created to last.

Practical Classics contains ten sections, each with essays on five different books. Sections are thematic awnings covering a stage of life, including youth, love, identity formation, work, and loss. I've organized the book this way to spotlight the "practical" component of what we're doing here. Great books in part derive their greatness by speaking to us at the formative moments of our lives. We probably haven't had enough of those moments as teenagers to see them this way.

Choosing the fifty books was a whole lot harder than deciding which awning to put them under, as any such project will invariably leave out dozens, if not hundreds, of deserving candidates. That's fine. *Practical Classics* is meant as a reintroduction, the beginning of a renewed relationship with great literature, not a comprehensive sweep through it. When we've parted company, it'll be obvious, should you wish to continue, what to read next. And if you know all the books I've chosen backward and forward, then you're already secure in your relationship with the classics and I've got nothing for you.

In choosing the fifty books, I combined syllabi from my own high school English teachers, the College Board's list of books most cited on advanced-placement English exams, and lists of canonical books cited in my two favorite texts on the subject, Clifton Fadiman's *The Lifetime Reading Plan* (1999 edition, the year he died) and Harold Bloom's *How to Read and Why* (2002). Data on the most assigned books in American high schools is not kept in any standardized way. As much as I would have liked to, I couldn't take what American high schools are currently assigning and revisit them, because there wasn't any easy way to know which books were being used. I also tried my best to include not only books a high school student of my generation would have read (class of 1991) but also books from a generation or two before and a few I imagine more recent graduates might have read. Much has changed since I was in high school English. It'd be thoughtless to hand you a reading list as though time had stopped.

I've taken four additional liberties with this list of books, the first three out of good faith, the last because I couldn't help it.

1. I have deliberately focused on books that have not only been deemed classics but that are generally regarded as vigorous but brisk reading experiences. While I realize not every great book goes down like chocolate milk, for our purposes, I begin with those that do and leave it to you to graduate to the stuff that goes down like single malt scotch if you choose. My assumption: you are a busy person making room in an already full life for great books. Since there are many of them, it's only fair for me to ask you to begin with sprints instead of marathons.

   The books in *Practical Classics* will mostly be in the two-hundred- to four-hundred-page range. I don't see length as a measure of quality, but I can't in good faith recommend thousand-page tomes to readers trying to take time out of a busy life for my suggestions. It feels pushy, like asking for a nine-hour first date.

2. For that reason, I've also stuck to books strong on narrative and story, so plan to see more novels and plays, fewer treatises. I don't argue for a moment that Gibbon's *The Decline and Fall of the Roman Empire* or Newton's *Principia* are not great and important works. But statistically, they stand a good chance of simply not being your cup of tea. As human beings, we are all preconditioned to appreciate story, so that's where I'll stay.

3. I've included a single essay on the complete works of Shakespeare and overlooked texts from the ancients and Middle Ages entirely. All are as essential to the well-read person as oxygen. But whereas I feel one can have near-weekly contact with Shakespeare (through local productions, Hollywood adaptations, and Tweets® from @tinyshakespeare), the same cannot be said for Homer or Sophocles or Terence or Chaucer. Their influence is undeniable. But that influence is both so far in the past and so endemic to who we are now as to be imperceptible. Another book will have to speak for them.

4. Sprinkled throughout *Practical Classics* are essays on kinds of books that were not assigned to me in high school but that I hope are assigned now. We are far too attached to the moldy idea that only certain kinds of literature are worthy of being studied by teenagers. And that's just plain stupid. If we're trying to reincorporate the classics into our adult lives, let's include classics wrongly labeled as "genre" or "pop literature"—mysteries, science fiction, and graphic novels. Erecting arbitrary fences does nothing but make the whole reading endeavor a lot less fun.

Along this line, I've made an effort to include great works by authors who are not male, Caucasian, European, or American.

All these authors are legends on their own and don't need my endorsement. But I don't intend to hand you a book of recommended readings by authors who all look just like me. And I'd be selling you short as readers to think that's what you wanted.

I've made sure each essay is not an argument for a book's quality (that is assumed) but rather is an argument for how its greatness can be useful to the life you are living now. Former *Paris Review* poetry editor Meghan O'Rourke wrote in her memoir, *The Long Goodbye*, that part of her understanding of her mother's death was obsessive rereadings of *Hamlet*. For someone in Ms. O'Rourke's line of work, this makes perfect sense. A truck driver might seek to understand his or her mother's death via a long road trip. Were my mother to pass away, I'd probably cope with repeated viewings of *The Simpsons* and an open jar of peanut butter. The point: making an argument for the practicality of great literature does not undermine its greatness; it supports it.

Since classics are almost always viewed in retrospect, I've considered who the authors were as people and how history has regarded them and their work as fair game. I make note of how the books have been adapted and reconstituted throughout time and whether you should watch the movie instead.

That isn't a crime. It *would* be a crime to miss out on great books entirely because they cast too intimidating a shadow or remind us of who we used be. I used to be a self-righteous brat. I am beyond grateful to know a little bit better now. Let us enjoy these books now, not just because they are great, not just because they are useful, but because we are now in a position to enjoy them much, much more.

They haven't changed. We have. We are ready for them.

PART 1
YOUTH AND GROWING UP

1
THE MIDLIFE CRISIS
OF *HUCKLEBERRY FINN*

Mark Twain was forty-one years old when he began work on *Adventures of Huckleberry Finn*. He had a wife, three children, and was about a dozen books into his career. He'd been famous for over a decade and largely wrote *Huck* during summers at his sister-in-law's farm, where an octagonal writing studio had been built especially for him. He led a comfortable and contented life but struggled for eight long years to give Huck Finn, a supporting player in one of his earlier books, *The Adventures of Tom Sawyer*, a starring role. Nearly fifty years old when he finished *Huck*, Mr. Twain had spent the first decade of his middle age on the novel now credited with inventing our archetypes of American boyhood.

Adventures of Huckleberry Finn was published in the winter of 1885 but takes place, like *Tom Sawyer*, a good half century before that, in the pre–Civil War, pre-industrial Missouri where the author grew up. The year before *Huck* arrived, Twain had completed his first memoir, *Life on the Mississippi*, about his service as a riverboat captain when he was a young man in his twenties. A spell of nostalgia had likely seeped into that eight-sided room. And since we typically join Huck's adventures as kids or in high school English class, we probably remember those adventures now under that same spell—as Mr. Twain's love letter to childhood and an America from long ago.

That way of looking at *Huck Finn*—as boyhood tale and song of a more innocent nation—is very true, but like many of Twain's own fables and folktales, it is true as much in spirit as in fact. Rereading

Huck Finn reminded me that it's a book as much about hard lessons as it is about carefree summers, a quiet affirmation of maturity as well as a celebration of youth. Raft adventures on dangerous rivers and the loyalty of friends are nostalgic crack. But holding fast just under *Huck*'s brisk pacing are truths applicable long after we've traded fishing poles and corncob pipes for mortgages and job interviews. And if we ask classics to keep offering gifts even while we change and they don't, then this contested "Great American Novel" is inarguably one of our most generous. Mark Twain did indeed write *Huck Finn* looking back, but he wanted us to read it looking forward.

Even if you haven't read *Huck Finn* in a long time, you can empty your pockets of its images right now—Huck and Jim on a raft pointed southward on the Mississippi; darkly comic standoffs with con men and criminals; an opening pronouncement that the reader "don't know me, but that ain't no matter"; and a conclusion at which point Huck must choose between "civilis'ation" and "lighting out for the territory." Clifton Fadiman wrote that "*Huckleberry Finn* is our *Odyssey*," America's epic poem to itself, which seems about right.[1] The novel is structured as a journey—as timeless as Homer, *Don Quixote*, or *The Wizard of Oz*—and Huck's torment over the stability of home and clean clothes versus a wilder, unblemished America beyond the next river bend describes exactly the torment of the American soul since the country's founding. Is America a country of CEOs in great cities or of cowboys on Great Plains? Of grown-ups with responsibilities and delayed desires or children with dreams and wide-open spaces where we chase them?

The latter sounds a lot more fun, but read five pages from *Tom Sawyer* and realize that fun is a lot of what Mark Twain left out in the sequel. The world of Tom Sawyer is whitewashed fences, schoolboy crushes, and hunts for buried treasure. The world of *Huck Finn* (also the fictional St. Petersburg, Missouri, probably just a few years later) is abusive fathers, human bondage, and murderous family feuds. If this is our nation's past, Twain seems to be saying, it seems a violent, dangerous place. We might miss it, but do we want it back? Isn't it better that both we and it have grown up?

This metaphoric tug between the innocence of youth and the self-knowledge of adulthood has made *Huck Finn* a subject of argument since its first birthday. The book was gloriously reviewed in Europe and trashed in America, where critics found its prose vulgar and its aspirations overblown, and they thought Huck was an irresponsibly drawn hero for children. Louisa May Alcott, who had written soft-core pornography before *Little Women*, scolded, "If Mr. Clemens cannot think of something better to tell our pure-minded lads and lasses, he had best stop writing for them."[2]

But that was only the beginning of the book's troubles. For over a century, *Huck Finn* has remained one of the most banned books in America, censured by school boards, libraries, and entire towns. Early on, the complaint was that Huck was a bad role model for kids. Following the book's canonization as a Great American Novel in the 1950s and during the civil rights movement a decade later, *Huck Finn* became Exhibit A in the discussion of whether Mark Twain had grappled with slavery as a defining issue in our nation's history or had chickened out by dressing up race in the boyhood rags of loyalty and friendship. With Toni Morrison being pro-Huck and Jane Smiley against—as just one example—the case of *Huck Finn* continues to divide American literature to this day.

Whether *Adventures of Huckleberry Finn* is a progressive or racist book is only one, tired way to read it. I prefer to imagine that Twain saw his novel not as an attempt to undo the terrible, tangled mess of racism but as an acknowledgment of how deeply racism is a part of us and the challenge that presented for a nation coming into its own. If a teenage boy is so tormented over even a basic understanding of bigotry and prejudice—two decades before Appomattox and the Fourteenth Amendment—how difficult it must be to confront these old fears and intolerances as adults. Whatever the result, Twain says, we must try.

There's something equally readable about *Huck Finn* among both high school students and adults, thanks to crucial choices Twain made in relying on his best approximation of an assortment of

American vernaculars—Southern working class, African American, Creole—for the characters instead of using more Eurocentric, "literary" prose, which was the fashion at the time. It has been overstated that, with *Huck Finn*, Mark Twain was the first writer to speak to Americans in a voice they heard each day, even if James Fenimore Cooper had addressed many of Huck's central themes a good half century before in his novel *The Last of the Mohicans*. But Cooper's writing is tangled, opaque, like freeing oneself from a wet raincoat. *Huck Finn* is divided into short chapters so focused on plot that, in several instances, what happens stands alone and adds nothing to the greater story. Combine that with prose that feels like conversation instead of a sermon, and you can glimpse why *Huck Finn* did for American literature what Bob Dylan would do for American popular music: elevate it to art by making it more essentially itself. We read Twain much more today than we do Cooper, with both young and middle-aged enthusiasm, in large part because he is more fun.

It's fair to say that, without *Adventures of Huckleberry Finn*, the entire genre of "road movie" or "road novel," an odyssey through America doubling as a journey of maturity and understanding captured by the seminal work of Jack Kerouac or films like Barry Levinson's *Rain Man*, might not exist. The mythic America shot through the music of Woody Guthrie and Bruce Springsteen owes a great deal to Twain. It's also difficult to imagine the Southern tradition of folk humor handed off first to Flannery O'Connor and, much later, to Roy Blount Jr. and comedian Jeff Foxworthy, without Mark Twain. That *Huck Finn* itself seems resistant to adaptation (none of its two dozen film versions are memorable, though the 1985 musical *Big River* does an adequate job) corroborates that its true legacy is as much in its disciples as its descendants.

As teenagers we will probably get assigned *Adventures of Huckleberry Finn* in school and return to the same old battlefields of youthful innocence and the wake-up call of racism. As adults, we should reread it to see both how far we've come and how the challenges of our young life may haunt us still. *Huck Finn* is a boy's story that endorses adulthood, effectively saying, Aren't we better for having grown up, gotten older, and learned a thing or two? I recommend it often to chronically worried parents of teenagers. Huck Finn, based on real-life boys from Mark Twain's childhood, lived in scarier, more treacherous times than our families ever will. If Mark Twain was any example, they turned out just fine.

2
CANDIDE SAYS RELAX. THEN GET TO WORK.

Two centuries after its birth, *Candide* by Voltaire remains one of the most widely read books ever written in the French language. It still shows up on plenty of US high school reading lists probably because (a) it's a quick read, (b) it's funny, and (c) Voltaire was an inspiration to and favorite author of Washington, Jefferson, and Franklin, making it an easy pairing with the American History class down the hall.

Candide also has an astonishing sweep of sex, violence, and human misery within its short 140 pages. This little novella shows up almost as much on banned books lists as syllabi and bears the distinction of slipping the statement "Let's eat a Jesuit for dinner!" into English.[1] If that isn't the name of a Christian punk band by now, a lead guitarist somewhere is asleep at the switch.

I first learned of *Candide* while sitting through an unfortunate summer stock production of it in the Berkshire Mountains of Massachusetts, the kind of night at the theater where you voluntarily give yourself an ice cream headache afterward to forget it. Leonard Bernstein had adopted the novella for Broadway in 1956, with a libretto by Lillian Hellman and lyrics by many of the great writers of the time, including Dorothy Parker and Richard Wilbur. Though initially a box office dud, subsequent revivals made *Candide* a mainstay of the American theater and a particular favorite of high schools and university drama clubs. The accepted reason for this is that the songs of *Candide* land squarely within the range of a young voice. I like to think it's also because the story of *Candide* has a lot to teach us about being young, even if we can't quite understand those lessons until we're a bit older.

Candide is the eponymous tale of a young man raised in privilege and taught by Dr. Pangloss, a world-famous philosopher whose chief lesson is that right now we are living in the best of all possible worlds as "things cannot be other than they are, for since everything was made for a purpose, it follows that everything was made for the best purpose."[2] By chapter 2 (and the chapters are short), Candide is living in the worst of all possible worlds—exiled, broken, sold into slavery, and a world away from his home and his love, the lady Cunégonde. The remainder of the novella is the *Odyssey* on a gallon of caffeine— short chapters; characters who appear, vanish, then reappear like a Dickensian benefactor; plus a narrative with enough twists to dizzy a Hula-Hoop®. Before I lost count, I'm quite sure Candide and the several friends he makes along the way are beaten, sold into slavery, and condemned to die no less than fifteen times each.

Voltaire meant this book as both cold satire (Candide's travails are ridiculous but are told without an ounce of sympathy) and a philosophical hit job. Voltaire modeled the clownish Pangloss on the philosopher Gottfried Leibniz, who a generation before had coined the term "best of all possible worlds." A few years before *Candide* was published, an earthquake struck Lisbon, Portugal, killing thousands. Adherents of Leibniz's ideas argued that even the death and destruction of Lisbon was as it should be and that the world remained perfect as God had designed it. The siege Voltaire laid on this thinking with *Candide* seemed to be saying, "It always seems like the best of all possible worlds, if you're not the one the world just kicked in the head."

The triumphs of *Candide* are often viewed as a trio—the author's quick, pitiless wit at full gallop; the victory of the thoughtful Enlightenment philosophy over its smug, clueless older brother; and being the forerunner of the coming-of-age novel. A coming-of-age novel is also called a *bildungsroman*, a name impossible to pronounce and therefore of no use at cocktail parties.

It is this third unpronounceable victory that we will concern ourselves with here, as it reveals both the trunk and elephant of Voltaire's accomplishment. *Candide* certainly has a great deal to teach us about being young and stupid, about not questioning what we've been taught, and about believing we bear no responsibility for our destiny. We might not get that message in the dead middle of youth, just as a young fish doesn't yet understand water, but for a young person struggling much and learning some, the message is an archetype because it is identified with and not just remembered.

For adults, however, *Candide* tosses two more lessons our way: (1) The world is larger than we perceive it, and (2) hard work is its own reward. If I had known either of these as an adolescent, (1) I probably would have had a date to the prom from another school, and (2) I probably wouldn't have made myself miserable by writing every term paper the night before it was due.

Lesson number 1: Voltaire casts Pangloss as a well-intentioned but misguided idiot, a figure of broad, pathetic comedy. He's not evil, not the villain but rather the stupid best friend, Sancho Panza with a mortarboard and high opinion of himself. And Voltaire is careful to mock not what Pangloss is saying (that "best of all possible worlds" thing) but under what circumstances he says it.

The inclusion of a real-world event (the Lisbon earthquake I mentioned earlier) makes all the difference: optimism isn't the issue. Optimism that is willfully blind to the situation of others is just cruelty—misguided, childish cruelty in professorial robes.

We use *childish* as an insult usually when someone is acting bratty and unreasonable. At the heart of that childish behavior is the belief that life exists only for me, and the worldview I've constructed in that moment has no room for anyone else's. Anyone else's worldview is just in the way of *mine*.

This is the Panglossian (look it up, it's in the dictionary) idea, an "unwarranted optimism," which Voltaire argues we should grow out of; as grown-ups we should know better.

Lesson number 2: *Candide* begins and ends in a garden; the first is an obvious Edenic paradise that Candide is expelled from, and the second is a simple farm where the protagonist and his friends will live out their days working the soil. Candide himself ends the novel with the line "We can discuss it later. First we must work the garden."[3]

Voltaire here seems to be both supporting and attacking the philosophical school of which he was valedictorian. We see his support for hard work, prudence, and reason in the ideals of the Enlightenment and in the lives of Thomas Jefferson and Benjamin Franklin, two of Voltaire's biggest fans. And yet Voltaire is also presenting the heady philosophical arguments and debates he presided over in glory for the better part of his life, the kind every late-night conference in a college dorm room has mimicked since.

Voltaire seems to be saying that it's not enough to be a Professor Pangloss, that satisfied high ideals and well-thought-out opinions are enough. Hard work requiring something more than hard thinking makes us humble, reminds us that we are part of something larger, reinforces that the world isn't waiting for us or our great ideas but is rather going on about its way. It's our job to till our part of it.

What a bizarre argument for modesty and hard work from one of the most famous men of his time. Voltaire was in his sixties when he wrote *Candide* and already a celebrity all over Europe. When he died two decades later, his lifetime output made Joyce Carol Oates look like a slacker—essays, plays, poetry, novels, and 102 volumes of letters. Yet outside philosophy and political science departments, we mostly know him through a few great quotes ("Man is free at the instant he wants to be") and for *Candide*, this slim novella that would resemble a shed among skyscrapers if lined up next to the remainder of his bibliography.

Clifton Fadiman thought this irony rather sad—an immense achievement represented by a quick, mean satire that a reader could swallow between breakfast and lunch. I prefer to see it as one of the great testaments to Voltaire's genius—the ability to pack this much gold into a pouch rather than a vault.

And maybe that's the best reason, besides hard work, besides humility, and besides a macro-rather-than-me perspective, to read *Candide* as a grown-up, particularly if we are the parent or mentor of teenagers. It shows us how much can be said with just a few correct words, a few vivid examples. And it reminds us that sometimes saying nothing works just as well.

3

A SEPARATE PEACE AND THE DREAM OF BEST FRIENDS FOREVER

A *Separate Peace* was my mother's favorite book in high school. She graduated in 1964, five years after its publication, from a midsized public high school in northern New Jersey. As far as I know, she didn't have any friends who went to elite private schools like the Devon School of New Hampshire, which is almost the entire world of *A Separate Peace*. The novel's characters were the class of 1943, a generation older than my mom. So it was less their biographies than their circumstances (coming of age during war) and decisions (loyalty to one's peers over more abstract concepts like "school" or "nation") that spoke to my mother as a teenager in the opening months of Vietnam and that has kept *A Separate Peace* an important book to her since. When I told her I had not read it in high school and thus hadn't made a place for it here, she insisted (nicely) that I fix this immediately.

I had only heard of *A Separate Peace* as an older brother to stories of young men at uniformed private schools—*The Chocolate War*, *The Paper Chase*, *Dead Poets Society*, *School Ties*, and *Rushmore*. I knew it to be somewhat autobiographical (author John Knowles had based Devon on Phillips Exeter Academy, from which he graduated in 1945) and that its characters lived in a contained, homogenous world—male, white, northeastern, and a half-generation older than the Baby Boomers. I understood their struggles to be of a certain midcentury American sort. Will I honor my school, country, and destiny by succeeding in this rarified educational environment? Should my loyalties lie with my friends, my future, or my country? These last questions are why my mom still remembers being five years old and seeing her mother sob as she watched the McCarthy hearings on television.

I would have related to perhaps 60 percent of *A Separate Peace* had I been assigned it in high school. I had already read of and formed solidarity with characters like Holden Caulfield and Sal Paradise, who both came to life around the same time in history. But I was also a high school student in the late 1980s, before the Internet, the casualness of the term *Silicon Valley*, and America becoming a nation of many colors. So what would an average sixteen-year-old of today (the terms *average* and *today* probably mean neither white nor northeastern nor private-school dwelling) do with this book now? What could I do with it as a grown man? Perhaps you can see yourself in the struggles of an eighteenth-century Scottish farmer or an empress of Ming China. You have a stronger imagination than I do.

John Knowles does not make it easy for the twenty-first-century adult reader, even if that reader is in a hurry and sees the novel's modest two hundred pages as a blessing. *A Separate Peace* does not shout its intentions or help you locate them via loud, blinking plot points. Its tone is measured, sad, and a bit concealing. The story is less about event than mood. Where we are—in setting, in history—and how the characters interact with their environment are as important as what happens to them. If this novel were played on a bugle, it would be "Taps" not "Reveille." It feels like it should be read in the rain or at dusk, never midday.

The narrator is Gene Forrester: introverted, studious, insecure. His generation of students attends to both the rituals of high school—sports, classes, friendships, and rivalries—while the threat/ obligation of military service in World War II looms just beyond the campus gates. Gene's best friend and roommate, Phineas (called "Finny"), is also his polar opposite—voluble, gregarious, an effortless success at everything he tries. The adult Gene tells the story in flashback while visiting the campus fifteen years later. A horrible accident invades his memories. While playing a game involving a leap from a tall tree, Gene might or might not have intentionally shaken the branch Phineas was standing on, resulting in an accident that crippled his friend for life and ultimately resulted in his death. The reason for Gene's action is unclear, other than perhaps a rivalry he perceives that his best friend does not.

Phineas believes World War II is a scheme cooked up by adults to make the young fight the battles of the old. Gene has not decided where his loyalties lie strongest, to friends, to school, to country, or to his future. *A Separate Peace* ends with a campus visit by military recruiters and Gene signing on with the Army Air Force. And though the novel's final pages bring us back, however obliquely, to the adult Gene Forrester, Knowles tells us almost nothing about him—what he does for a living, whether he is married or has children, where he lives, how long he served in the military, or even why he is back at his high school. It is fifteen years later—after World War II and Korea, in the time of *On the Road* and Elvis Presley. Who is Gene Forrester now? By telling us nothing, Knowles whispers that our narrator may be a very sad man who has never let go of losing his best friend when he was barely old enough to drive and has built no future for himself since then.

I don't think Knowles wants us to go to the mat over Gene's guilt or innocence. An adult narrator and a dead best friend can remind us that actions, even those that are silly and juvenile, have lifelong consequences. The oblique question of Gene's role in the accident indicts the character's allegiances. If Gene did injure Finny, what is he "winning" when Finny clearly does not see any competition between them? And wrapped around the novel's world is World War II, which asks the characters to see their lives in relation to something outside the only universe Knowles grants them.

Loyalty seems to be the connective tissue here. Misguided loyalty, Knowles seems to be saying, is a tragic but inevitable part of being young. When you are young, your world feels as small as Devon does to its students. The act of youthful loyalty is the act of defining yourself in opposition to something. Example: I am a nerd as much as because of who I am as who I am not (i.e., the guy who beat me up last week after study hall).

Anyone who remembers an endless argument in high school over the inherent superiority of your favorite band/sports team/ political point of view understands this. Loyalty is not only who or what you choose to believe in; it is fundamental to your own conception of yourself. Rejecting an "other" is a form of both self-defense and blind edification. We don't realize that tearing down an "other" is just as much about how powerfully uncertain and afraid we are about ourselves.

Knowles takes us to this scary place in a final three pages. His prose is significantly firmer and more declarative than the rest of the book, but his conclusions are as elusive as mist.

> No one else I have ever met could do this. All others at some point found something in themselves pitted violently against something in the world around them. With those of my year this point often came when they grasped the fact of the war.
>
>   . . .
>
>   All of them, all except Phineas, constructed at infinite cost to themselves, these Maginot Lines against this enemy they thought they saw across the frontier, this enemy who never attacked that way—if he ever attacked at all; if indeed he was the enemy.[1]

How many "enemies" do you have now versus when you were in high school? I bet the very thought of keeping even a skeleton crew of enemies feels exhausting and silly. You probably believe that one can be loyal to one's own friends, ideas, and interests and let others have theirs—that one of the liberations of maturity is that you can be "for" something without having to devote equal energy to being "against" its opposite. The young Gene and by extension the stunted world of *A Separate Peace* cannot allow for this and snuffs it out. Looking at the bare-bones sketches of the adult Gene, it's unlikely he has learned this.

How does World War II fit into this? I'm not quite sure. Knowles certainly thinks it's important, but it intrudes on the Gene/Finny story, then disappears like an annoying party guest. I never got the sense that Knowles made up his mind where it fit in. Best I can conclude, it's a stand-in for the immaturity of loyalty I mentioned earlier. Maybe Knowles is saying this isn't about vanquishing enemies but knowing and appreciating who your friends are. But I'm really not sure.

A Separate Peace makes just about every list of great coming-of-age novels. And yet it contains very few of the scenes we now associate with the genre—no tyrannical parents, laughable teachers, or madcap pranks. No one references an "honor code" or is saving up to buy a car. There also isn't a single female character in this novel, which also precludes dances with a neighboring girls' school and adolescent heartbreak.

I think this is on purpose. By trapping us at Devon, Knowles emphasizes the brutal tribalism his characters bring to this idea of loyalty. When we read this book, we are older than the boys at Devon. Hopefully we see ourselves standing outside the school gates as adult Gene does, but in a much larger, accepting world.

As adults we choose different loyalties, those of partner, parent, equal member of the household. A loyalty to a job might mean you love that job. Or it might mean you just need it. Loyalty to friends is a nice idea, our adult selves say, but it feels like a second or third priority as we grow older, a holdover from adolescence that is a bonus, not fundamental to adulthood.

In adulthood we hope to have a different kind of relationship with our own Finnys, one free from the shackles of our young, limited minds. We don't need their unquestioning devotion or their accomplishments to measure ourselves against. We need them to be themselves; let us be ourselves and remind each other that we are loved for who we are, not what we are yet to be.

I thought of my best friends when reading *A Separate Peace* and the rewards of those relationships now. I wanted to send them each a copy of Knowles's book with an inscription saying, "Look at our story! Isn't it great that Gene and Phineas got to be grown-up friends too?"

4
OWNERS OF OUR LONELY HEARTS

I remember first being told of *The Heart Is a Lonely Hunter* by a woman I worked with at a summer job. I was twenty-five; she was a few years older. We got to talking about favorite books, and she mentioned Carson McCullers's debut novel, which she had read about seventy-five times as a teenager. "What teenage girl did not relate to Mick Kelly in *The Heart Is a Lonely Hunter*?" she said to me by way of explanation. "She feels trapped, without friends, wants to go somewhere else, be a musician, or do other great things she can't in her stupid hometown. That's the story of every teenage girl who doesn't get asked early to the prom!"

At the time, I probably felt the same about Peter Hatcher in Judy Blume's *Tales of a Fourth Grade Nothing*, which I had read about seventy-five times as a preteen. I only knew *The Heart Is a Lonely Hunter* by title (it has, like everything Carson McCullers wrote, a magnificent title). My colleague's explanation led me to believe that *Hunter* was a novel about a teenage girl. One quarter of it is, which is apparently reason enough for this book to have spoken to teenage girls for the last seventy years and to be assigned continuously by their English teachers. Other reasons include (1) that the author was only twenty-three when she wrote it, barely out of adolescence herself, and (2) *Hunter*'s inescapable feeling of loneliness, as heavy and omnipresent as muggy air. As teenagers we spend almost all our time around people our own age. And yet, I've never met someone who would not describe those years, at least some of them, as lonely.

We lose much of this "protagonists as pals" relationship as adult readers. I've found it harder to see the struggles of a character I related to at seventeen than at thirty-eight. I even feel that way now about characters exactly like me. My grown-up life is too present, too "here," and frankly, I've worked too hard to arrive to want to escape into literature about someone like me. I'd rather disappear into a world not so much like mine, one where the music I hear evokes fresh feelings and emotions and a sense of what I don't yet understand and could learn. Whether those sensations make my heart sing or scare the heck out of me, they should all make me feel alive rather than comfort me as a reader. If I'm honest, that is what I really want when I pick up a book. The adult me picks up a book to be shaken, not given a hug.

I first read *The Heart Is a Lonely Hunter* around age twenty-five and again last Wednesday. It has no hugs to give. It is a sad, empty heartbreaker of a novel about small people with the equally small but absolutely human desire to be understood. No one does in the little Southern town they inhabit. Up the highways and across the plains of America, a depression is ending and a war is on its way. America is about to enter the most prosperous decades of its history. In the distance is a faint hum of a better tomorrow. The novel's main characters—Mick, the teenage girl; Dr. Copeland, the African American physician; Biff Brannon, the town diner owner; and Jake Blount, an alcoholic laborer—will never see it. Their fates as written by McCullers will fall short in giving them even the most basic happiness and comfort. Each life will end in violence, ineptitude, shattered dreams, and simple disappointment. That all of them seek counsel in John Singer, a deaf mute who lives at Mick's family's rooming house, underscores what musician Jim White described in a radio documentary about *Hunter*: "This novel is a photograph with a hole in the middle. In that hole is a question mark . . . the characters all want to be heard by a man who cannot speak."[1]

These are not bad people, nor are they innocent victims of circumstance. That's the mean little trap Carson McCullers has sprung on us when we look for just which character will be our stand-in. Each of them is a little bit responsible for their own isolation and unhappiness. But the universe of the story, what the author describes in her opening chapter as "along the streets . . . the desperate look of hunger and of loneliness,"[2] imprisons the characters like plants in a terrarium. We want to scream out, "Can't Mick take music lessons and still work at Woolworth's? Can't Dr. Copeland love his children and be a Marxist too?" But McCullers renders our protests silly, even mute. There is no outside, no other, no alternative to this small town. Mick is a teenager with younger siblings and an incapacitated father. Dr. Copeland is elderly and sick. Biff Brannon can't exactly yell, "Get happy!" to his customers. Alcoholics Anonymous had just been created and was too new to help Jake Blount find his way out of addiction.

Though written by a very young person, *Hunter* doesn't read like the product of a young talent. McCullers has made up her mind about the human condition. Connection with others is impossible. Trying is futile. In a review of *Hunter* for the *New Republic*, Richard Wright remarked, "This is not so much a novel as a projected mood, a state of mind poetically objectified in words, in sentences whose neutrality makes Hemingway's terse prose seem warm and partisan by comparison."[3] I don't think that's quite true. The language in *The Heart Is a Lonely Hunter* is not warm but full-blooded, bristling if not cuddly. The prose succeeds in being vigorously alive yet composed and certain of itself at the same time. I remember pausing at least ten times and asking myself, "Could a person one year past college really write with this level of confidence?"

Or maybe that's exactly how a young person would write, certainty coming from a lack of experience, a poverty of perspective. We have a different kind of writer working here than the others in this section—Maya Angelou in *I Know Why the Caged Bird Sings*, Mark Twain in *Adventures of Huckleberry Finn*, even Voltaire in *Candide*. All these writers were middle-aged adults writing about young people becoming adults. They speak with distance and with sympathy to the gauntlet of growing up but with the wisdom that says, "It's a helluva lot better over here in adulthood." McCullers makes no such claim.

She's instead saying, "There's nothing at all waiting for you out there. The escape of growing up is pointless. No one will understand you any better than they do now. Your heart will always be lonely. 'Hunting' for a better tomorrow is a waste of time."

McCullers grew up in Columbus, Georgia, a town much like the setting she chose for *Hunter*. As a young woman, she felt like a prisoner of both geography (her mother led a literary salon, and Carson had been a talented pianist; neither avocations held much respect in Columbus) and biology (in poor health her whole life, McCullers would die at age fifty from a series of strokes abetted by alcoholism. Her body had betrayed her dozens of times before). *Hunter* was written in Charlotte, North Carolina, after McCullers had married a young soldier and sold a few pieces of autobiographical fiction to national magazines. Published in 1940, it was an instant success and announced the debut of a major new talent. Though by far her most popular book, many scholars contend McCullers's best work was yet to come with her third novel, *The Member of the Wedding*, in 1946.

McCullers's output (four novels, a short-story collection, two plays, and an unfinished autobiography) have been bought, adapted, studied, and read almost continuously since their publication. *Hunter* is on *Time* magazine's "All-TIME 100 Novels" list and was adapted as an Oscar-nominated film in 1968.[4] But there remains some debate over whether Carson McCullers was one of the twentieth century's great American novelists, a literary anthropologist of the American South on par with William Faulkner and Flannery O'Connor, or whether she simply didn't live long enough or produce enough to achieve those heights. Her champions in life (Tennessee Williams, Richard Wright) and in death (Gore Vidal, Graham Greene) are a trustworthy all-star team. Her detractors (Arthur Miller said of her work, "moving but a minor author. And broken by illness at such a young age"[5]) have a point, even if it seems like a petty one. Ralph Ellison and Nathanael West have been canonized for producing less; West for writing on an equally intimate and epic-less scale.

Reading *The Heart Is a Lonely Hunter* as an adult puts you in a tough spot. In many of our favorite books, we love the characters. In others, we don't but instead love how the characters make us feel, what they do, who they allow us to be while we are reading. Here, McCullers has compassion for her characters and therefore for their predicaments. But she also, without pity, exposes their unhappiness and isolation as evidence of the fraud that is the human connection. Do we take our joy from the skill she displays in doing this or admire that she did it at such a young age? Do we relate to her characters' longing despite their outcome? How excited are we to welcome this beautiful fiction into our lives if its message is essentially "trying to make life better will only make you miserable"?

There isn't an easy answer. Graham Greene said he loved McCullers's work because "she has no message."[6] I don't love it for that. I understand but do not seek out the merciless outlook she has on our fate as human beings (although to be fair, *The Member of the Wedding* has a happy ending and also stars a teenage girl). I love instead the sheer fullness of McCullers's imagination, that her books inhabit the lives of people removed from her in a half dozen ways— men, African Americans, the elderly, people trapped in a place she herself had long since left—and yet these lives feel real enough to touch or hurl to the ground and break. If that isn't the essence of writing great fiction, I'm not sure what is.

I am still glad I welcomed in *The Heart Is a Lonely Hunter* and that it led me to McCullers's other books. At times I see her as that difficult friend you keep around for difficult reasons. She's that friend who is reckless, sharp, and alive. We might not choose to imitate her or trust her with our house during a weekend away. She's here for a different purpose. She reminds us of the fundamental kinetic energy of being alive, of a kind of unchained zeal we all had or felt before we decided that life was also about responsibility, tact, and cable bills.

We feel this in *The Heart Is a Lonely Hunter*. Its voice is confident, rich, a little arrogant. The lives of its characters are much less so: their pain is sloppy and random. They are simply making a go in the same unforgiving world we inhabit. Their pain is what makes them relatable even if we haven't experienced it ourselves, even if doesn't comfort us when we read about it.

A young Carson McCullers has reminded us of something we most fully grasp after getting our own hearts broken a few too many times: mistakes and ugliness make us more human, more like each other, more relatable. They're as elemental and real as our own lonely hearts pumping blood.

5

HOW THE UNCAGED BIRD SINGS

Have you read *I Know Why the Caged Bird Sings*? If so, have you read it recently or was it assigned to you a long time ago by a teacher? Do you know the book I'm talking about? If the answer is yes, did you just follow up with "You must be kidding me"?

I'm going to recommend you give it another look, here, right now. You're probably closer to the age Maya Angelou was when she wrote this autobiography (forty-one) than how old she was in the book itself (seven through seventeen). I'm going to suggest a whole other layer of riches to discover in *Caged Bird* upon second meeting that you might have missed in the first. Like any coming-of-age story, this book has something to tell us about growing up but just as much about getting to be grown up. It speaks to us about the telling of our own story and the living we do after it has been told.

Read it again with my blessing. Then call me Admiral Obvious leading a fleet of U-Idiot Boats.

Eye rolling. Several pairs. Saying "There's a lot to learn from Maya Angelou's most famous book!" feels about as daring as prescribing sleep for exhaustion. Since the publication of *I Know Why the Caged Bird Sings* in 1969, Dr. Maya Angelou has gone from being a very popular author (*Caged Bird* has never gone out of print and was nominated for a National Book Award) to an institution as inevitable as morning following night. She's written over thirty books, has at least that many honorary degrees, has been awarded medals and commissions by three sitting presidents, was Bill Clinton's inaugural poet, and is Oprah Winfrey's mentor. Now eighty-four, she still gives nearly a hundred lectures a year and has been called "a national treasure" as many times as Mount Rushmore. She is as omnipresent in American literature as a hot mug of tea and at least that well liked. To recommend (re)reading her most famous book sounds both easy and unfair to a hundred other well-deserving but lesser-known authors. Unfair, because Maya Angelou needs another cheerleader like the Oscars® need another "salute to the movies" montage. Easy, since Maya Angelou is, as the *Guardian* newspaper put it, "in the inspiration business" (complete with her own line of Hallmark® cards). Learning from even her most regarded book feels like succumbing to a cliché. What's next? Tearing up at orphans?

Hear me out. I reread *I Know Why the Caged Bird Sings* this winter, nearly twenty years after my first go-round with it, and was rather surprised at what I found. I'm no more a young black girl growing up in the South of the 1930s now than I was when I first read the book in college. So I didn't exactly "hear my own story" in Angelou's the way Oprah has famously said she did, nor did I feel a world of literary possibility opening up as many African American, feminist, and memoir writers did upon the book's publication. Rightfully called a trailblazer in 1969, *Caged Bird* had exposed and broken taboos long before I read it in 1992. At that time, I was just on the other side of not feeling like a kid anymore; about to enter the wide, unknown world of adulthood; and missing the town of my birth. *Caged Bird* was a book about growing up. I was growing up and scared about it. It spoke to me.

Now I am an adult around the same age as Dr. Angelou was when she began work on this book. She has lived a second remarkable life in the forty years since, including five additional volumes of memoir chronicling her life's first four decades. The final sentence of the final book in the series is the first line of *Caged Bird*.

> I thought if I wrote a book, I would have to examine the quality in the human spirit that continues to rise despite the slings and arrows of outrageous fortune.
>
> Rise out of physical pain and the psychological cruelties.
>
> Rise from being victims of rape and abuse and abandonment to the determination to be no victim of any kind.

Rise and be prepared to move on and ever on.

I remembered a children's poem from my mute days in Arkansas that seemed to say however low you perceive me now, I am headed to higher ground.

I wrote the first line in the book which would become "I Know Why the Caged Bird Sings."

What you looking at me for? I didn't come to stay.[1]

I Know Why the Caged Bird Sings was the beginning of a literary endeavor, the close of one chapter of the author's life and the beginning of the next. She didn't intend it to begin a series. And though most critics see the remaining five volumes as varyingly paler shades of *Caged Bird*, their presence and that of Maya Angelou herself as an icon changes how I as an adult see this book. As a college student, I read it as a tale of childhood, a story of survival over trauma, an embodiment of a time and place in America. I even imagined writing my own *Caged Bird* one day about a round Jewish boy growing up in the 1970s in the (not-so) little town of Ann Arbor, Michigan.

Now I/we have the sweep of Dr. Angelou's eighty years of life before us. *Caged Bird* now seems equally a statement of liberation through wisdom, of freedom through an understanding of our past as only one part of our story, a song of praise to not just putting in time but to being grown-up and wise enough to recognize how far we have come.

Maya Angelou had been writing poetry and plays for much of the 1960s but hadn't given much thought to book writing. In 1968, her friend Dr. Martin Luther King Jr. was murdered on her birthday. The leadership of black politics would soon pass from King and Malcolm X to Jesse Jackson, Shirley Chisholm, and Barbara Jordan, from the spiritual "We will get there someday" to the more practical "We are here now."

Despondent and heartbroken, Ms. Angelou accepted a dinner party invitation later that year at the home of cartoonist Jules Feiffer. In attendance were her escorts and friends, James Baldwin and

Robert Loomis, an editor at Random House. The guests had been sharing stories of their own childhoods when Ms. Angelou joined in. Afterward, Mr. Loomis remarked to Mr. Baldwin that Maya Angelou should write an autobiography but then challenged her to "write an autobiography as literature."

It's a good basic description of a chief asset of *Caged Bird*, especially for someone reading it now. Central to the story are several pivotal events: young Marguerite Ann Johnson (she became "Maya Angelou" as a singer in early adulthood) is raped by her mother's boyfriend at age eight and rendered mute by that act of violation; later she gets pregnant at age sixteen, after her first experience of consensual sex. Frank telling of events like these, shocking in 1969, is not uncommon in the memoirs of today. And except for these, *Caged Bird* is a story not really told through event but rather through the inflection that captures those events and the setting that holds them. Angelou gives us many more ordinary days than special occasions. Her pacing is deep breaths instead of quick pants.

She also does not lunge for metaphor and detail but seems to select it, carefully, off the kitchen table. Her language is what I like to call "plainly lyrical," adorned without feeling fussed over and taken from the imagery of the everyday. There are few words an alert high school reader wouldn't understand. "A knife" works as well in metaphor here as "a scimitar."

In an interview with George Plimpton for the *Paris Review*, Dr. Angelou spoke of how she gets her prose this way. "I try to pull the language in to such a sharpness that it jumps off the page. It must look easy, but it takes me forever to get it to look so easy. I work at the language."[2]

Caged Bird took Maya Angelou two hard years to write. She worked to make the language feel natural. It is not hurried or demanding or trying to impress you. It is confident, serene, and wise even when it is angry. And anyone who writes fiction knows, as Nathaniel Hawthorne says, that "easy reading is damn hard writing."[3]

The last sentence in the book's opening chapter is "If growing up is painful for the Southern Black girl, being aware of her displacement is the rust on the razor that threatens the throat. It is an unnecessary insult."[4] It is stern, smoldering, but levelheaded. It is the language of maturity.

A grown-up Maya Angelou wrote this book looking back. She worked hard and polished until her fingers hurt. That's the easiest explanation for its wise, assured air. But reading it four decades later can easily get you tangled in larger contradictions beyond its covers: Should we take *Caged Bird* on its own, as a story of a place in time and in the author's life, an author who had only this book in mind while writing it? Or do we account for it being the first volume of a much larger story? Can we avoid Dr. Angelou's standing as an icon and receive the gifts of *Caged Bird* as a book outside the persona of its author?

I'm going to ask you to hold contradicting ideas in your hands at the same time. All by itself, *Caged Bird* is a book of reflection. The author had already lived the entire life captured in her six volumes of memoir by the time she wrote volume number one. By the time *Caged Bird* was born, the author's son was a grown man. She had lived all over the world, written, danced, sung, and been mentored by several of the great men and women of twentieth-century America. She may have written *Caged Bird* about a young Southern black girl, but she is speaking to us light-years from that point and knows it. And that's the voice we hear. This is the story of a little girl told unmistakably in the voice of the woman she has become. That little girl, so alive on the page, is also a long time gone.

The book's title, taken from a poem by Paul Laurence Dunbar, tells us this. The "caged bird" in Dunbar's poem "Sympathy" sings:

> When his wing is bruised and his bosom sore,—
> When he beats his bars and he would be free;
> It is not a carol of joy or glee.[5]

Angelou rewrites the poem. Her version ends like this:

> But a caged bird stands on the grave of dreams
> his shadow shouts on a nightmare scream
> his wings are clipped and his feet are tied
> so he opens his throat to sing
>
> The caged bird sings
> with a fearful trill
> of things unknown
> but longed for still
> and his tune is heard
> on the distant hill
> for the caged bird
> sings of freedom[6]

That "caged bird" has already freed herself by the telling of her own story, by working at that telling, by having lived and "moved on and ever on." In telling the story of childhood, Maya Angelou has also written a statement about the pride of arriving in maturity.

Now add in Maya Angelou the Celebrity. It would seem difficult to separate the "lessons" of this book from Angelou herself. Angelou is a one-woman factory of "lessons" and has published just as many "wisdom books" (label from *New Yorker* writer Hilton Als) of short essays and life lessons as she has memoirs.[7] An adult reader can easily feel like a chump thinking about what they've learned from reading *Caged Bird* when seen amid the rest of the author's output. The industry of Maya Angelou practically demands you learn something.

That's usually where Angelou's detractors begin. And they are not wrong. They look at Angelou's books as likeable manipulations instead of art and assert that her fame gives her a free pass from the standards other writers have to reach. Novelist Francine Prose criticized what I called Angelou's plain lyricism as "murky turgid, convoluted."[8] Professor John McWhorter in the *New Republic* cites Angelou's breaking down of barriers as pioneering, but he wonders "how readers can find art in these books."[9] In an unrelated review for the *New York Review of Books*, Ian Buruma criticizes his subject's over-reliance on sentimentality and triumphant victimhood by sneering that the author "even throws in a bit of Maya Angelou poetry for good measure."[10]

All true. All important, but not a skunk at the picnic. Read *Caged Bird* on its own, but remember the writer who wrote it, where she was in her journey, not to becoming a giant celebrity, but to becoming herself.

In an interview on the eve of President Barack Obama's election, Maya Angelou said, "Growing up means taking responsibility for the time you take up and the space you occupy."[11] She has done this, I think beautifully, in *I Know Why the Caged Bird Sings* and has created what I see as the canonical second life for the coming-of-age story. We read these books as young people to hear our own story, to meet a friend in the author, someone like us. We read them as grown-ups with an emphasis on the words "of age." We read them to witness a journey into maturity and understanding, to see ourselves, along with the author, becoming ourselves.

PART 2
IDENTITY

6
REAL INDIANS PLAY
ROCK 'N' ROLL

I didn't read Sherman Alexie's books in high school. His first short-story collection, *The Lone Ranger and Tonto Fistfight in Heaven*, didn't come out until 1993, when I was already a junior in college. By then political correctness and identity politics were in full swing in American education, and being familiar with the literature of ethnicities different from yours was not only part of a balanced cultural diet but was also a political imperative. To not think so could be seen as racist or, worse, unfashionable.

I started reading Sherman Alexie for exactly the opposite reason. I heard him on a radio interview discussing his second novel, *Indian Killer* (1996), about a Seattle murderer who scalped his victims. I like crime fiction, but I liked this guy even more—he was cocky, hilarious, and had no use for the careful politeness I'd come to associate with conversations about race. He joked about how Indian boys pretended to be mystics to impress white girls, how as a kid he'd idolized Jimi Hendrix as much as Crazy Horse, and how he used the word *Indian* without shame and expected his interviewer to do so as well.

Sherman Alexie wasn't out to shock NPR audiences when I heard him that day. He'd just arrived at our twenty-first-century definition of *identity* about ten years earlier than most of us. It was clear to me on that day that, to Sherman Alexie, we are all some messy combination of what we were born with, the surroundings that had seeped into our skin, and the desires and shortcomings—lust, jealousy, sadness, and longing—that made us all human. Blended, fluid iden-

49

tity was a given, W. E. B. Du Bois's "double consciousness" multiplied to infinity. The question on Alexie's mind seemed to be "OK, now what?" That we not only inherited an identity but could also shape it was liberating but ominous with the weight of responsibility—which sounds an awful lot more like life in the 2010s than in the 1990s. Now this thing called "identity" shape-shifts one tweet/status update/ friend request at a time.

Sherman Alexie's books are now taught in high schools all over America. *The Lone Ranger and Tonto Fistfight in Heaven* is his most famous (it became the movie *Smoke Signals* in 1998), but the follow-up, *Reservation Blues* (1995), is his most prescient. His second work of fiction and first novel, *Reservation Blues* examines the short life of Coyote Springs, a rock 'n' roll band made up of young Spokane Indians. At first glance, it's kind of an Indian version of *The Commitments,* another first novel about a band that's really more about growing up and the loyalty to friends we feel strongest right before the call of adulthood. But Alexie is up to a lot more than that premise suggests: he uses Coyote Springs as a little laboratory to investigate these different kinds of identity. What criteria do we use to define ourselves? How do we react when someone else imposes identity upon us, even if that "someone else" is an entire country? What kind of risks do we run if identity is fluid, instead of fixed?

Reservation Blues opens with Thomas Builds-The-Fire, a thirty-year-old Spokane Indian who lives on the Spokane Reservation in Wellpinit, Washington, picking up hitchhiker Robert Johnson. Yes, that Robert Johnson, he of the blues guitar and the selling his soul to the devil at the crossroads, the African American hero to three generations of white musicians. Johnson has apparently faked his own death and has been hiding out from the devil since. He cannot play guitar for fear of being discovered and deliberately tries to abandon the instrument each time he moves on. This time, he leaves the guitar in Thomas Builds-The-Fire's truck. Thomas takes it and decides to start a band with his friends on the reservation, Victor Joseph and Junior Polatkin.

Alexie names each chapter after one of the band's songs ("Treaties," "Urban Indian Blues") and includes the song lyrics at the beginning of each chapter. We immediately wonder what Coyote Springs sounds like. The band first becomes known around the reservation and later the state by playing "a mix of blues, rock, pop, gospel, rap, and a few unidentifiable musical forms"; in other words, playing American music.[1] The inclusion of Robert Johnson (who is on the reservation to visit Big Mom, a Spokane elder who was also a music teacher to Janis Joplin, Jimi Hendrix, and many of the saints of American song) does two things: we see that Coyote Springs, composed of the descendants of the first Americans, is an ingredient in the great gumbo pot that is the history of American music; traditions brought in from elsewhere congeal and combine to form something wholly unique. Also, Alexie has used American music as a metaphor for the struggle of identity itself: to be both unique and to belong to something larger.

The members of Coyote Springs are acutely aware of the shopworn identities Indians have been given by others. They joke about vision quests and Custer and smallpox blankets. Victor scowls at Thomas for believing in the good luck of eagle feathers. The band's backup singer, Checkers Warm Water, fumes at the empty machismo of Indian men by sneering to herself: "I'm super Indian Man. Able to leap tall HUD houses in a single bound. Faster than a BIA pickup. Stronger than a block of commodity cheese."[2]

Alexie also gives each character multiple pages of dream sequences, where Indian iconography of wild horses and scalping collide against the modern world of skyscrapers and television sets. It's here, in this cliché of a "vision," where the author lets his imagination free but makes his strongest point: We are as free as wild horses in a world of conflicting images, sounds, cultures, and identities. But we bring into that world our history, our story up until that point. We are not trapped by that history. But we don't have the comfort of certainty, of community and belonging, either.

Reservation Blues could have fit into this last section as a coming-of-age novel. The characters are on the young side, unmarried, a bit lost. There's a little sex, a lot of drinking, and a sweet love story. It's also an "Indian novel," which is the other reason I'm sure a lot of high school teachers, particularly in the Southwest, Northwest, or in schools that call themselves "progressive," assign it. To me, it's one of the most "American" novels of the last half century. That the characters are "Native Americans" is only a small part of why. America is a young country of reinvention and multiple selves, where identities mix and combine as easily as paints in a can. That's a rather obvious thing to say, and Alexie doesn't stop there. This is a novel not just about the fluidity of identity but also its consequences: there is great safety in knowing you are Indian or Irish or Japanese and having someone else tell you what that means. There is great fear of the unknown, in "leaving the reservation" even if the reservation is our hometown, a longtime job that no longer serves us, a dysfunctional but comfortable relationship, or simply our own mind and an expired idea about ourselves.

You will not be surprised by what happens to the members of Coyote Springs. They don't change all that much, and when several of them do "leave the reservation," we understand why. Alexie does not tell their story at the eye level of each character but rather in the dark, lonely sky above them. We are up there with Alexie, looking down and listening to an Indian band play American music, borrowing the guitar of a blues legend. The neighboring Indians think they aren't acting Indian enough while the local parish priest thinks the band has a better future in the church choir. Indian, black, Christian, native. Blues, country, pop, rock 'n' roll. "Identity" is the wind that whips through the story, landing and disrupting a dozen different ways. But the story feels quiet and inevitable instead of charged with struggle and drama.

"Sherman Alexie is a Spokane/Coeur d'Alene Indian." That is the opening line of Mr. Alexie's author biography for his first four works of fiction. Following the 1998 release of *Smoke Signals*, his bios would become a simple list of his literary accomplishments. Each book was still about Indians, and Alexie spoke of himself in interviews as an Indian. But as his stature grew, the awards accumulated (*Reservation Blues* won the American Book Award. A National Book Award would follow a decade later for his young-adult novel *The Absolutely True Diary of a Part-Time Indian*). As Sherman Alexie grew older, his public identity seemed to become the many-sided thing he'd spoken of that July afternoon when I heard him fifteen years ago. He's now as likely to talk about being a father to sons, a committed political liberal, or a basketball fan. It's all in the context of "being Indian," but "being Indian" is a lot more kaleidoscopic than the phrase would suggest.

This is where most of us are in the second decade of the twenty-first century, the freedom of an identity no longer defined exclusively by race, sexuality, geography, religion, or age. Some of those old skins still haunt us, *Reservation Blues* says, but even more, it says with freedom are both the joy and the fear that we are all human, with all the joy and pain that comes with it.

Reservation Blues is one of Alexie's longer works, at a little over three hundred pages. It reads fast but serene, like a long drive with the windows down. You will finish it quickly but will most appreciate the experience if you read it when you have some uninterrupted time. This also feels to me like a novel to read at night. I'm not sure why.

I am comfortable saying that just about anyone would like *Reservation Blues* at any time in life—except maybe people who are quite satisfied with where they are or are held captive by their own fear. They could see this novel's quiet mission as strange or even threatening. The remainder of us who are searching or even content to be on our path will love it both as literature and maybe as a code breaker of how we can understand ourselves, even while wearing Indian beads, listening to country music, loving basketball, reading across time, and dreaming about the rightful and ultimate home of Robert Johnson's guitar.

7
THE AUTOBIOGRAPHY OF MALCOLM X: YOURS AND MINE

Malcolm X was thirty-nine years old when he was murdered in the winter of 1965. At that age, he had lived more lives and assumed more identities than most of us will do in twice that time. In just the two years before his death, he resigned from the Nation of Islam ministry he had brought to national prominence, toured Europe and Africa as a foreign dignitary, made a pilgrimage to Mecca, converted to Islam, lectured on college campuses throughout the United States, started a new organization called the Organization of Afro-American Unity, and underwent a profound change of heart. In a letter to *New York Times* reporter M. S. Handler around that time, he wrote, "Some of my very dearest friends are Christians, Jews, Buddhists, Hindus, agnostics, and even atheists— some are capitalists, socialists, conservatives, extremists . . . some are even Uncle Toms—some are black, brown, red, yellow and some are even white."[1] This was a very different man from the one who had, two winters before, called the assassination of John F. Kennedy a case of the chickens coming home to roost—just retribution for a government insensitive to the unfair treatment of its citizens.

During those last two years, Malcolm X had also begun work on his autobiography in collaboration with journalist Alex Haley. He had predicted to Haley (a prediction captured in the autobiography's final pages) that he would probably not live to see the book's publication. Not only was he right; his murder also meant history would never know what iteration of Malcolm X would have come next. "My whole life has been a chronology of changes," he wrote earlier in the autobiography, a statement that could be exactly right or a sizable understatement.[2] He was clearly not a man who stayed put for very long.

The choice to commit his life to an autobiography right before his assassination did give Malcolm X one final identity: icon. *The Autobiography of Malcolm X* sold six million copies in its first decade of publication and has remained in print for nearly a half century. Malcolm X was the subject of an acclaimed film biography by Spike Lee in 1992 and of a Pulitzer Prize–winning biography by Manning Marable in 2011. The autobiography is now required reading in high schools everywhere. Since the author did not think he would live to see it published, we can safely assume that this story was meant to capture not just who he had been but also how he wanted history to remember him.

"Everyone finds in Malcolm X the Malcolm X that he or she needs," said a recent *New York Review of Books* article.[3] That's a compliment to the book's depth but is also its greatest mystery. Who is the Malcolm X we are supposed to remember? Civil rights hero or eloquent bigot? A person in a constant state of transformation and learning (the book's final pages include a lengthy statement of regret about X's lack of formal education and his eagerness for more study[4]) or "a life strangely and pitifully wasted" by myopia and distorted fanaticism, as the *New York Times* said in its obituary?[5] Malcolm X is now immortal, but is he immortal for who he was when he was lost or who he was becoming when found? Perhaps both?

To some extent, the answer depends on when the reader and *The Autobiography of Malcolm X* first meet. When I read it in high school, my mind was fixated on the question of whether this Malcolm X was someone to be looked up to or feared (X's successor, Louis Farrakhan, and his eloquent anti-Semitism were news at the time). If this was what had become of whatever good Malcolm X had done, I wondered how much good he'd actually done. For a teenager, everything is about right now, or maybe next semester, and how something squares with your own worldview because you don't yet understand what or if anything lies beyond it.

As an adult, I was compelled to revisit the autobiography when I heard an hour-long documentary of it last year. The public radio program *Studio 360* had made the book into an episode of its "American Icons" series and turned its attention to how much the story of Malcolm X parallels other great American stories of humble origins ending in national prominence, of reinvention and transformation, of identities shed and donned like suits of clothes.[6] The life story of Malcolm X was a sequence of identity shifts dictated by, but ultimately transcending, circumstance: bright kid, foster child, hoodlum teenager, prisoner at age twenty, self-taught jailhouse scholar, religious convert, national spokesman, husband, father, outcast, foreign dignitary, Muslim, murder victim, icon. I've probably missed a few. But seen in this way, how different is the story of Malcolm Little of Lansing, Michigan, from that of Robert Zimmerman of Hibbing, Minnesota (Bob Dylan), Cassius Clay of Louisville, Kentucky (Muhammad Ali), or Marguerite Johnson of Stamps, Arkansas (Maya Angelou)? America is a country that both brands us by skin color and birthplace but also says that identity is a fluid concept.

There was great power in that concept for this adult reader of the autobiography. All the chapters of Malcolm X's story are part of who he was, but none trapped him in who he became. The chance to reflect upon this idea via the printed word, in this case, is an argument that circumstances are not the final verdict on our lives, that we may not yet know who we are becoming, but the omnipresent opportunity to become something or someone else is its own kind of freedom.

It helps that Malcolm X has written his story in a way that leaves no room for nostalgia. Minus a few moments of reflection, this book heads in exactly one direction: forward. Losing who he used to be was the only way Malcolm X saw to be able to continue living. There's a particularly sad moment in the autobiography where he runs into his old friend Shorty from his days of petty crime, and the two have nothing to say to each other. Malcolm X doesn't say so, but it requires a coldness of the spirit to break cleanly with old friends and past lives and never look back. Many of us assemble our identity from where we came. *The Autobiography of Malcolm X* is the merciless other half of that choice.

I know how difficult it is to look past Malcolm X's earlier life of hostility and bigotry even if he felt terrible about it later and spends almost the entire last chapter of the autobiography saying so. Marable's biography also points out that Malcolm X trafficked in half-baked logic and other easy prejudices like sexism and anti-Semitism when his powers of articulation failed him.[7] He was at times too proud a man and too immature a thinker, too ashamed of who he once was to admit when he wasn't yet wise enough for the wisdom asked of him.

That may tarnish Malcolm X as a hero or reaffirm him as a villain in your eyes. It just reminds me that he was a person, a person who knew how far he had come from being a hood named "Detroit Red" and who felt he still had a long way to go. The responsibility for getting there, for whatever new identity he would assume next, would be his. The line I repeat to myself from the autobiography is the last one: "Only the mistakes have been mine."[8] Admitting error without shame is a sign of a maturity and wisdom long fought for and built on, like layers of earth. It's fair to say that Malcolm X had arrived at some plateau in his own human development when he wrote his story, even if he knew he was just getting started.

As a reading experience, *Malcolm X* is smooth, lyrical, and structured like an archetypal tale of struggle and redemption. Much study has been devoted to both its accuracy and to Alex Haley's role in the book's construction. At the time writing began, Haley was a newly working journalist after leaving twenty years of military service; he both wanted and needed a bestseller. In the beginning of the relationship between the two men, Malcolm X was still working for the Nation of Islam and immediately distrusted Haley and his moderate politics. And though their relationship evolved as the events of the two men's lives did, the reading experience does not feel damaged by those fits and starts. *Malcolm X* moves at the assured, colorful stride of a great modernist novel, like E. L Doctorow's *Ragtime* or Ralph Ellison's *Invisible Man.* You'll be eighty-five pages in before you realize you're hungry from missing dinner. But I'll leave it to you to decide the issue of who gets credit for that (to my mind, Haley's mastery is keeping himself invisible) or if it matters to you.

Rereading the autobiography places you in esteemed company. President Barack Obama read it as a young man coming to terms with his own biracial, fatherless childhood. Author Bell Hooks first read it as a university student and cited it as a seminal book of her political awakening. *The Autobiography of Malcolm X* has been on the shelves of the White House for several administrations. Its reviews on Amazon are almost uniformly positive, even from students assigned it by teachers. The same cannot be said for *The Great Gatsby* or *Catcher in the Rye*, where opinion is fiercely divided.

As it should be. Malcolm X's story is, at heart, a story not of race or religion but of growing up, of self-awareness, and of identity always changing even when we feel it lashes us to a post. We are all on that path as well.

8

EDITH WHARTON: *"INNOCENCE IS FOR WIMPS"*

The children of Warren Buffett are on record as growing up not knowing their father was a billionaire. I believe them for two reasons. (1) Buffett never spent money like it was all that much fun, and (2) wealth—earned, inherited, or stolen—is now an optional (like sports fandom) rather than a fundamental (like ethnicity) part of American identity. Buffett still lives in the same house in Omaha he purchased for $30,000 in 1957 and would probably call himself "a Nebraskan" or "an investor" long before "a billionaire." Expecting the same modesty from his billionaire American predecessors like John D. Rockefeller or Conrad Hilton seems absurd.

Edith Wharton grew up Edith Jones in a city and nation ruled by the billionaires of its day—New York City during its first industrial boom, the "Gilded Age" of the 1870s—where enormous and sudden wealth had elbowed its way into the American conception of itself. Her family had so much money that they begat the phrase "keeping up with the Joneses." But the Jones family was of English stock, not Dutch, like New York's first settlers. Wharton has a withering joke about this in her most famous novel, *The Age of Innocence* (1920): that one could be seen as less American if one's roots went back to the wrong generation of settlers and if your money had come along too quickly like it had for the Scottish Carnegies or the German Protestant Rockefellers.[1] "It seems stupid to have discovered America only to make it a copy of another country," a character remarks in the 1993 film adaptation of *Innocence* with at least a gloved handful of irony.[2]

Edith Jones knew where she came from and was proud of it. But she saw her roots as one part, not the entirety, of what her life could mean, and she struggled with the extent to which the issue of her roots affected her creativity. How much of her identity belonged to the life she was born into versus the life she made for herself? To what extent do we hold onto where we come from after we are no longer citizens of that land? And how much does it matter that we still benefit from that citizenry? These are the questions at the heart of central characters of *Innocence*, even if their author had largely answered these questions for herself.

The Age of Innocence is the story of Newland Archer, a young lawyer from one of New York's most powerful old families. He's engaged to marry May Welland—whose family prestige rivals his own—when he meets her cousin, Ellen Olenska, who has just left her husband, a Polish count. Newland and Ellen fall for each other, a relationship attempted, anguished over, but never begun. In the end, not much has changed, and Archer declines, even years later after May has passed away, to see Ellen.

Those who read *The Age of Innocence* in high school may focus on the elements of the story that ring true for them—loving someone you can't have, being trapped by a society you had no part in creating, being told to behave in ways demanded yet unexplained. But this makes it sound as though Wharton condemned the world of her childhood in *Innocence* by having it smother the desires of her characters, as if Archer and Olenska were a grown-up version of Romeo and Juliet. The absolute command the author has of this world's every mannerism and furnishing could suggest its oppressiveness. No one uses words like *damask* and *gilt cornice* with a raised eyebrow like Edith Wharton does. No one could, without knowing every inch of the universe in which they lived.

Edith Wharton was also a long way away from this universe. She was fifty-seven years old when she wrote *The Age of Innocence*, her twelfth novel. She was a famous author, living in France free from a loveless marriage, and not one for nostalgia or sentimentality. The "Age" in question—her childhood in 1870s New York—was long over, buried in time by financial panic, immigration, the coming of the automobile and motion pictures, and a world war. Her life may have been the better for the Age of Innocence dying, but Wharton was no fan of modernity, and in a letter to a friend she called it "simply awful—a kind of continuous earthquake of motors, busses, trams, lorries, taxis and other howling and swooping and colliding engines."[3] She neither wanted her past back nor celebrated the change that had done away with it.

Wharton gives the characters of *Innocence* the same wisdom she herself had earned. Newland Archer and Ellen Olenska are not star-crossed lovers. Newland and Ellen know what they want, what they are doing, and what they can't have. They recognize that the world they inhabit will not change for them, as well as their own limitations in breaking free from it. Even May Welland—first a naïve child, later a cunning operator—is defined by an acceptance of the rules of the game she was born playing. The title *The Age of Innocence* is chosen with a knowing arch of the eyebrows. The characters do not possess anything of the kind.

Accepting one's lot and letting it define you, though, are two very different things, and here is where Wharton and her creation part company. If there is a tragedy to be found in *Innocence*, it is Newland Archer's unhappiness, not at ending up with the wrong woman but at never accepting his own choices. Newland cannot make a decision about how much of his world he wishes to have define him. Who is he: An Archer? A man? A lawyer? A New Yorker? A nineteenth-century billionaire? Archer's wife, May, has accepted that her life will be defined by the expectations of her family and its reputation. Ellen Olenska has done the same: her identity will be largely colored by leaving an unfaithful husband. Archer is a man, with more choices than both of these women. And yet he is constantly shuffling his sense of self between profession and standing, between obligation and desire, between who he would like to be and who he thinks he cannot be. He is unhappy because he is a grown man who has not decided who he is.

His creator did not make this mistake. Most women of Wharton's time and standing became wives, mothers, hostesses, and philanthropists, their power derived not just from wealth but from an understanding of their rarified world and its customs. Edith Wharton held onto that understanding her entire life but used it to birth and maintain a writing career. She became one of America's most respected novelists, the first woman to win a Pulitzer Prize, friend to Henry James and Sinclair Lewis, a war correspondent, a divorcée (when such things were rare), and a literary expat in Europe a decade before Ernest Hemingway and Ezra Pound. She also relished decorating her mansions, being driven around by chauffeurs, and using the connections her wealth gave her to take her places her contemporaries could not go. Wharton wrote many of her finest books in bed, tossing pages on the floor for a secretary to pick up and copy.[4] She was famously snobby and self-assured, and, by the writing of *Innocence*, she had probably earned that right.

We have all been Newland Archer more often than we have been Edith Wharton. We have all had to decide if we work better as team players or by ourselves; where family ranks alongside career and passions; whether we are countrymen or regionalists, citizens or human beings, and in what order and when. We are more often uncertain than swift about those choices.

The Age of Innocence does not argue that there is a right answer. Edith Wharton does not critique where she came from, and she recognizes the value her upbringing provided—comfort, security, and, most important, clarity about your identity if you chose to accept it. "There are worse things than boring convention," said satirist P. J. O'Rourke of the novel.[5] Wharton's disdain (the tone of *Innocence* is that of an elderly aunt telling you what a disappointment you've become) is reserved for not being honest with your choices by avoiding them. Newland Archer's pain is in direct proportion to his unwillingness to act on his own circumstances. Wharton accepted her circumstances but as the theme rather than totality of her story. It's a choice that gave us Edith Wharton the novelist instead of Edith Jones.

I'm surprised that I enjoy *The Age of Innocence* as much as I do. I don't care for love stories, forbidden or public, and lean toward fiction set in the present or recent past. Corsets and blue-patterned china give me a headache. I'm also talky, Jewish, and the son of two psychologists. Which means novels featuring emotional repression and not saying what's on your mind—the printed version of Merchant/Ivory movies—leave me cold. I want to charge into the characters' drawing rooms, knock a tea service to the floor, and scream, "Say what you mean or I'm sending you all to a twelve-step meeting!" In fact, I probably said exactly this to the people around me in the half-empty screening room as I watched Martin Scorsese's 1993 adaptation of *The Age of Innocence*, my first exposure to it, fifteen years before I read the novel.

And yet, I remember something writer Amy Tan said about this book and why we can relate to it, despite the closed world it inhabits— that "we're all concerned about belonging. We're especially concerned when we don't belong and don't know why."[6] I know, then, why I've read it several times, why I recommend it to friends in the anteroom of huge life decisions, especially when not deciding seems a better solution than action. Most huge decisions are fundamentally about what order we choose to place our priorities and which ones make up the different parts of ourselves. Are we alone or members of a group? Are we what we create or who we already are? These are the struggles of identity. The only right answer, says *The Age of Innocence*, is to decide and find where you can work toward the best set of consequences. To not decide is one kind of identity but no real life at all.

9

THE US YET TO COME

Margaret Atwood was a shadow figure at my high school, an author I heard only a little about, but I could tell there was much, much more. I knew she was Canadian. I knew she wrote both novels and poetry. And I observed that everyone at school who read her was female.

It was the early 1990s. Third-wave feminism was ascendant. The women at my high school who were vocal about their feminism were equally vocal about their loyalty to Margaret Atwood. One of them read the Atwood poem "This Is a Photograph of Me" at graduation. Most swore by the Atwood novels *Cat's Eye* (1988), which had been published around that time, and *The Handmaid's Tale* (1985), which had just been made into a movie.

It is *Surfacing*, however, the author's second novel (1972) that I find popping up on more than a few high school reading lists these days. An explanation for its popularity could be its audible resonances with other canonical works of feminist literature—the merging of nature and the female body in Kate Chopin's *Awakening*, the iconography of imprisonment and madness in Charlotte Perkins Gilman's *Yellow Wallpaper*, and the fiction that whispers autobiography in Sylvia Plath's *The Bell Jar*. *Surfacing* was also first published in Canada in the early 1970s, smack in the middle of the women's movement, which made it a formative, if lesser cited, text of feminism's second wave and the latter days of '60s activism. Or it could be its equally firm themes of our relationship to the natural world, to our romantic partners and family, and to the country of our birth that give *Surfacing* fodder for dozens of English class discussions beyond second-wave feminism and the identity politics that would emerge a generation later.

I gave *Surfacing* another look recently and kept coming back to that word *identity* and the particular way Atwood takes it on—how we see ourselves relationally and adopt identities, with us sitting on one end of the seesaw from lovers, family, country, and nature. I've heard this is characteristically a very female perspective (that old chestnut about men seeing themselves in hierarchies and women in webs of relationships), but I think Atwood is up to something larger than gender here. And it isn't very optimistic. Atwood seems to be saying that our relationships with others both clarify who we are and dwarf us. While the world is vast, we are small and incomplete. But that struggle, with all its powerlessness, is one of the only fail-safes of being human. Animals can only be themselves and have their relationships defined at birth. It is our relationships, frightening and humbling as they may be, that give us personhood, even as they also remind us of how little that matters.

Surfacing is the story of an unnamed woman, her lover, and a second couple traveling to a cabin in the wilderness of Quebec where the narrator grew up. Her father now lives there and has gone missing. The four spend about a week searching for him, and we see that one couple, David and Anne, have a marriage largely based on manipulation and power plays (in a petty, awful scene, David forces Anne to take off her clothes in front of their friends). The narrator and her lover, Joe, live together. Joe wants to get married. The narrator isn't sure if she even loves Joe and is haunted by the memory of an affair with a married man and a resulting aborted pregnancy. The conclusion of *Surfacing* involves the protagonist left behind in the cabin by her friends, wanton destruction of the cabin, and a kind of animalistic transformation I had heard about and saw coming, but it still shook me.

Nothing here, not even the bizarre conclusion, feels like closure. We have a nameless narrator searching for a missing father, in one relationship that has stalled, and with her memory occupied by another. Atwood continually returns to images of incompleteness, of transitions interrupted, of voids and phantom limbs. The cabin abuts a river where the two couples look for the missing man in canoes. The narrator swims and dives there. The term *surfacing* is linked back to fish and sea creatures, to something appearing that has not yet fully arrived yet, to something growing into itself. And yet Atwood keeps her gaze riveted on the missing, on the "not yet happened."

"All around us, the illusion of infinite space and no space." This is how she describes the small world (cabin, lake, woods) of the novel, making it somehow feel vast. "The obscure shore which it seems we could touch, the water between an absence. . . . It's like moving on air, nothing beneath us, holding us up, suspended."[1]

Suspended is the opposite of *surfacing*. The latter implies movement, potential energy, and possibility. At least somewhat, Atwood's title is like a photo negative. *Surfacing* can mean coming into one's own but also imply that a great deal is missing of "one's own."

There is a lot more here. Atwood dips her hands into an emergent Canadian nationalism of the period (David scowls at American tourists, calling them "bloody fascist pig Yanks"); our sensual yet violent relationship with nature (a lifetime theme of her work: Atwood's father was a biologist, and she and her siblings grew up working alongside him in the Canadian wilderness); and the spiritual implications of a woman discovering her place in the world by visiting a now-missing chapter of her past.[2] The novel clocks in at a bit under three hundred pages, and while the themes are as dense and multilayered as soil, Atwood's prose remains light, lyrical, and exact, rays of sun creating a lattice through tree cover.

Surfacing is therefore a book to sink deeply into, to stop, breathe, reread favorite passages, and continue at the pace of a nature walk. Very little happens, so the inclination (often mine) to let your eyes skip along the surface is understandable. Try not to. You'll be missing the best sentences, which are deep in paragraph thickets instead of on the eye level of plot. Also, I'd save this one for a weekend alone or some other prolonged solitude. It doesn't feel to me like a novel to read with others around.

I can completely understand how a reader would come to *Surfacing* even now and still read it as a novel about a woman's understanding of her own power, a surrealist manual of female liberation with the line "This above all, to refuse to be a victim" from the final page as a kind of manifesto.[3] As a man, I also look at *Surfacing* as a story of the challenge of understanding oneself; of assembling and reassembling different identities, be they gender, geography, or genus; of seeing what still-incomplete version of yourself emerges. There's probably still a lot under the waterline you won't know, which tells me that *Surfacing* may also be a useful novel to read at moments of important life decisions, when you can feel yourself stepping out of who you once were into who you will be.

Margaret Atwood was just getting started when she wrote *Surfacing*. Ahead lay nearly fifty books, every literary award imaginable, and the informal designation as one of the giants of twentieth-century literature, a Canadian Philip Roth or John Updike. And yet she is not complacent on her throne. Margaret Atwood has three hundred thousand followers on Twitter®, shows up regularly at writers' conferences, and is currently developing mobile apps to facilitate interaction between authors and their fans. Whereas Norman Mailer and Updike ended their lives bemoaning what had happened to their profession, Margaret Atwood seems to want to have a hand in shaping it. The identity of "important novelist" seems too small for her. Even at age seventy-two, more is surfacing.

10

AM I A MAN OR AN ANDROID?

Sometime in the very near future, there will be a sequel to *Blade Runner*. In that near future, a teenager will see *Blade Runner 2*, or whatever it will be called, and not know that what he is seeing is a continuation of a landmark now listed in the Library of Congress's National Film Registry as "culturally significant" and worthy of preservation for all time. I'm not being a cynic by supposing this. The very near present has provided more than enough evidence that some teenage viewers of the movie *Titanic* did not know it was based on actual events, that *Footloose, Hairspray,* and *The Karate Kid* existed before the invention of the mobile phone, or that *Prometheus* was a prequel to anything, least of all the 1979 classic *Alien.*

Continuing in grouch mode, I'd have to assume that same teenager would have no idea that *Blade Runner* is based on the 1968 novel *Do Androids Dream of Electric Sheep?* by Philip K. Dick. This teenager might, if he is a stone-cold geek in the lives-in-one's-science-fiction-imagination sense. Or if he goes to a forward-thinking high school, he might have come across Philip K. Dick in English class. Science fiction has a far more prominent place in high school curricula than it did in my day, and all the evidence I've seen indicates that, along with graphic novels, this will only continue. The first teachers to include science fiction in their classes most likely visited the work of the genre's most-respected-by-the-laypeople practitioners—Isaac Asimov, Robert Heinlein, Ray Bradbury, Kurt Vonnegut, Ursula Le Guin, Arthur C. Clarke, and Philip K. Dick.

I'm also going to assume that if people in their forties read Dick in high school, it was of their own choosing and not assigned by a teacher.

But all signs point to this reality changing in the very near future. Dick's novel *Ubik* was named one of *Time* magazine's 100 Greatest Novels in the English Language in 2005.[1] Two years later, he became the first science fiction novelist to have his work included in the Library of America. Hollywood cannot adopt his stories fast enough, with seven movies released in the last decade. Ursula Le Guin called him "Our Homegrown Borges."[2] Novelist Jonathan Lethem has been on a Dick promotional tear as of late, editing (with Pamela Jackson) the author's previously uncollected writings in a nine-hundred-plus tome called *The Exegesis of Philip K. Dick* and doing radio interviews about his thirty-year infatuation with the author. Two of those essays appear in Lethem's 2011 essay collection *The Ecstasy of Influence*.

Philip K. Dick lived to see only the prologue of this success. He died of a stroke in March of 1982, three months before the release of *Blade Runner*. Upon release, *Blade Runner* was considered a box office disappointment. Nonetheless, Dick scholars trace the beginning of his recognition in America (his books had sold well for a long time overseas) to *Blade Runner*. Although Dick passed away having written forty-four novels and hundreds of short stories, it was recognition by the movies that first brought his worlds into public consciousness.

You cannot, then, separate *Do Androids Dream of Electric Sheep?* from *Blade Runner* any more than you could *Jaws* by Peter Benchley from *Jaws* by Stephen Spielberg. *Blade Runner* may be only loosely based on *Androids* and is more than a little influenced by screenwriters Hampton Fancher and David Peoples, director Ridley Scott, groundbreaking special effects, and simply by being made almost twenty years after its source material. But despite these differences, both *Androids* and *Blade Runner* have the same beating heart. Both are works of art about identity crisis and what it means to be human. Their mirage-like complexity actually underlines what they have in common.

Androids may be nearly two hundred pages, but, meat-to-fat, it's a short story in a novel's skin. In the very near future, earth has been rendered uninhabitable by war. Citizens are sent away to live on other planets and are given robot servants as a kind of going-away prize. However, a few of these androids are advanced models, practically identical to humans, and they have returned to earth where their presence is illegal. The police have specially designed bounty hunters whose job it is to "retire" (a.k.a. kill) androids who have come back home. This novel takes place over a twenty-four-hour period during which bounty hunter Rick Deckard must retire six of these Cadillac®-level androids. He's also fallen in love with one of them.

The "sheep" of the title refers to humankind's coveting of animals (most of which are now extinct) and building cheaper replicates of actual ones. *Blade Runner* dispenses with this plot entirely and instead simply focuses on Deckard and his bounty hunting. The movie was a visual revelation, credited with perfecting a style referred to as "a retro-fitted future," which would show up later in movies like *Dark City* and *The Matrix*, but is not easy to follow.[3] Characters appear without explanation, certain scenes seem unnecessary, and a much-reviled voiceover from the Deckard character was added at the last minute when test-screening audiences did not understand what was going on.

Preparation for this essay was my third viewing of *Blade Runner*, this time directly after reading *Androids*. I realized that the plot of neither is complicated—essentially 20 percent setup and 80 percent chase scene, which leaves us free to focus on the themes that are less simple but that are really the internal core of both.

"You will be required to violate your own identity," Deckard is told late in the novel. "At some time every creature which lives must do so. It is the ultimate shadow, the defeat of creation."[4] *Androids* takes identity as a question of missing pieces: what makes us human is not permanent but an orchestra in which some instruments can be playing or silent. How easily can humanity be manipulated, obscured, even ascribed to something that isn't actually human? This was no doubt a newer, sexier question in 1968, but it's hardly stale now: let us not forget that Steve Jobs revised the original Macintosh design repeatedly so it would more closely resemble a human face, and when TiVo® first appeared in the late 1990s, it was often referred

to as "a member of the family." Anyone who has taken it personally when a cell phone has stopped working has engaged in adding
humanity to something that doesn't have any.

There's plenty to chew on with those basic questions alone, and
Dick makes sure you don't miss any of them. Jonathan Lethem has
pointed out that Philip K. Dick's prose can be hopelessly tangled,
even within a single page. You get plenty of that here in *Androids*.
Dick sounds an awful lot like someone who has so much to say he
doesn't care if you have stopped listening. Because of that, his larger
philosophical points can come across as a bit intrusive and lecture-y,
as if he had to throw on the narrative brakes just to explain what the
story meant. I'd recommend when you get to a point in *Androids*
that sets your mind turning to either put the book down or speed
past it to where Dick resumes the plot. Otherwise it can feel like he's
shouting in your ear.

Blade Runner has the advantage of being heavily visual and dialogue sparse. It hits you first emotionally and afterward sends the
wheels in your head spinning. "Identity" in *Blade Runner* is less about
missing a part and more tied to longing, the sorrow and emptiness
of not understanding who you are but wanting it anyway. "Maybe
he just wants to know what we all do," says Deckard about his dying
android adversary, "how much time we have left."[5] Humans are the
only animals who know they are going to die. That could be about
cognition, or mortality, or consciousness, or many other things. *Blade
Runner* doesn't answer but rather stays with the emptiness of how that
feels. The piece played on the film's score during the scene where
this question is asked is called "Tears in the Rain."

Both *Androids* and *Blade Runner* raise a cask of questions compared to the tumbler I've just offered up. But I think those questions
begin at the same source: that of who we are, how we know it, and
what not being able to act on that definition feels like. Start there,
and beyond the intrusiveness of Dick's prose and the film's rusty sen-
suality, the skies of both book and film start to open up.

You could also begin with Dick's more acclaimed novels like *Ubik* or *Man in the High Castle*. He wrote forty-four books and hundreds of short stories, so starting from zero will feel somewhat like standing at the foot of Big Rock Candy Mountain and being told, "Here, have dessert." I think the teenagers of now and the very near future will begin with *Androids* but could just as easily start with his other works turned into popular movies, like *Minority Report*.

"Reality is becoming more like a Philip K. Dick novel all the time," claimed a 1979 *Rolling Stone* interview with the author.[6] I think that's true in ways not anticipated. *Androids* feels very much like a novel written in 1968, a psychedelic fantasy with the ice water of violence thrown over it. *Blade Runner* feels less like the Los Angeles of 2019 and more like the Hong Kong or Mumbai of today, crowded, junk-filled, breathtaking progress leaving a populace in Middle Ages poverty. But I think this claim is dead-on when we look at what makes up our conception of ourselves, a vapor cloud of data, preferences, relationships, and reputational points held together by devices that have become members of our family. The evidence of our identity, of the traces we will leave when we are gone, is increasingly at a distance from our own bodies. That may simply feel like the way of things. Or it may feel like a present that would have seemed like outrageous fantasy when Philip K. Dick was alive. *Androids* is a good place to interrogate that feeling and decide if Dick's look at it is the kind of encouragement that tantalizes or irritates. If the former, take the first step into more of Dick's work. And no need to wait for the sequels. They'll be here soon enough.

PART 3
THE INNER AND THE OUTER WORLD

11
IF THIS *LIBRARY* IS PARADISE . . .

I have always imagined that paradise will be a kind of library.
>   —Jorge Luis Borges, *Dreamtigers*

That quote from Jorge Luis Borges is an old favorite of book lovers who probably have also imagined paradise as a library. Or maybe as a giant bookstore that never closes and serves bottomless cups of quality coffee. Borges's quote has been stuck on ceramic mugs, silk-screened on T-shirts, committed to bronze plaques, and slapped on every third tote bag you get for becoming a "Friend of Insert Library Name Here."

The paradise-as-a-kind-of-library line first appeared in a 1960 essay by Borges called "El Hacedor" (The Maker). In 1960 Borges was already a well-known poet and translator in Latin America and was in the fifth year of his term as director of Argentina's National Public Library in Buenos Aires. A year later, at the age of sixty, he would share the first Prix International with Samuel Beckett and come to the attention of book lovers around the world.

Borges had been a library junkie for a long time before that. The son of an academic family educated by English-speaking tutors, Borges had worked for a branch of the Buenos Aires Municipal Library in a working-class neighborhood of the capital. The under-resourced branch had so few books that the young Borges was able to finish his duties in about an hour and spend the remainder of the day out of sight and among the shelves, researching, reading, and writing.

It was around this time that Borges published the short story "The Library of Babel"—which would be among his most influential—in his first collection "The Garden of Forking Paths" (1941).[1] Adopted from his own essay "The Total Library" and a mere nine pages (this is actually on the long side; Borges's longest story is only fourteen pages), "Babel" is a sinister take on our love of libraries and our dearest wish to just be alone with our books. Borges isn't mean or judgmental about it. But "The Library of Babel" takes this wish that so many readers have and asks the kind of questions that make an eternity spent reading sound like a bad dream: If we build a world of our dreams, what happens once we live there? What happens if this world includes other people, with their own nonsense and human failings? And the real humdinger: If we create our own paradise, aren't we still going to be flawed, all-too-human creatures once we get there?

Stop the library, please. I want to get off.

I first read this story many years ago in the 1962 English-language Borges anthology *Labyrinths* and reread it a few evenings ago while waiting for a group of friends to arrive for dinner. When the first guest arrived, she took one look at *Labyrinths* and called it "the one book that defined my undergraduate career." I had been given *Labyrinths* by my parents for my fifteenth birthday after expressing an interest in mazes, Spanish, and M. C. Escher's artwork, probably not in that order. Hearing the paradise-as-library quote drove me back to "The Library of Babel," as I was positive that it contained that sentiment.

It contains nothing even close to it. "The Library of Babel" is told as a short historical summation of the universe as an infinite library by a nameless narrator, nearly blind (as Borges was becoming when he wrote it) and close to death (as Borges was not; he would live another forty-five years). The narrator is old, alone, and scared. He's leaving this brief testimonial of the kind of place the library is for reasons that are not quite clear but contain a low hum of horror. "Perhaps my old age and fearfulness deceive me," the narrator admits. "But I suspect the human species . . . is about to be extinguished, but the Library will endure: illuminated, solitary, infinite, perfectly motionless, equipped with precious volumes, useless, incorruptible, secret."[2] From that alone, Borges's library doesn't sound like anywhere I'd want to spend an afternoon, much less a lifetime.

This library contains an infinite number of hexagonal galleries, each gallery with twenty shelves containing thirty-five books each. Each book looks the same—410 pages long, 40 lines per page—but with differing symbols on their spines. The symbols "do not indicate or prefigure what the books will say," and the narrator uses humankind's attempt to decipher these symbols as a first step toward knowing the contents of the entire library and thus the entirety of what can be known.[3] The human race lives within this vast library, its galleries connected by short staircases and hallways that contain rooms for sleeping and using the toilet. When a person dies, he is "thrown over the railing," which borders the galleries.[4] "Over the railing" is infinite nothingness where a body falls until it has decomposed and been blown apart by the wind.

The universe as library does not mean everyone keeps peacefully to a gallery with their nose in a book. The bulk of the narrator's story is not so much how we have made a mess of paradise but how our most basic and human attempts at understanding it—really, the all-too-human process of understanding our world—have led us to some very dark places. The narrator speaks of a legend long ago in which a man posited that no two books in the library are the same, so the library itself must contain all human knowledge. The result was first celebration, then chaos, as library dwellers dashed through the galleries, looking for the answer to all of life's mysteries. They collided and clashed, often violently, with fellow searchers. An oppositional sect arose a bit later in history that argued that while the library might contain no two identical books, it must contain redundant copies, "works which differ only in a letter or a comma."[5] All those near-copies were simply getting in the way and needed to be removed and destroyed, this group decided, an act that resulted in mass libricide. Finally a corollary legend: in order to know what is contained in the library, someone must have done the cataloging and written it down somewhere. The library must then contain one book, written by one person, that has everything in it. The library's cataloger must therefore be a kind of God. The search for him is more vaguely sketched than that of the clashing pilgrims of yesteryear. But the narrator follows that story with at least two references to an unexplained recent outbreak of suicides within the library. When I read that, I had to put down the book and shudder.

"The Library of Babel" contains many of Borges's lifelong fascinations—mazes, bibliophilia, the subjective retelling of history, and fiction as a kind of elegant lie. Not surprisingly, it's also one of his most utilized and referenced stories. Mathematicians, physicists, and visual artists have tried to both quantify and capture exactly how many books are in the library and what their arrangement might look like if committed to canvas. The idea of the infinite library shows up in both Umberto Eco's novel *The Name of the Rose* and in the Discworld science fiction series by Terry Pratchett. The infinite library is often cited as a prescient metaphor for the Internet and what can happen to humanity when all the knowledge it could ever want is only a (digital) gallery away. "There can be no more perfect case of information glut," wrote James Gleick of "The Library of Babel" in his 2011 bestseller *The Information: A History, A Theory, A Flood.* "The persistence of information, the difficulty of forgetting: No knowledge can be discovered there precisely because all knowledge *is* there."[6]

In revisiting these hexagonal galleries, I was reminded of one of the simplest, least shakable facts about visions of paradise: once we get to Eden, we are all still dumbly ourselves, capable (guaranteed, actually) to make the same silly mistakes out of vanity, greed, and fear that we make right here on earth. Only in paradise, we delude ourselves into thinking that living in paradise means paradise within as well. It never does. We bring ourselves into the garden, into utopia, and into the library. And then we are terribly upset when it no longer looks like paradise—even if we are the reason.

During a particularly hard day of work, I've been known to fantasize about storming away from my desk, finding the nearest comfortable chair, and spending the rest of the day reading. My wife and I have been known to spend most of a vacation reading, intercut with rich food and naps at 2:00 p.m. One of reading's first glories is the escape hatch it gives us from wherever we are now. But that can't be all it is or else a book is just a variation of hiding in the closet from monsters. I like to think we read to lead more active, engaged lives, so that the world both inside and out becomes richer, a place we want to be, not hide away from. Borges's "The Library of Babel" reminded me that perhaps the unstated best quality of paradise is the opportunity to leave when you want to and go back to living.

12

STAYING OUT OF THE *BELL JAR*

I didn't select *The Bell Jar,* Sylvia Plath's only novel, for this book because I read it in high school. I actually hadn't heard of it until graduate school, when I was assigned *The Silent Woman* (1994), a biography by journalist Janet Malcolm on the shaping of Plath's posthumous reputation. Of the twelve students in that class, nine had read *Ariel,* Plath's second and final volume of poetry. I was the only one who had not read *The Bell Jar* in high school.

What I knew about Sylvia Plath before that point could have fit under a bell jar and left room for a dozen bells: I knew she had committed suicide at age thirty by sticking her head in an oven and had made sure her kids sleeping upstairs would not be harmed by the act. I knew that at the time of her suicide, she was separated from her husband—another poet, named Ted Hughes—and that feminist intellectuals often took up Plath and her work as a cause. And I knew that the phrase "in the Bell Jar" had entered everyday speech to mean "in a fog of sadness, often of one's own making." Look for it at about minute forty of the iconic 1990s movie *Reality Bites.*

I expected, then, to read *The Bell Jar* and find a lightly fictionalized retelling of the author's own self-destruction. *The Bell Jar,* based very much on Plath when she was in her twenties, was published a month before her suicide, first in England under the pen name Victoria Lucas. It was not released under Plath's name until 1967 (after *Ariel* had brought her work renewed attention) and not in America until 1971. Even though *The Bell Jar* was written several years after the events described (including Plath's 1953 suicide attempt while in college), I knew enough about the author to not expect that the story of her stand-in, Esther Greenwood, would be one of redemption and healing. That would be separating the world of Plath's art from her own life.

That can't be done. Plath's own life and her writing have been married with a welding torch. "Sylvia Plath belongs to that curious band of poets—it includes Chatterton, Keats, Rimbaud—whose fame is inextricably bound up with their lives," wrote Al Alvarez, a fellow poet and friend of Plath's.[1] Many of those poets, Alvarez argues, also died young and dramatically, but few incorporated death of this kind into their work. Ernest Hemingway, Hart Crane, and Virginia Woolf were, along with Plath, three of twentieth-century literature's terrible losses to suicide. None of them wrote about the act in any meaningful way like Plath does in *The Bell Jar*.

But *The Bell Jar* is no two-hundred-page letter of "good-bye cruel world." It is a fierce and furious story of struggling to live, not making peace with how to die. The author of this book has no trouble getting out of bed in the morning, even if her narrator cannot. This is as much the story of Plath's ambition as it is of her illness. Her prose is first like a hot needle—jabbing, insistent, and alive—then blunted and exhausted by its own fury.

That fury I didn't expect. It felt like getting slapped by a stranger.

Esther Greenwood is much like Plath was in her twenties: an intern at a successful magazine, attending a respected college, and slowly losing her mind. Esther is ambitious, talented, and arrogant. She hates New York, tolerates the other girls in her program, and believes working for the magazine (along with its uncomfortable outfits and dreary parties) is an annoying rest stop on the way to a meaningful literary career. Here Plath writes Esther with fast, chilly confidence. Each line feels as though Esther is ordering a waiter back to the kitchen.

At the novel's halfway point, Esther completes her internship, returns home, and begins to unravel. She cannot sleep, cannot read, and wants help from no one. Doctor's appointments, therapy, electroshock treatments, hospitalizations, and several suicide attempts follow.

Here Plath's sentences feel like slush under slow tires, tired, short paragraphs that can barely hold their heads up. The novel ends with Esther entering a room where her doctors wait; they will ask her questions and determine if she is ready to leave the hospital. Without sympathy, for Esther or for us, Plath ends the story without telling us what happens.

Esther Greenwood is not easy to like. Plath has made the character cold, self-righteous, and dismissive of just about everyone who shows her kindness. She throws away flowers her mother sends her while at the asylum and blows off the only peer in the asylum who shows her friendship. Esther begins *The Bell Jar* as a brat and concludes it as an older brat who has gone through hell but not changed much. I don't wish pain and suffering on anyone. But Esther Greenwood does not earn much sympathy. And there is a ferocity to Plath's choice of writing her that way that can feel almost mean.

You can find a feminist parable or an important work about mental health in *The Bell Jar* if you're looking for it. But what I found is not just a portrait of patriarchy or of sickness but also one of conflict—of a culture with unfair expectations for a young woman, yes, but also of Esther Greenwood making an impossible attempt to both live within those expectations and reject them. That her mind is making it hard to do much of anything is just salt in the wound.

In an appreciation of *The Bell Jar*'s fortieth anniversary, writer Emily Gould wrote, "Like many American girls, I first read *The Bell Jar* when I was around 14. The parts I found most striking then were about Esther losing her virginity and related archetypes of passage" (our narrator loses her virginity, is fitted for a diaphragm, and holds her friend's hair as she throws up).[2] Did other readers feel, as Esther did, imprisoned by the warring forces of their own dreams, of society's expectations, and of their own minds plotting against them? I have never been a teenage girl, but something tells me that that three-way tug-of-war doesn't fade with each generation. It just changes forms.

I certainly felt crazy as a teenager. But was my craziness as bad as being "blank and stopped as a dead baby" with "the world itself is the bad dream"?[3] To me, yes. Your inner and outer world are dangerously close together at that age, and it's difficult to imagine the horrible things in your head not coming true or a world beyond your own where those things simply don't matter all that much. That your mind is often not fully developed enough to make that distinction is some kind of cruel trick of nature.

So why read *The Bell Jar* now, if I'm past all that? Why not read the first half of the novel, then abandon it at the library? Why did I finish *The Bell Jar* in a day and wish it were a hundred pages longer?

Because Esther Greenwood and Sylvia Plath wanted to live—richly, wisely, and well. That attempt, be it confused, arrogant, or misplaced, is a noble one. Sylvia Plath was writing some of her most lauded poetry until a week before her suicide. Had Esther Greenwood not wanted to go on, Plath would not have ended her novel with Esther inquiring after and planning for her future—even if we don't get to find out the result of her meeting with the doctors. David Rieff, Susan Sontag's son, said in a radio interview how angry his mother was when she found out she had terminal leukemia.[4] Susan Sontag wasn't angry that she was sick, Rieff explained, but at the fact that she loved to be alive and that her illness would steal that from her. She died that way, angry, because she desperately wanted to keep living. Decide for yourself if dying angry is the best idea. It's hard to find fault with being angry because you love being alive that much.

The idea of imprisonment that Plath lays bare in *The Bell Jar* is not based simply on the notion that women in mid-twentieth-century America lived under the boot of patriarchy. Plath's bell jar actually had four sides—her ambitions, society's expectations, her illness, and her nonacceptance of the first three.

Just saying that makes me uncomfortable. In my own reading of *The Bell Jar*, I have tried to not diagnose Sylvia Plath's illness or guess at her motives for killing herself. (1) I am her reader, not her biographer or therapist. (2) While author and novel are impossible to separate, I viewed this novel as a reading experience. *The Bell Jar* is a great reading experience, even if you know nothing of Sylvia Plath and her fate.

Earlier this winter, I was at a party and someone asked me if I was planning to include *The Bell Jar* on this reading list. I said I hadn't considered it. Another person in that circle of conversation said she remembered reading it in high school, as did every other girl she knew. "*The Bell Jar* is for teenage girls what *On the Road* is for teenage boys," she summarized. Jack Kerouac's *On the Road* had been my favorite book as a teenage boy.

I thought about the comparison. Published six years before *The Bell Jar*, *On the Road* is a book about youth, about liberation, about America opening like the great gates of Oz, welcoming you to find your true self.

"The only people for me are the mad ones," wrote Kerouac. "The ones who are mad to live, mad to talk, mad to be saved, desirous of everything at the same time, the ones who never yawn or say a commonplace thing, but burn, burn, burn, like fabulous yellow roman candles exploding like spiders across the stars."[5]

On the Road was Jack Kerouac's breakthrough novel. He died at age forty-seven, a slow suicide of alcoholism and self-hatred, but he had a good decade or so of fame and a few more great books in him before then.

What we have of Sylvia Plath is mostly reverberation: *The Bell Jar*, two collections of poetry, a volume of letters, and a raft of biographies and head scratching. New examinations of her mental state and of Ted Hughes's affairs (the man had trouble keeping his pants on) arrive annually. They do not interest me very much.

If you can, ignore the gossip and blame and what-if-ing. Take Ms. Plath's one great novel about battling worlds inner and outer that cannot be reconciled, a book that rages at its own predicament, and weigh those predicaments against your own. Can you imagine having both ambition and duty and also not getting it right all the time? Can you imagine falling short, knowing that those in your life will still support you and that you'll be able to be better tomorrow?

If you can, take *The Bell Jar* as a great novel that could have been the beginning of a great life and breathe with relief at your own. I would not read *The Bell Jar* right before life's next big chapter but rather in the middle of one, where the heights you want to reach are imaginable even alongside the mistakes you've made, where the voices in your head may disagree with circumstance but are, on most days, calm.

13

YOU MAY FIND YOURSELF TRAPPED IN ALEXANDER PORTNOY'S HEAD . . .

P hilip Roth's third novel, *Portnoy's Complaint* (1969), pins us against the frontal lobe of its main character, Alexander Portnoy, and then locks the exit. We're trapped in the head of a nutcase, watching his nutcase thoughts flow from his head out his mouth without filter in a nearly three-hundred-page monologue to his therapist. The therapist gets one line, the last one. The rest belongs to Portnoy. If he has left a single thought out in this counseling session, I fear it would reveal him as having landed from a distant galaxy. Or as actually being President Zachary Taylor. Or as saying, "Ha! Ha! This has all been a joke. Please read the actual story of my life in Philip Roth's next novel." *Portnoy's Complaint* has joy, bile, racism, bodily functions, masturbation, and more than few pairs of befouled underwear. And that's only in the first few chapters.

While still in those opening chapters, I was tempted to throw my body against the wall of Alexander Portnoy's head and run screaming in any available direction. Or collapse from exhaustion. Philip Roth has written Portnoy (perhaps the most famous character of his early career; novelist Nathan Zuckerman holds that title in later books) as one of twentieth-century literature's most exasperating companions. His giant monologue has enough digressions, exclamation points, excuses, and wildly offensive bluster (a chapter titled "Cunt Crazy" is barely as bad as the remainder of the novel) to make the *Ring Cycle* seem like a lullaby. Imagine how exhausting it would be in real life to listen to one manic mind throw off sparks for the audible equivalent of three hundred pages. In fiction, the only escape is to stop reading altogether.

I made that mistake many years ago. A college professor recommended *Portnoy* along with Roth's first book, *Goodbye, Columbus*, after I'd turned in an essay about family dynamics at a Passover Seder table. It was 1993, and I had the completely false idea that every Jewish person at my mid-Atlantic university but me had a nasally voice, loved *Seinfeld* and complaining, and carried a passport from some town in northern New Jersey I'd never visited. I already felt imprisoned in what I imagined was a collegiate, latter-day version of a Philip Roth novel, and I wasn't about to devote my reading hours to replaying it. I resigned, then, from reading *Portnoy's Complaint* in self-righteous disgust after about ninety-seven pages. Would an African American reader hang in there for ninety-seven pages if the main character ate watermelon, drank malt liquor, and played basketball? Did I have to spend that much time with Alexander Portnoy, age thirty-three, an accomplished city administrator who is paralyzed with guilt over wanting to sleep with blondes, who is uptight about the size of his wang, and who resents his hardworking, beaten-down parents and their nagging at him to settle down and start giving them grandchildren? If this wasn't self-hating nonsense, what was? And did I owe it my attention?

I really missed the point. Several of them. Yes, *Portnoy's Complaint* is a novel about self-hating American Judaism, about the voicing of sexual taboos in the 1960s, and about classically Freudian lusting for one's mother and awkwardness around one's own desires. It has enough cursing, misogyny, and detailing of bodily functions and orifices to have been banned in school districts throughout America and in several foreign countries. If something about all that excites you as a reader, you're probably waist-deep in love for Philip Roth already. If it all seems curiously alienating at first, like a tactless party guest who doesn't know when to shut up, try looking at the novel this way: *Portnoy's Complaint* is a few hours trapped in someone's head. The narrator is as recklessly unreliable as a teenager with a new driver's license. One example of many: Portnoy says to his therapist, "If he [Portnoy's father] ever uses the word nigger in my presence again, I will drive a dagger into his fucking bigoted heart." He then uses the same slur and several variants just pages later.[1] The novel is also entirely contained within a single therapy session. We're trapped in that office with Portnoy and the therapist, Dr. Spielvogel, where Roth has aided us in both culturally and legally violating the confidentiality of his characters. And since one character does all the talking, we're getting a subjective version of his autobiography (the one he chooses to tell Dr. Spielvogel), but, given the setting, it's probably more than he would tell you upon meeting you at the gym or even if you became friends.

What is Mr. Roth up to? To me, *Portnoy's Complaint* reads like he's having jolly good fun with the act of creating fiction, of drawing us toward the protagonist and then repulsing us backward, of allowing us to eavesdrop and then horrifying us while we do so.

He opens the novel with straight-faced conventional narration ("She was so deeply embedded in my consciousness that for the first year of school I seem to have believed that each of my teachers was my mother in disguise"[2]) and does not reveal we're in a therapy session until a good dozen pages in. Before that, we think we're just in a story. Then we realize we're being told a story and that we're in the room witnessing the telling. Later (around page 97) we realize that only one person will be talking, so we are also inside that person's head.

This nestling of modes of storytelling gives me the same charge I get out of watching movies about movie making and listening to songs about going on tour with the band. The things we love ignite curiosity about how they're made. And one of the most fun parts of this is weaving the process into the final piece of art—the way Phil Spector used "the studio as an instrument," or Alfred Hitchcock appeared as an extra in his own movies, or the photographer Weegee would include the railing he leaned against to get the shot within the frame of the photo, so you not only saw the image but could imagine him taking it too.

Portnoy's Complaint is a master class at showing how a story shape-shifts based on who is telling it and under what circumstances. It's a big reason why I felt the delight rather than pathos of Philip Roth when I read the book this time around. He is writing (hilariously) about a person in pain. He is having enormous fun in the writing of it. The joy in the process of creating narrative, of storytelling, is as embedded in *Portnoy's Complaint* as the paint on the therapist's office walls.

Portnoy's Complaint made Philip Roth into a giant celebrity, an enemy of an older, more conservative Jewish establishment, and a hero to their baby-boomer children. The book is on both *Time* magazine's and the Modern Language Association's lists of the best novels of the twentieth century and was made into a not-great movie in 1972 (Roger Ebert called it "a true fiasco"[3]). *Portnoy* the movie was directed by legendary screenwriter Ernest Lehman, which I believe was its biggest problem. For a story so much about the weaving of narrative and the confinement of space, perhaps a stage director would have been best. Given the narrative power I saw on the TV series *In Treatment,* which also takes place entirely in a therapist's office, a remake of *Portnoy* would not only be possible but welcomed.

If your high school was loosey-goosey enough to assign any part of *Portnoy's Complaint* (I'm sure mine was; it just never came up), it was probably an excerpt tucked about 80 percent of the way into the brick-sized *Norton Anthology of American Literature.* The included passages were carefully selected to remove all the impurities and nasty bits. In the twenty years since I've been in high school, Alexander Portnoy penetrating a lump of liver is probably no big deal.

I wouldn't read this book before or after a session with your therapist or anytime around a visit with your family. Or while eating, because you'll just end up choking from all the titters and giggles that come about every six paragraphs. It strikes me as a great after-lunch, pre-anything-productive weekend novel, a spirited ride through a troubled, hilarious mind. The author is having a great time opening the door for you. When I put the book down, I was overjoyed I'd given it a second try, that I had much more Philip Roth to look forward to, and that Alexander Portnoy's issues were his to sweat, ours to enjoy, and they belonged to an inner world safely not our own.

14

CANNERY ROW: WHERE EVERYBODY KNOWS YOUR NAME

John Steinbeck opened his twelfth novel, *Cannery Row* (1945), with the book's most famous line: "Cannery Row in Monterey in California is a poem, a stink, a grating noise, a quality of light, a tone, a habit, a nostalgia, a dream."[1] The most important items in that list are the last two. We know Steinbeck wrote the novel inspired by the decade he lived in Monterey (1930–41). Since that time, Steinbeck moved east, spent time in Europe as a World War II correspondent, and then returned to Monterey in 1943. On his return, he found his second marriage faltering and himself—now a wealthy, famous author—alienated from his old home and friends. He wrote *Cannery Row* out of longing for the place that held part of his youth, now gone.

That's an obvious argument for reading the novel with a little age and maturity at your back. But *Cannery Row* is still read a ton by students and people in their early twenties. And sitting at the book's center is a good reason why: *Cannery Row* is a story of communities, of bonds formed when a small group of people think the people nearby are the whole world. It's a place we've all been, at a high school cafeteria table, a college dorm, and perhaps one's first job, when everyone you know seems just as poor, confused, and powerless as you are. It's a place we look back on with fondness in adulthood, when marriages and children are often the focus and when friends are seen less frequently than family. As adults, we often consider these tribal memberships part of our past.

Cannery Row is a short novel made up of shorter episodes in which not a lot happens. We see the principal characters living their lives: Doc, the biologist, who collects and sells marine life; Dora, the madam, who runs the local bordello called the Palace Flophouse up the road; Lee Chong, the neighborhood grocer; and Mack, the leader of a group of itinerant men (known as "the boys") who sleep where they can, drink, and work in the canneries when they need to. The narrative consists of Mack having the idea to throw a party for Doc, the community's most beloved member, screwing it up, then trying again for Doc's birthday and succeeding. Steinbeck intercuts about every third chapter with a fable about a minor character from Cannery Row's unspecified past. That minor character might show up again on the edge of another scene or not at all. The effect is to give the community a history outside simple nostalgia, a "before" that existed even if the narrator did not live it.

Cannery Row is an interdependent world. "The boys" travel in a pack. The working girls Dora employs look out for one another. When characters go off on their own (as Doc does on a fishing trip just before the disastrous first party), bad things follow. The image and metaphor Steinbeck returns to is that of the tide pools just off the shores of town, an ecosystem of individual species who form something greater when living among each other. Indeed, no one on Cannery Row is alone much at all, and no one seems to want it any differently.

As very young people, we find ourselves in these sorts of communities—through school, neighborhoods, and activities—because we can't imagine a world bigger than what we know. As teenagers, we gather in tribes to lessen anxiety. We don't yet know who we are, and a tribe not only gives us an identity now but also supports us as we're finding out. The later manifestation of this same tribe are the college freshmen who travel in groups of twelve like juries on recess. The tribes become looser and nocturnal but no less important when we take our first job, meet after work in the same bar, and seem to date only people in exactly the same situation as us.

The John Steinbeck who wrote *Cannery Row* was not this young, but a very sad man in his forties. He was far from home, about to get divorced again, and he missed his old friend Ed Ricketts (the inspiration for Doc) and the decade they had spent in Monterey together. Earlier novels—*Tortilla Flat* (1935), *Of Mice and Men* (1937), and *The Grapes of Wrath* (1939)—had brought him wealth, critical acclaim, and the attention of Hollywood and Broadway. He still felt part of himself missing. It seems that by writing *Cannery Row,* John Steinbeck wanted not only California back but community back as well.

This kind of hazy nostalgia is not just naïve; it is dangerous, as anyone who has bet on the past never changing will tell you. And yet we probably talk too little about this moment of realization, one we all have and for which life leaves us completely unprepared. Nobody tells us that belonging to what seems like an unbreakable tribe is largely the domain of the young, and that at some point, time has a way of retiring most of our tribes. But if someone had told you that in the middle of your tribal membership, would you have believed him? Or would you have thought "nothing lasts forever" is something a sad, old person in his forties says?

Playwright Arthur Miller and Steinbeck were good friends. Miller had great respect for Steinbeck as a writer and called his prose "like opening paintings."[2] As a person, Miller found Steinbeck a bit of a naïf: "That man was always so moved with everything. . . . He agonized about everything. . . . He always reminded me of an adolescent . . . there was something of a country boy about him . . . there was a blessed naïveté here."[3]

That's one explanation for the bruises Steinbeck's reputation has sustained since his death in 1968. Biographies have blamed his decline, which had already begun during his lifetime, on Steinbeck's West Coast roots, the popularity of his books, and his poor handling of politics (Steinbeck, lefty and pro-worker in so many of his novels, was also hawkish on the Vietnam War, an inconsistency he either didn't notice or didn't explain very well).[4] Even after winning the Nobel Prize in Literature in 1962, John Steinbeck had the lingering reputation as a writer who'd had an incredible run early on and now could not grow up. His best-regarded books (*The Grapes of Wrath*, *Tortilla Flat*, *Of Mice and Men*) had all been written in his twenties and thirties and were, without fail, set in his boyhood home of California's Central Valley. Long after he had moved east, he continued to write about Monterey and Salinas as if his heart ached for the young man he once was there. His tone was often mythic and sunbaked, which felt both appropriate to his novels' time and place but also made it seem like he couldn't help reaching for meaning when there wasn't any. "A kind of sentimental gruffness was Steinbeck's constant temptation," wrote literary critic Roger Sale.[5] Even *East of Eden* (1952), which Steinbeck considered his greatest work, was seen, perhaps unfairly, as both overreaching and as territory he'd covered before.

That *Of Mice and Men*, *The Grapes of Wrath*, *The Red Pony*, and *The Pearl* are standard texts of high school English throughout America can speak to Steinbeck's place as a great American writer as well as confirm the slight: Steinbeck, like Walt Whitman, had all of America in mind as his readers, but, too self-involved and grand to know it, he was really the great storyteller to the American adolescent.

There's a lot of blessed naïveté in *Cannery Row* to be sure: of places where special things happen and memories dwell, of everyone around you knowing and looking after you, of nothing mattering outside your circle of friends. If people are important to you at all, your lists of favorite books, movies, and music contain at least one strong example of this theme (my list has *The Commitments* and *Crooklyn* and the song "Thank You Friends" by Big Star, if you're curious). Now we could argue that those feelings are evidence of a forty-one-year-old Steinbeck, eleven novels into his career, working far below his capacity. Or right at his capacity, sadder still. Or we could argue that Steinbeck put his finger on the near-universal wish of life in this twenty-first century that he did not live to see, that of greater connection, real belonging, and a sense of relationships that are enduring—and voluntarily so.

John Steinbeck published a less-acclaimed sequel to *Cannery*

Row called *Sweet Thursday* in 1954. The two books were combined and adapted for the screen in 1982 and for the stage in 1995. Since 1958, shortly after the collapse of the commercial fishing industry in Monterey, Ocean Avenue, home of Doc's marine lab, was renamed Cannery Row in honor of the book. The last cannery on the row closed in 1973 and was reopened in 1984 as the site of the now world-famous Monterey Bay Aquarium. The Cannery Row Foundation looks after the area's history, as the aquarium and nearby wildlife and water sports have made the area one of California's most popular tourist destinations.

Cannery Row is not assigned to high schoolers as often as *Of Mice and Men* is, which is responsible for half the total Steinbeck books sold each year, or *The Grapes of Wrath*. Most of the fans of *Cannery Row* I know read it on their own after coming to Steinbeck through a different novel or after visiting Monterey. If I were the Cannery Row Foundation, I'd promote a "Best Friends Vacation Package," with the novel thrown in as a giveaway. *Cannery Row* is one of the better literary testaments to friendship and informal community I know. And while it is a novel focused on the past and not the present, I see in that past a reminder that our tribes don't forcibly disband once we get married, have families, or grow older. Rather, they fade from lack of energy and time. To have even a bit of them back is entirely possible. It just takes work now. Back then, before a whole lot of life happened, it just took walking down to Doc's.

15

MY FAVORITE BOOK OF THEM ALL

Sales are limited primarily to journalism schools.
—Mike Weiss,
"Randy Shilts Was Gutsy, Brash
and Unforgettable . . ."

That was the fate the *San Francisco Chronicle* lamented in 2004 regarding perhaps the greatest book written by one of its own: *And the Band Played On* by Randy Shilts, the definitive look at the first decade of the AIDS epidemic in America. Shilts, the paper's national correspondent and first openly gay staff member, had spent four years in research and reporting, accruing personal debt and publisher rejection. Since its eventual publication in 1987, *And the Band Played On* has sold nearly a million copies, has won fistfuls of awards, and was made into an HBO movie in 1993. Historian Gary Wills wrote, "This book will be to gay liberation what *The Feminine Mystique* was to early feminism and Rachel Carson's *Silent Spring* was to environmentalism."[1]

The Feminine Mystique and *Silent Spring* still find their way into the high school classroom as testaments not only to the pioneers who wrote them but also to the movements they birthed and inspire. Read in the present, they manage to reach backward, look forward, and reflect on "now" all at once. "Sales . . . limited primarily to journalism schools" reduces *And the Band Played On* to a vocational textbook, as if *Casablanca* were shown only to students in bartending schools.

This is a shame. If a toehold in classrooms is the straightest path for a book to achieve continuing relevance, the reasons *And the Band Played On* doesn't have that toehold are varied but all unfair: logistical (it is an intimidating 650 pages and only twenty-five years old); bigoted (it is about the AIDS epidemic and includes descriptions of gay sex); small-minded (it argues that the American medical establishment dragged its feet on researching AIDS because the suffering occurred among society's least empowered, which is a small-minded person's notion of liberal hogwash); and confused (does it belong in a current-events class, history, gay and lesbian studies, medical ethics, or only journalism?). I fear though it may suffer from simple myopia, as worthwhile books of historical journalism do with each passing year, nonfiction books about a concluded period can seem so yoked to that period that we view them as safely buried time capsules. *The Emperor of All Maladies: A Biography of Cancer* by oncologist Siddhartha Mukherjee won the 2011 Pulitzer Prize in General Nonfiction. Would it have won if its subject had been smallpox or influenza?

Why have I included *And the Band Played On*? Because it must be included. *And the Band Played On* is one of the great works of journalism of the last century and not just for the reasons you think—depth of reporting (staggering), vividness of characters (heartbreaking), and fervor of prose (like fire). Reading *And the Band Played On* changes you, molding your consciousness like liquid glass with the flame of its rage and conviction. But it also awakens you to exactly what a book is capable of, reminding us that we occupy this world with others and that they suffer as we do. We may not be able to change the circumstances of their suffering, but we are not entitled to be ignorant of it.

It is a book so angry it burns to the touch yet never releases us from the source of its pain: the unfairness and cruelty of deciding that one person's life is worth more than another.

Randy Shilts was the first American journalist with homosexuality as his full-time "beat." When Shilts began working at the *San Francisco Chronicle* in 1981, AIDS had already begun appearing in the city's gay neighborhoods and among its addict population, though it was largely unacknowledged by the national media. Shilts published his first book in 1982, *The Mayor of Castro Street: The Life and Times of Harvey Milk*, about his friend Harvey Milk, America's first openly gay elected official.

And the Band Played On would come five hard years later. By then, America knew of what was once considered only a disease of the promiscuous, the addicted, and the chronically ill. Rock Hudson had died from it. Elizabeth Taylor and Princess Diana made raising awareness and money a crusade. Randy Shilts was convinced that such efforts were too little, too late, that by the time the medical establishment and halls of government cared, thousands had been left to die because of what they injected, how their blood clotted, or whom they slept with.

Randy Shilts was not a brilliant prose stylist, and his sentences sometimes flow with the lyricism of meat cleavers. His gift was that of a fearless, thorough reporter with an unshakable sense of conviction. *And the Band Played On* made him rich and well known—he openly sought this fame—but it also made him enemies in his own community. In the book, gay activists and business leaders who refused to acknowledge the role sex clubs played in spreading the disease get the same frontal assault as government and medical inaction. Gay business owners and community leaders accused Shilts of being a traitor to his own kind.

Though I was too young at the time of its first publication, *And the Band Played On* nonetheless appeared at a crucial time in my reading life. I was twenty years old, a junior in college, hacking my way through a particularly cold autumn in Baltimore. I had declared my major "Writing Seminars" (which just meant creative writing in all its forms) and was busy positioning myself for a career in journalism via internships and independent studies. Terrified of the end of school only eighteen months away, I had no time for any book that didn't hold the answer to my future. I also hadn't read for pleasure since the ninth grade and did not see the point.

It was 1993, and I had grown up with AIDS on the nightly news. Rock Hudson had already died from the disease, as had Queen lead singer Freddie Mercury, a personal hero. Rudolph Nureyev and Arthur Ashe had passed away earlier that year. The HBO movie version of *And the Band Played On* had just been released. I had not seen or heard of it.

In early November, shortly after midterm exams, a friend loaned me the book. I do not remember why. In fact, I remember little other than her saying, "You must read this" and "it's easy. The chapters are short," which was true. When I gave the usual arguments—too busy, lack of interest, mystification at reading being pleasure and not punishment, she looked at me and asked something no one had before or has since. "I'm asking you to read this, to make time. This book is that important to me."

I set down the huge, intimidating book next to my bed and did as I was asked. I read one chapter, two to five pages, each night until I finished. It took the remainder of the school year, but when I finished, through the anger, the shock, and the sorrow, I said out loud to an empty room: "This is what I've been missing."

I have not stopped reading since.

I owe *And the Band Played On* and Randy Shilts my whole adult life. This book has played some part in why I became a writer, why I live in San Francisco, why I value books the way that I do. More than that, it reminds me that we live our lives among others and that we may share nothing with them but DNA. I was not an AIDS sufferer and didn't know any AIDS sufferers. I was too young to understand the extent of the injustice being perpetrated against those who had the disease in the time period Randy Shilts covered. I found out about the AIDS Memorial Quilt at the National Mall in Washington in 1996, the day after the quilt was last displayed.

Still, I reread *And the Band Played On* every few years. I've given every important person in my life a copy. It is the only answer I have when I am asked, "What is the most important book to you?" And if it were it up to me, every high schooler would be given a copy too, so they could witness its power and the power of books in general without the same ignorance and resentment of them that I had. And each year, I leave a copy of it at the AIDS Memorial Grove in San Francisco in honor of Randy Shilts, who perished from the disease in 1994.

We are all busy people who must make time to read. It is worth asking why we would spend our time reading 650 pages about a disease that continues to kill hundreds of thousands of people a year, most of whom are poor, brown-skinned, and far away—people we will never know. My best answer: I believe that great literature (and music and film and theater) is exhilarating, no matter how sad its subject. It reminds us of the bottomlessness of human creativity and passion, of what we can accomplish, of how rich our stories are, of genius like Randy Shilts's, and of how great books can free us from our own sillier, smaller selves.

Like a thaw of a long winter, these books awaken us to what it means to be alive. Every time I reread *And the Band Played On*, even all these years later, I am awakened again.

PART 4

LOVE AND PAIN

16
PRIDE AND PREJUDICE: JANE AUSTEN FOR THE CLUMSIER SEX

Here's what happens in Jane Austen's most popular novel, *Pride and Prejudice*: The Bennet family has five unmarried daughters. The parents must pair them off to suitable husbands to secure financial well-being, as was the custom at the time. Middle child Elizabeth spots handsome Mr. Darcy at a ball, where Darcy acts like a stand-offish jerk. The two run into each other at various social functions, and romantic bobbing and weaving ensues. Other Bennet sisters have their own mating dances at the plot's periphery. Elizabeth takes up with a more handsome soldier for a time but comes around to Mr. Darcy's tight-lipped charm, and during a long, soulful walk, they confess their mutual love and agree to marry. The end.

If that sounds like just your kind of story, (a) you're probably a woman and (b) you've probably read it already. If it sounds like any form of entertainment with the word "chick" in front of its title, there's a reason for that too: Jane Austen is the godmother of the form. Her six novels of men and women tossed—often gently, sometimes with great force—by the whims of the human heart are the DNA of *Waiting to Exhale, Steel Magnolias, Sex and the City, Bridget Jones's Diary, Clueless,* and *Twilight*. Virginia Woolf, who idolized Austen, called her "the most perfect artist amongst women."[1] But the "amongst" Woolf spoke of were other writers, a laughable miniature of Austen's influence. Today, it would be fair to call Austen the finest artist among any literate person with two X chromosomes and the beneficiary of the biggest career aftershock in the history of modern literature.[2] And it's the aftershock that best explains why Austen's novels are read mainly by women and but shouldn't only be.

Jane Austen never published under her own name while she was alive. Each of her books simply had the byline "A Lady," owing perhaps to her standing as a daughter of a respected church official and to the limited freedom of her gender. Austen died at forty-one, having never married. She had never left England, and she called her also-unmarried sister her closest friend. And yet Austen's father insisted his daughters get the same classical education as his sons; her brother Henry later acted as her business manager and literary agent. It would be Austen's nephew James Edward Austen-Leigh's *Memoir of Jane Austen* who reignited interest in her novels fifty years after her death, and literary scholars A. C. Bradley and Lionel Trilling who fanned the flames in the early twentieth century. Austen's novels haven't gone out of print since, but it would be several more decades before her books would be indispensable to women readers everywhere. Before that, Austen's historical endurance was mostly due to men in positions of intellectual and cultural power who admired her.

Where did those men go? For over a century, Austen has been regarded as one of the most important novelists—male or female—writing in the English language. But find a Jane Austen fan these days, and, in just about all cases, you will be looking at a woman.

But that's today. The Jane Austen Society of North America was founded by two men and one woman thirty years ago (although now there is exactly one man on its eleven-member editorial board). In 1924, Rudyard Kipling published "The Janeites," a short story about World War I veterans who were crazy about Austen. Walter Scott, E. M. Forster, and many other novelists not known for their enlightened attitudes toward women swore by Austen's talents in the prime of their careers. These days, Austen scholars tend to be women, their students tend to be women, and the devoted are drawn to annual celebratory tea parties and swooning visions of Colin Firth emerging damp-chested from a lake on British television. Today it surprises no one that Mr. Darcy, whom Firth played, was voted in 2003 as the fictional character English readers would most like to take on a first date.[3]

What happened? How did Jane Austen maintain her seat in the pantheon of history's great writers regardless of her gender and simultaneously birth chick lit and chick flicks—entertainment created for women but also used to denigrate their interests and concerns? This cloven literary legacy would amuse no one more than Jane Austen herself. Austen certainly did not scoff at the romantic travails of her characters (despite England's life-and-death struggle with Napoleon during her lifetime, romantic travails were pretty much all she wrote about), but she also deliberately positioned herself as observer and not as a "gal pal." Austen's prose does not giggle or nod approvingly when you ask it, "Do you think he likes me?" Instead, it views its own world beneath arched eyebrows and ironic asides falling like a lady's intentionally dropped handkerchief. Jane Austen is a wit but a very dry one. She loves her heroes and heroines but finds how much trouble their hearts cause them amusing, even a bit ridiculous. To her we are all fools in matters of love, but she forgives us because it's also what makes us actors in the grand comedy of our species.

That's usually how I like to tell men (or, more likely, the women in their lives eager to convert them) to begin with Jane Austen. Look past the frilly dresses, blue-and-white china, and "Will they finally kiss?" anticipation. Those things were the set dressing of Austen's narrow world, and she didn't pay them much attention either. Instead, focus on how her books are filled with good people trying to be right and proper and failing because they find other good people kinda sexy. The struggle to maintain one's dignity in situations that don't warrant it is the basis of all great comedy, and Austen knew this in her bones. So go ahead and blame her for the whiny Bridget Jones. But can we not also credit her with embodying so much of what we love in the great British comedy of Charlie Chaplin, *Monty Python*, Peter Sellers, and Douglas Adams? Or their children in the colonies like *The Kids in the Hall*, *Saturday Night Live*, *The Office*, or the films of Judd Apatow?

So while many fans argue that *Emma* is the most accessible Austen novel and the best place to begin, I say, why screw around? Grab *Pride and Prejudice*, her most popular, and jump in with both feet. *P&P* is the most "Austen" of Austen books, so you'll be able to hold a conversation, if that's as far as you wish to go. Its several film adaptations also provide ample cheat sheets (the 2008 version starring Keira Knightley is more than adequate and runs two hours instead of six), as does the loony 2007 book adaptation *Pride and Prejudice and Zombies*, which is exactly what it sounds like.

Bear in mind that Jane Austen wrote to amuse her readers as much as herself, so *Pride and Prejudice* would best accompany you in moments of intentional rather than needed relaxation—weekends instead of lunch breaks, a hammock over a moment in a bathroom stall. And consider food pairings, as fans have done for decades. A 2003 BBC poll named *Pride and Prejudice* England's second-favorite novel behind *Lord of the Rings*, so a fair trade with your partner might be Austen for Tolkien and then crumpets downed with a tankard of Elvish wine.[4]

17

MARRIAGE COUNSELING FROM HENRIK IBSEN

These days, a production of Ibsen's *A Doll's House* is likely to resemble a concert of jazz standards: it is as much about the singer as the song. You know this play even if you've never seen it or read it, just like you know *Rhapsody in Blue* even if you didn't know that the tune you've heard a million times was called *Rhapsody in Blue*. Although only a century and change old, *A Doll's House* is now considered such a staple of theatrical history that UNESCO has placed author Henrik Ibsen's original manuscript on its Memory of the World Register, a program that preserves documents of "world significance and outstanding universal value." The play has been performed pretty much continuously since its debut in 1879 at the Royal Theatre in Copenhagen, and the central role of Nora Helmer is one of the half dozen characters an actress feels she must tackle in her lifetime. Nora Helmer may be a comparatively younger creation, but she still sits at a table with Antigone, Medea, Lady Macbeth, Arkadina, and Gertrude.

You may never have heard of *A Doll's House*. But even basic familiarity with theater and its conventions will cause the play to seem distantly familiar, like a third cousin. That's because even if you went to a production tomorrow (there is likely one nearby), you're watching *A Doll's House* for what this particular company does with a story much older than when Ibsen thought it up more than 130 years ago.

Henrik Ibsen wrote the play in the spring of 1878 but wanted to structure the plot as an archetypal tragedy, with beats and arcs as old as Sophocles or Shakespeare. If you know Oedipus pokes his eyes out and King Lear loses his mind, you'll get wind of what's happening to Nora and her marriage to Torvald Helmer over three acts before it actually happens, even though Ibsen leaves her fate uncertain rather than horrific (spoiler: Nora walks out on her husband and children as her husband castigates then forgives her for forging a bank note to get him out of debt).

"A woman cannot be herself in modern society," Ibsen wrote, since it is "an exclusively male society, with laws made by men and with prosecutors and judges who assess feminine conduct from a masculine standpoint."[1] The 1870s were the latter days of the Victorian era, and the Norway of Ibsen's birth and inspiration was even more parochial than mainland Europe. Back then, wives didn't keep secrets from their husbands, didn't bail them out of debt behind their backs, and sure didn't decide to leave their marriages and families behind to, in Nora's words, "see if I can find out who is right, the world or I."[2] Plays of the time didn't carry on about a married couple and their secrets for ninety minutes, only to have the wife split town as the finale. In fact, the prevailing style of theater making of the time was the "well-made play," a tightly plotted domestic comedy or drama of errors with everything wrapped up neatly at the end. *A Doll's House* looked exactly like a well-made play until its final moments. When Nora walks out the door of the house she shares with her husband, Torvald (the play takes place entirely on one set, the house), her last gesture is to slam the door. It is, as one critic called it, "the door slam that reverberated across the rooftop of the world."[3] *A Doll's House* was controversial from the moment the first curtain went up in 1879 and remained so for decades afterward.

It sure isn't nowadays. As you read or see *A Doll's House*, you're probably twitching in your seat for when the flighty Nora will grow a spine and punch her narcissistic twit of a husband in the kisser. The women's movement of the 1970s embraced Nora as a heroine ahead of her time and Ibsen as a playwright who understood the plight of women better than the generations of playwrights he influenced. Although Eugene O'Neil, George Bernard Shaw, and Arthur Miller, among others, have all called themselves students of Ibsen's genius, few have written female characters with the agency and power Ibsen gave to his.

Ibsen based the plight of many of his female characters on that of his mother, who suffered terribly under her husband's alcoholism and incompetent business practices. Nora Helmer is based on the Danish novelist Laura Kieler, who had a renowned career in literature after leaving her husband over an attempt to rescue him and their family from debt. But in an address to the Norwegian Association for Women's Rights made near the end of his life, Ibsen said he "must disclaim the honor of having consciously worked for the women's rights movement."[4] His focus in *A Doll's House* was human suffering in a situation that does not allow a human being—in this case a woman—to succeed at being herself.

Could Nora have left her husband earlier? Was the door she slammed at play's end, as Elizabeth Hardwick has argued, open all along, at least within herself? "The truth is that Nora has always been free," Hardwick wrote in the *New York Review of Books*. "It is all there in her gaiety, her lack of self-pity, her impulsiveness, her expansive, generous nature."[5]

"What ifs" are questions we have the luxury of asking as contemporary readers of *A Doll's House* even though Ibsen may have left room for them without quite meaning to. His plays often seem to catch characters in transition, and he drops the curtain just as another crucial part of their story is to be revealed. Elizabeth Hardwick again: "We would like to go back with (another Ibsen heroine) Hedda Gabler and forward with Nora Helmer."[6] Not knowing leaves room for the reader to guess, even to fantasize. And since Ibsen wrote for the stage, incompleteness also leaves the work open for adaptation, revision, even mutation. A perfect "well-made play" needs to have its shell cracked to feel like more than a faithful retelling. An Ibsen play, normally with a single set and a lot of unknown possibilities beyond the bounds of the plot, has left itself more room to change over time.

Nora's unknown fate and history's response to it points us to questions we can't avoid when reading great literature from long ago. What to do with drama that comes from values and norms that no longer apply? How much can we feel for the plight of Madame Bovary if adultery is still disgusting but not life-ending? What do we take from the illicit romance of Newland Archer and Countess Olenska in *The Age of Innocence* if being divorced no longer has the stain of disgrace it did in 1870s Manhattan? Where does our heart finally land in Nora's story if we don't quite see how this "little lark" (as Torvald calls her) is as trapped in a cage as the story makes her out to be?[7] Beyond interpretation by great actors and directors, where is the drama of Ibsen's drama?

I put the drama in what Ibsen has to say about marriage. I don't doubt for a moment that Nora and Torvald love each other, that they are good parents, and that perhaps at one time they saw their lives headed in the same direction. Now set aside the mores of the day, which Ibsen submits imprison them both. We have two people in the most intimate of human relationships completely unequipped or uninterested in knowing anything about the other. Torvald probably didn't feel he had to, and Nora probably thought her responsibilities lay elsewhere. But the two have made the mistake of committing to each other as members of an institution rather than as people. They've not yet shown any interest in each other as human beings but maintain great passion toward their roles in the abstraction known as marriage. It happens to be Nora who realizes it and has the play's most devastating line: "Does it not occur to you that this is the first time you and I, husband and wife, have had a serious conversation?"[8]

It has not occurred to Torvald. Nora isn't talking about how bills get paid or what schools the children will attend or even, on the face of it, serious subjects like what will happen when one of them dies. She is talking about the serious conversations anyone in a substantive relationship has had: This is what I need, these are my dreams, this is what I want my life to be, and most importantly, this is how being married to you helps make these things happen.

This kind of open communication would have been weird in Ibsen's time, the last gasp of when marriage was seen more as an arrangement of interests, with everyone taking to their roles like employees. But it's also a reminder to any of us in the audience of *A Doll's House* now. Within our relationships, how many of us have committed to being good partners, good providers, and strong parents without giving our full attention and interest to who the other person actually is? From a century ago, Ibsen seems to be telling us that danger lies that way, that we cannot succeed as a couple without an investment in the other person as a person first.

Ibsen was fifty-one years old when *A Doll's House*, his seventeenth play, premiered. He was living in Italy, rich and successful, and had been married for twenty years to Suzannah Thoresen, who really must have been something. Mrs. Ibsen had worked as a translator to bring the work of German playwrights to Norway, and she helped run her stepmother's literary salon. Suzannah held her own with her husband and was one of the several women in the playwright's life who ignited his imagination. Elizabeth Hardwick argues that Hedda Gabler, the lead character of a later Ibsen play of the same name, is a more complete character than Nora. Quite a few Ibsen admirers call 1884's *The Wild Duck* the height of his achievement. I like *A Doll's House* because it was my first meeting with Ibsen. Also, the play is fast-paced, to the point, and throws us right in with one of the Norwegian master's primary concerns, how men and women relate to each other and what happens to their sense of the other's humanity when coarser, uglier forces are introduced. It might seem like a rather simple line of inquiry from the man commonly referred to as "the finest playwright since Shakespeare" and a national hero of his native Norway. Its simplicity and endless interpretations since its birth 133 years ago are a testament to its power—like certain ageless songs that singers keep on singing.

18

EYES ON LOVE

The next time you're in a restaurant, look around the room for any table of two or more people. I guarantee you will be able to tell which group is talking about love and relationships without hearing a word of the conversation. Their bodies will be leaning slightly forward, their heads pointing a little toward the table's center. They'll be smiling, usually out of one side of their mouths, probably with slightly raised eyebrows. The body language of "I am now talking about someone I have been or wish to be naked with" is unmistakable; it is a subject every person on earth encounters, yet we still act as though it's totally unique and special to us. That body language says, "This is a private subject but needs to be said out loud in order to be real."

"There is no agony like bearing an untold story inside you," goes the often-quoted line by Zora Neale Hurston.[1] The untold stories of Janie Crawford, protagonist of Hurston's finest novel, *Their Eyes Were Watching God* (1937), are the three big love affairs of her life, the three husbands she has walked away from or buried. Janie is a grown woman who has returned to her hometown (and Hurston's) of Eatonville, Florida. There she runs into her best friend, Pheoby, and one evening, "full of that oldest human longing—self-revelation," begins to tell the story of her life.[2] That story is divided into three sections, each one matched with the love affair central to it. The novel is this untold story, being told in order to make it real.

The unbreakable bond between love and its testimony is the slow-beating heart of *Eyes*, Hurston's second of four novels. It had been out of print for many years when a 1975 article, "In Search of

Zora Neale Hurston," in *Ms.* magazine by writer Alice Walker revived interest in Hurston and her work.[3] Walker's article coincided with the rising profile of African American authors like Toni Morrison and Maya Angelou, as well as with the growth of black and women's studies departments at universities. *Eyes* has been in print ever since. In 2005, the book was selected for *Time* magazine's list of one hundred great novels of the twentieth century and was made into a film produced by Oprah Winfrey.[4] Eatonville, Florida, now has an annual festival honoring Hurston's life, work, and memory.

If your college had a black or women's studies department, that's likely where you and this novel would have met, if you're of a certain age. Nowadays, however, *Eyes* sits on American-literature reading lists in both high schools and colleges, alongside *Walden, Adventures of Huckleberry Finn,* and *To Kill a Mockingbird.* And while Hurston no doubt had a reader just like herself in mind (I'll explain this in a minute), the urge to tell one's story through one's love affairs is universal, even though it might embarrass us a little to do so out loud.

Hurston was both a participant in and a beneficiary of the Harlem Renaissance, the African American arts movement of the 1920s and '30s, and she counted writers like Langston Hughes, Jean Toomer, and Countee Cullen as friends. *Eyes* was published at the movement's tail end. Despite these kinships, Hurston didn't think much of the Harlem Renaissance's emphasis on artists of the north (Hurston was a Southerner and proud of it) or its attempt at a kind of urbane sophistication she saw as taking the blackness out of black art. Hurston wrote *Eyes* in Haiti on a Guggenheim Fellowship to research Obeah practices in the West Indies, one of many sponsored trips she took as a folklorist of African and African American traditions. To her, the culture African Americans had created themselves had worth on its own and didn't need rationalization or apology to gain acceptance from white America.

Accordingly, *Eyes* seems to have been written in two distinct voices. The third-person voice of Zora Neale Hurston is supple, aristocratic, and quietly sexy, like a Duke Ellington composition. It's not fair to call it "a white voice"; it is more like one removed from the soil where it first grew. It's the voice in which Hurston introduces the novel's title, as Janie and her third husband, Tea Cake, huddle for safety from a hurricane. "They seemed to be staring at the dark, but their eyes were watching God." It's the voice in which she concludes the story: "She pulled in her horizon like a great fish-net. Pulled it from around the waist of the world and draped it over her shoulder. So much of life in its meshes! She called in her soul to come and see."[5]

These are sentences that can be intoned with straight shoulders. They could be read aloud from behind a lectern.

When Hurston's characters talk, a much more colloquial voice emerges. Hurston makes them sound, well, like how these characters would have talked.

Janie and Tea Cake meet:

Tea Cake: "Good evenin', Mis' Starks."
Janie: "Good evenin'. You got all de advantage 'cause Ah
    don't know yo' name."
Tea Cake: "People wouldn't know me lak dey would *you*."[6]

Hurston got plenty of flak for having her characters talk this way. Ralph Ellison called her use of vernacular "a blight of calculated burlesque."[7] Richard Wright was equally unkind, saying the characters "swing like a pendulum eternally in that safe and narrow orbit in which America likes to see the Negro live."[8] Other black artists didn't like how Hurston's method of creating black fiction seemed to romanticize a rural, backward African American experience from an earlier, less enlightened time. Hurston, headstrong and iconoclastic, thought this criticism was nonsense.

Eyes was not much of a commercial success, and Hurston never attained the level of recognition during life that came after her death. Though she would publish four novels and dozens of stories, plays, and essays, Hurston was notoriously bad with money (the publication deal for *Eyes* saved her from eviction) and was constantly scrambling to stay afloat. Near the end of her life, she had to pawn her typewriter, and she died in a welfare motel at age sixty. Her papers were in the process of being consigned to an incinerator when a local police officer who had read Hurston's work saved them. When Alice Walker visited Hurston's hometown in 1973, Zora Neale Hurston, who had once been grouped with African Americans like W. E. B. Du Bois, Langston Hughes, and Jelly Roll Morton, did not even have a marked grave.

All that has changed now. As scholar Henry Louis Gates wrote, "Hurston, like Moses, has indeed crossed over."[9] Both the concerns of *Eyes* and its first champions in afterlife would make it seem like a novel with a specific kind of reader in mind. But there is something more elusively magisterial in this book that held me like an embrace. Under the leadership of Hurston's imagination, I don't feel that *Eyes* is anything like gossiping about last night's date over brunch or spying on other people's bedroom business or even reducing one's life story to a series of affairs. Hurston instead reminded me that love is the set of poles on which we string the story of our life. Love isn't the sum total of our life, but it reveals not only who we gave ourselves to but who we became when we did. Even though love shapes who we are, it does not steal us from ourselves. Love is the map. We have planned the journey.

The daughters of *Eyes* are novels by Carol Shields, Doris Lessing, and Terry McMillan. Each of these writers did some of their finest work by focusing on a protagonist capturing her autobiography highlighted by love affairs. Writer Azar Nafisi calls this "the weapon women have always had. Let me tell you my story, and by telling her story, she takes hold of her life."[10] It's not a weapon invented by Zora Neale Hurston, but her methods—conversational, crafted, loose, and sculpted all at once—are something special. And they seem to resemble the rapidly turning pages of emotions we feel both in love and when we are under the spell of recounting it.

In case you were wondering, Zora Neale Hurston had two unsuccessful marriages and several passionate love affairs, one of which was the basis of Janie and Tea Cake's romance. I've asked myself if *Their Eyes Were Watching God* is a good "breakup" book, a good "I just fell for someone" book, or a better "I'm reflecting on relationships past and present" book. Perhaps all of them. Your body language will probably say something while reading it, without you actually saying a word.

19

I'VE BEEN YOUNG AND AFRAID, JOYCE CAROL OATES. THANK YOU FOR ASKING.

"**B**e careful of your young desires," cautions Joyce Carol Oates's short story "Where Are You Going, Where Have You Been?"—her most anthologized and most read piece of work among high school students. "They can make you a target for dangerous older men."[1] It breaks my heart a little to think high schoolers have been reading this incredible piece for a half century not just on its merits but because high school teachers saw it as a kind of public-service announcement.

"Where Are You Going, Where Have You Been?" is lean and fierce at eighteen pages; reading it is like looking a rat in the eye. It was published in Cornell University's literary magazine *Epoch* in 1966, and if you can look past the scattered references to vintage cars and weekend radio shows, the tale is timeless. A teenage girl named Connie likes to go out with her friends and flirt with boys. Her mother disapproves and wishes Connie would be more like her plain, employed older sister. Her father is largely absent. One night, a no-longer-teenage boy named Arnold Friend spots Connie and shows up at her house the next weekend while her parents and sister are away at a family barbecue. He asks Connie to come for a ride, and when she puts him off, Arnold Friend makes it clear that she is coming whether she wants to or not. Oates ends the story without telling us what happens to Connie, only that she barely hears Arnold Friend's voice because it was "taken up just the same by the vast sunlit reaches of the land behind him and on all sides of him—so much land that Connie had never seen before and did not recognize except to know that she was going to it."[2]

What we have here is *Little Red Riding Hood, Beauty and the Beast, Phantom of the Opera*—choose your death-and-the-maiden parable. It's one of Oates's favorite literary instruments—allegorical short fiction like that of Hawthorne or Poe that borrows heavily from the dark places of fairy tales and fables. In this story she blends in a second genre—headline-y true stories of crime and violence. Oates went on to write novels inspired by the unsolved murder of child beauty queen JonBenét Ramsey and the mysterious circumstances surrounding the death of Marilyn Monroe. The character of Arnold Friend in "Where Are You Going" was based in part on "The Pied Piper of Tucson," Charles Schmid, a thirty-year-old man who in the mid-1960s had a habit of partying with blonde high school girls and then murdering them. He was tried and convicted in 1966, and, though the case received significant national news coverage, it does not seem to me to be as well remembered as the case of Richard Speck, who murdered eight student nurses in Chicago that same year, or as the Manson Family killings just a few summers later. What has kept the name "Charles Schmid" around is eleventh-graders reading the Joyce Carol Oates story with a villain based on him. When she wrote this story, Oates was in her late twenties—younger than Schmid—about the age of a student teacher, with a novel and a short-story collection to her credit. Arnold Friend drives a gold convertible and stuffs his boots to appear taller, just as Schmid did.

Life magazine ran a story about the case in 1966 called "The Pied Piper of Tucson," considered a classic of crime reporting.[3] Even so, the article uses the "is this the kind of town awful things could happen in?" chestnut that journalism can't seem to help resorting to when covering human-made tragedy. Since the Schmid killings also took place in the mid-1960s—during the early days of the Vietnam War, after the urban riots of 1964–65, and around the time of the civil rights marches to Selma, much of the coverage of Schmid carried the melancholy tone of lost innocence, of a simpler time giving way to an age of more common brutality. The fact that Schmid's victims were teenagers undoubtedly had much to do with that too.

"Where Are You Going" was made into a movie in 1985 and retitled *Smooth Talk*. It starred a pre-Oscar®-nominated Laura Dern as Connie and a pre-dad-on-*Everwood* Treat Williams as Arnold Friend. The film was not a box office success, but it received generally positive reviews. A notable exception was noted feminist film critic B. Ruby Rich, who disparaged *Smooth Talk* as a tired return trip to "Blame the Victim Land," where young women cannot enjoy sex but instead must be punished for desiring or even gently exploring it.[4]

Though she doesn't say so, Rich pointed to something bigger happening in movies at the time. From the late 1970s to the early 1990s, American cinema had a small bumper crop of movies about young people, particularly teenagers, who seemed to live in a world without adults and who paid dearly for believing they were more grownup than they really were. Beginning with *The Warriors* (1979) and followed by *Foxes* (1980), *The Outsiders* (1983), *Rumble Fish* (1983), *The Legend of Billie Jean* (1984), *River's Edge* (1986), and *Permanent Record* (1988), each of these movies is implicitly trafficking in a kind of cross-generational fear. At this point, baby boomers had kids of their own but also strong memories of what they were like as teenagers. What becomes of youth rebellion when the world is a much more dangerous place for it to happen in? Why does the world seem so out of control now that the young people are running wild? *Smooth Talk* is a filmed one-act play, a small-town microcosm of this larger cultural anxiety.

Oates splits her story into two uneven parts. She takes only five pages to introduce Connie, her family and friends. Twice that many pages are spent on Arnold Friend and his emotional violation of Connie on the front porch of her family home. Oates has a great few lines that make us feel the switch being thrown between parts 1 and 2.

> They went up through the maze of parked and cruising cars to the bright-lit, fly-infested restaurant, their faces pleased and expectant

as if they were entering a sacred building that loomed up out of the night to give them what haven and blessing they yearned for.

Further down, same page:

> [Connie] drew her shoulders up and sucked in her breath at the pure pleasure of being alive.[5]

One sentence later, Arnold Friend appears.

Oates has chosen this pivot point very carefully. The devil appears right as the maiden feels most alive. But for Connie, that feeling of life lighting her up inside is the signal that brings Arnold Friend out of the darkness—confidence in both her own sexuality and, just as important, a sense of control over it. Lust and desire may be that place in our experience where "aliveness" and "control" part company (I'm sure the same argument has been made for leaping out of an airplane). That place holds the ultimate thrill and terror all at once.

It's a duality most artists I encounter would prefer to explore separately: love as the great energy source of our existence, the loss and misunderstanding of it as our great sorrow. Here the two are actually so intertwined that they even resemble each other.

I remember an argument I've had several times about the legendary Patti Smith song "Because the Night" and why I think her version is a six-course feast and the early '90s cover by 10,000 Maniacs is a pillow mint. The Maniacs version is champagne and roses, the chorus "Because the night belongs to lovers / Because the night belongs to us" is a seductive promise or a toast at the end of Valentine's Day. In Smith's hands, the song contains an element of fear, of losing control, of having to trust your lover but not quite knowing if you should. Look at the way Smith has written into her second verse the lines "The way I feel when I'm in your hand" (which implies possession, whereas *hands* might imply an embrace) and "Take my hand as the sun descends" (the sun "sets" in romance novels. The sun "descends" in an Edgar Allan Poe story).

This is the double-sided puzzle Oates gives the reader in "Where are You Going." Passion and excitement both bring us to life but also to the point where we are most vulnerable to dark forces outside ourselves at the same time. Cooler heads might prevail when we are older. But part of what makes this Oates's most enduring story is how common it is to the human experience of attraction leaving us blind to danger, of love being dangerously close to pain. That the story's title consists of two phrases, one expressing the present; the other, the past, suggests that, at any age, we are always in the process of learning. And how much it can hurt if we haven't learned yet.

20

THE SCARLET LETTER:
I DON'T LIKE IT EITHER

*T*he *Scarlet Letter* can't find a friend. Before writing this chapter, I had probably four dozen conversations about the idea of revisiting books from high school. A good 70 percent of those conversations included mentions of *The Scarlet Letter*, and each and every one followed up that mention with "Never, ever again."

I can't say I blame them. *The Scarlet Letter* is a fussy, airless, boiled cabbage of a book, light on plot and heavy on community values that were already moldy when Hawthorne wrote about them. Not much happens in this story. A high schooler would be right in saying that its three central characters spend most of the text standing around and sermonizing about morality, sin, and salvation. These were important issues in the Boston of the 1640s, where *TSL* takes place, and were apparently of great fascination to the author writing during the rapidly growing and changing America of the 1840s. In all likelihood, contemporary interest in Hawthorne's book has to do with the universal appeal of love and attraction, the wrestling match of desire and doing right, the sadness of wanting something you can't have. Otherwise, we don't have much of an explanation as to why *The Scarlet Letter* marches on as a staple of high school—a great agora of love, attraction, and wanting something you can't have—despite the novel's central crime seeming like no big deal today.

Hawthorne does not make it easy. His prose—exacting, starched, and with the breathing room of a made hotel bed—recounts the events of *The Scarlet Letter* with the verve of a court reporter reading

back testimony. He's chosen the human heart and its terrible long-
ings as his subject and manages to make them feel imperious and,
worse, administrative.

Even swaddled in puritan cloth, this story—indeed, any story—
could have been a thrilling read had it been captured in prose that
feels like clutching a string of firecrackers. Nicholson Baker's debut
novel *The Mezzanine* is 144 pages describing a man ascending an escalator while on lunch break. It's brilliantly written, and, boy, even as
you read, you're saying, "That is some fascinating escalator riding."
In the elemental act of seducing the reader, Hawthorne is as graceful
as a teenage boy on prom night.

Time has not helped. Whatever wisdom or reader's experience
I've gained in the two decades since I graduated from high school is
useless in bringing me onboard with *The Scarlet Letter.* The novel is a
scant 190 pages and felt like *Infinite Jest,* a "magnum opus" in all the
wrong ways. Single pages would lose me mid-paragraph. Passages of
adultery and lust drove me into the arms of household chores. And
Hawthorne's prose is a deadly hybrid: dull in delivery, then intrusive
to boot. He values the issues his book raises more than the people
who battle them out, and he communicates this by talking over and
louder than his characters.

The Scarlet Letter feels like either a sermon or an extended diag-
nosis swaddled in fiction. If my test of what books belong here is, at
its most basic, something you read in high school that you can enjoy
in adulthood, this novel does not succeed.

And here I am recommending it anyway. Not because of what we
can learn about the painful meeting of desire and judgment (I can
think of sixteen other books that do that with your pleasure foremost
in mind) but because of what *The Scarlet Letter* does not do. *The Scarlet
Letter* does not care about being a good read, at least not anymore.
But that doesn't make it a useless book. Its endurance as art, despite
it being so profoundly unlovable as fiction, raises perhaps the most
basic and central questions of reading beyond simple escapism: What
do we gain from reading difficult books? Does the author owe us a

good time or is reading like athletics, and we only get better by challenging ourselves?

That may seem like a rather ordinary candy-versus-vitamins argument about culture. And yet it remains as relevant as ever, perhaps even more so now. When we feel like we have increasingly less free time to read and, at the same time, increasingly more options of what to read, the question of "something I like versus something I will learn and grow from versus why not both?" is with us every time we finish a book then decide what to read next.

An overview: Hester Prynne is a young woman living in 1640s Boston who has given birth to a daughter supposedly while her husband is away at sea. She is convicted of committing adultery and forced to wear a scarlet letter *A* on her clothes as a badge of her misdeeds. Over the course of seven years, we discover her husband is an elderly physician, Roger Chillingworth, and her lover is the town preacher, Arthur Dimmesdale. Chillingworth discovers the affair and manipulates himself into caring for Dimmesdale when the preacher fails ill. Hester and Arthur plot to run away to Europe together. Roger finds out. Arthur becomes too sick to leave, confesses the affair, and dies. Roger dies a year later. Hester dies way after that and is buried with an *A* on her tombstone for reasons I don't quite understand.

This summary above was cobbled together after several Google® searches. Had I tried to put it together via a sustained reading of the book, I would have been buried alongside Hester Prynne, with a paperback copy of *The Scarlet Letter* laid on the headstone.

Although some of Hawthorne's early critics professed enjoying Hawthorne's short stories more, *The Scarlet Letter* was an instant bestseller upon its publication in 1850. D. H. Lawrence and Henry James both cited it as one of their favorite books. It's been adopted into every conceivable artistic medium multiple times. The 2010 film comedy *Easy A* is a fine place to get a taste of the novel playing itself out in the halls of a contemporary high school.

In a 2002 article for the *New Yorker*, novelist Jonathan Franzen submitted that there are two opposing models of the novel: the

Status Novel and the Contract Novel.[1] The Status Novel is a singular indication of the author's genius. Its aesthetic value exists independent of its likeability. The Contract Novel is an implied acknowledgment of a work of fiction as an act of communication. The writer is thereby creating art both for its own sake and also as something intended ultimately to be enjoyed by someone. As Franzen puts it (better than I did), "According to the Contract model, difficulty is a sign of trouble. In the most grievous cases, it may convict an author of placing his selfish artistic imperatives ahead of the audience's legitimate desire to be entertained. Taken to its free-market extreme, Contract stipulates that if the product is disagreeable, the fault must be with the product. You're the customer. You rule."[2]

Agreed. Whoever the reader was for *The Scarlet Letter*, he or she is long dead and so are their grandchildren. Hawthorne's greatness is on ample display in his short fiction, and I would recommend a Sunday morning with the stories "Young Goodman Brown" or "Rappaccini's Daughter" in a hot second. *The Scarlet Letter* feels like a week I will never get back and already miss.

So why is it here? Because I am no longer a teenager ruled by my fear of boredom. Because as an adult, I can decide that nothing that bores me is worth my time (It's my free market, right? says Franzen, backing me up) or that reading richly is like eating richly and living richly, that it comes from patience, time, and effort, and sometimes effort is a fucking drag. So much of a drag that few books are worth it. And while it's totally fair to say, "I don't care that this book has lived on for 150 years, it does nothing for me," those might be precisely the books that shove us into the next phase of our development as readers, that make us read wider and more ravenously and, I would submit, make us better readers for it.

The Scarlet Letter's inclusion here is more of a glyph, a stand-in for every book that once was or even continues to be too unappealing or hostile to you, the reader, to land on the top of your nightstand pile. I'd say for one of every ten books you read, contend with a difficult in-law like this one. They aren't there to be our friends, which is okay. Not every book worth picking up must be.

PART 5

WORKING

21

BARTLEBY IN THE BREAKROOM

You've got a Bartleby at your job. Their name may be Josh or Antonio or Sally, but feel free to mutter "Bartleby" when you pass them in the break room. "Bartlebys" are people who do their job just as asked until one day they decide there are certain tasks they simply won't do. They get away with it because (a) they work in a small, understaffed office and no one has time to argue with them; (b) they work in an enormous office and no one has noticed them; or, the most likely these days, (c) they have special skills that make them difficult to replace. Regarding (c): anyone who has submitted a project to the design or engineering department and had that department do 71 percent of what was asked with no explanation as to the missing 29 percent knows what I'm talking about. You've just interacted with a little bit of Bartleby sprung loose from pre–Civil War Manhattan and filling a desk near you here in the twenty-first century.

"Bartleby," of course, is the title character of the Herman Melville short story "Bartleby the Scrivener: A Story of Wall-Street" (1856), which Melville first published anonymously as two separate magazine articles in *Putnam's Monthly* (a predecessor to the *Atlantic*). Other than *Moby Dick* and perhaps the novella *Billy Budd*, "Bartleby" is Melville's best-known work and is considered one of the finest examples of the American short story form. It also shows up repeatedly on lists of great books and stories concerning the workplace. We'll focus on this second point.

The thirty-page "Bartleby" is narrated in flashback by an unnamed elderly lawyer. The lawyer hires a young man named Bartleby as his office's fourth copyist, or scrivener (this was how documents were duplicated in the days before the Xerox® machine). Bartleby is quiet and hardworking, and he appears to be without history—no family or friends, no existence before he answered the law office's "Help Wanted" advertisement.

For a while all is well. Then one ordinary day the lawyer asks Bartleby to perform a routine task, and Bartleby replies, "I prefer not to." The lawyer cannot make head or tail of this and submits the request again. Bartleby gives him the same answer.

From here, things slide downhill, first to strange, then to exasperating, and finally to absurd. When asked to do any task that is not copying, Bartleby counters with a mild "I prefer not to." When argued with, he says nothing. Eventually he tells his employer he is through with copying too. One strange night, the lawyer stops by the office to find Bartleby there, not working but doing, well, nobody really knows what he is doing. The door is locked, and Bartleby will not let his employer in. Before too long, the other three copyists are slipping "I would prefer" demands into their workplace interactions. The lawyer moves his business to a new location, but Bartleby returns to the old one and won't leave; "like the last column of some ruined temple, he remained standing mute and silent."[1] The building's landlord says this squatter is the lawyer's responsibility. The lawyer begs Bartleby, threatens, pleads, even offers to take him into his own home and look after him. Bartleby won't be moved and is arrested, then taken to prison. The lawyer visits him there, only to discover Bartleby has starved himself to death.

After "I would prefer not to," the story's most famous line is its last one: "Ah Bartleby! Ah humanity!"[2] The lawyer utters it after discovering a single biographical detail about his strange copyist: Bartleby used to work in the post office's Dead Letter Office. Melville then throws together a half dozen lines about what insight this discovery gives the narrator:

Dead Letters! Does it not sound like dead men? Conceive a man
by nature and misfortune, prone to a pallid helplessness, can any

business seem more fitting to heighten it than that of continually handling these dead letters and assorting them for the flames?[3]

I don't think we're supposed to buy the narrator's heartbreak. The tone here is markedly different, bordering on goopy, from the rest of the story, which has the cool recall of, well, a lawyerly summation. Also Melville has set up Bartleby as a room with a locked door. Bartleby unexplained is the source of the story's power. The narrator's flailing attempt at an explanation only underlines its futility, which is one of the things I think Melville was after: the sadness of not really knowing something, the pain of connections severed and relationships left incomplete.

Descendants of Bartleby have been reincarnated many times since his passing over 150 years ago. Albert Camus cited the story as an influence on his own tilted literary outlook. The comedy of Andy Kaufman is a descendant of Melville's silent copyist; Kaufman was known to stand on stage saying nothing, reading *The Great Gatsby*, or singing nursery rhymes. His art dared the audience to laugh, shrug, or stay baffled as to when the joke ended and real life began again. Chauncey Gardiner, the hero of the 1979 film *Being There*, played by Peter Sellers, is another enduring character entirely committed to a worldview that he doesn't bother to explain. As a result, others (including the president of the United States) graft their own meaning onto his cryptic phrases and actions. Bartleby has also been called an ancestor to the slacker. Essayist Sven Birkerts has offered the scrivener up as a model of idleness exemplifying contemplation and serenity rather than lazy avoidance of work.[4]

Melville was having a hard go of work when he wrote "Bartleby." Finishing *Moby Dick* had exhausted him, and the book had sold only moderately well. His next novel, *Pierre* (1852), had been a flop. One theory of biographers on what Melville meant by "Bartleby" is that the character symbolized a writer who is stuck with a project he has given up on (Bartleby refuses to work after copying morning and night at the beginning of his employ) and who cannot fit into an increasingly commercial society (that may be why Melville chose the subtitle "A Story of Wall-Street," even though Wall Street plays a supporting role, at best). In the mysterious scrivener, Melville may have seen a version of himself, a frustrated artist who cannot find space or welcoming for his creations.

A valid theory, but not a very useful one. "There's no place for an artist like me!" today seems to be an anachronistic, uptown problem in a time when there's a URL (if not an income) for just about every creative flight of fancy imaginable. Instead, Bartleby as a kind of workplace wraith seems far more relatable. Each of us has worked with someone we spent hours in proximity to, five days a week for months or years, and didn't really know at all. Perhaps neighbors or merchants are the only other people we see with such regularity who can still remain unknowable.

Not knowing usually leads me to create all kinds of nutty backstories—the polygamist in Human Resources, the ex–circus clown in System Administration, the serial killer working in Corporate Development. There are moments—office Christmas parties or smoke breaks in the parking lot—when someone you work with reveals something of themselves you didn't know, and, for a moment, they become a person instead of a ghost you catch sight of when looking up from your computer or coming out of the bathroom. That might continue until you graduate to being friends as well as colleagues. Or it might collide with your sense of what belongs at the office stays there and may never go any further than that.

I put down "Bartleby," wondering how well we really know the people we see every day at work. If I still worked in an office, I'd probably take a lunch break alone, maybe in the parking lot or at a bench down the street, read this story, then go back to work. I'd ask myself how strange it is that two-thirds of my day isn't spent with friends or with strangers but instead people who can seem less familiar by their daily presence.

"Bartleby" ends up on a lot of lists of "great books about work" and in more than a few melancholy essays about how contemporary writers don't focus on the workplace much anymore. Creative writing graduate programs are typically blamed for designing an environment in which a certain class of young writers has no idea what it's like to have a real job before their first book is published.

I don't think that's quite fair. We seem to have ceded the workplace to television and, to a lesser extent, the theater as being the best mediums to tackle the daily magnetic pulses of working. There we can have a popular sitcom called, simply, *The Office*, based on jokes about fixing the copier and inappropriate workplace behavior. Plays like David Mamet's *Race* (2009) can take place entirely in an office, something Mamet has been doing for thirty years with dramas like *Glengarry Glen Ross* and *American Buffalo*. Particularly sitcoms have stationary settings, regular, repeated characters and an indefinite ending, mimicking the composition of the workplace.

Idea for office mischief: Find your "Bartleby" and leave a copy of Melville's story on their desk. Spy on them and see if they read it. On the unlikely chance they do, I'd wager their first thought when setting eyes on Melville's classic is "I prefer not to."

22

THE WORK/LIFE BALANCE
OF SHERLOCK HOLMES

Are you a Holmes or a Watson? And by that I don't mean, are you a detective or a doctor, a boss or a first lieutenant, a violinist or a person with a gambling problem. I mean, are you the kind of person who sees their work as fundamental to their identity or the sort who works in order to make room for the things that really matter?

There are many ways to read the original Sherlock Holmes canon of four novels and fifty-six short stories that Arthur Conan Doyle wrote a little over a century ago—as puzzle boxes, second-wave crime fiction, postcards from Victorian London, or studies in homoerotic romance; perhaps even as fashion primer, if waistcoats and deerstalker hats flatter you (for me, hats yes, waistcoats no). But I've just emerged from a two-day Holmes binge, and the magnifying glass that Mr. Doyle's creation kept handing to me was turned to "work." What do Sherlock Holmes and Dr. John Watson show us about what we do for a living and how we choose to spend working hours?

I'm a relative newcomer to Holmes, having torn through a few stories in childhood as all reading kids seem to do and having seen a movie or TV adaptation when one came along. I believe there was also a Halloween costume of misaligned plaids and an empty calabash pipe sometime around 1983. But I hadn't read Sherlock Holmes at novel length or in adulthood until now. I'm in my late thirties, which makes me, according to calculations by fans of the characters, around the same age as Watson and Holmes. When I found that out, an absurd fantasy emerged that I could now relate to their worldly concerns the way I had been sure I could with Encyclopedia Brown, Boy Detective, when we were both fourth-graders.

The third Sherlock Holmes novel, *The Hound of the Baskervilles* (1901), was my beginning point for several reasons.[1] (1) It is the Holmes book that pops up most often on high school reading lists (if said high school is freewheeling enough to consider detective stories "literature"). (2) *Baskervilles* is the Holmes story I remember hearing the most about as a child, usually followed by a long howl at an imagined moon. (3) It was the first Holmes work of any kind Doyle wrote after killing off the character eight years earlier in the short story "The Final Problem." (4) The author had brought the character back due to overwhelming public demand. His heart was in writing historical fiction, which tells me that this was the first Holmes tale he saw more as professional obligation than artistic calling.[2]

Even if you know only a little about Sherlock Holmes, what happens in *The Hound of the Baskervilles* won't surprise you at all. Stranger comes to 221B Baker Street. Holmes makes rapid deductions, takes case with some reluctance, makes progress only to be held up by red herrings and potential suspects. Watson contributes both in insight, companionship, and heavy lifting. Case thought to be lost. Climactic showdown follows, after which Holmes explains everything. Pipe smoking and trips to the opera stuffed in plot crevices. Whole thing documented by Watson. The prose has the same elegant logic we hear when Holmes offers an explanation for a misplaced ashtray.

Here's the part that did surprise me: Dr. Watson does not practice medicine in *The Hound of the Baskervilles*. At all. Never sees a patient, diagnoses an illness, or makes a house call. Never even relays a bit of medical knowledge to help the case. He does a lot of other things as co-detective with, foil to, and agent of Holmes. But these are add-ons, avocations. It's completely unnecessary to call Watson "Dr." in this novel because he never acts as one.

Now I know that Doyle explains in the first Holmes novel

that Watson has retired from practice due to a war injury. Doyle himself was a doctor who had stopped practicing by the time he wrote *Baskervilles*. But I've also seen enough adaptations of Holmes (including the most recent film version starring Robert Downey Jr. and Jude Law) where Watson's profession is of great consequence to the plot. Here it doesn't matter at all.

Holmes, on the other hand, does not seem to exist outside his chosen profession. Yes, he is a man with carefully chosen hobbies (smoking, violin playing, opera going), but they are all there to give him time to chew on the case at hand. Early at the end of chapter 1, Holmes practically dismisses the Baskervilles case when the client, Dr. Mortimer, calls him not "a precisely scientific mind" but a "practical man of affairs."[3] Perhaps it is Holmes's ego taking a slap. Or perhaps Dr. Mortimer has unwittingly insulted Holmes by suggesting detective work is simply Holmes's job and not his reason for being.

Take the component parts of the character of Sherlock Holmes and try to remove any one. Minus the deerstalker cap, the obsessive cleanliness, the violin, or social awkwardness, we've still got Holmes. Now give him another profession. Can you picture Sherlock Holmes as a florist, a judge, a historian, or a doctor? How about if he still solved crimes like any number of literary or television gumshoes who are also novelists, physicians, or bored millionaires? Picturing Sherlock Holmes with another job is like picturing an eagle without wings.

Doyle made Sherlock Holmes a man who is his job and John Watson a man whose avocation/stand-in career is continually shuffling his titled profession off the page. Doyle had based Holmes on Dr. Joseph Bell, one of his teachers at medical school with remarkable powers of deduction. His own professional life bore more than a passing resemblance to Watson's—a chosen career with equally demanding ancillary jobs and hobbies. Doyle was still a doctor well into his career as a writer. He also ran twice for Parliament, was a noted political and social justice activist, and an avid golfer and cricket player. And though Sherlock Holmes made Arthur Conan Doyle both wealthy and famous, the author saw himself more as literary grandson to Sir Walter Scott.

Like Scott, Doyle wrote historical fiction, lots of it, but that's not how history remembers him. He would return to Holmes when he needed money or when the demands of his readership became too loud to ignore. But I get the sense that to Arthur Conan Doyle, his prized creation was not his passion, but a job.

This little trio of Holmes, Watson, and Arthur Conan Doyle represents three sides of a prism, splitting and combining the connections between work, meaning, and legacy. The enduring love we have for Holmes is completely tied up in his skill as a detective. Our affection for Watson is yoked to his relationship with Holmes, a workplace relationship as intimate as marriage. Doyle wanted to be remembered as a particular kind of writer, yet he succeeded at being another type and managed to fit in a very rich life outside his profession. Arthur Conan Doyle is a real person who could no more control how we regard him a century later than he could fate. But he smuggled in to his most famous creation—the one he downplayed and even resented a bit—a twin portrait about work and its relationship to our identity. And perhaps telling the stories of Holmes from the point of view of Watson was Conan Doyle's own way of examining his feelings about being compelled to write tales in which his heart, like Watson, was not the primary actor.

The place of the Holmes novels in history adds a whole other series of clues. Doyle had been inspired by the stories of Edgar Allan Poe featuring detective C. Auguste Dupin, published nearly a half century before Sherlock Holmes. However, Dupin and his contemporaries in French literature were amateur sleuths who solved crimes as a hobby. It was the invention of Sherlock Holmes that made the professional crime solver an icon of popular literature. Indeed, Mr. Doyle had done such a convincing job that he would receive letters by the armful from readers who thought Sherlock Holmes was real and wanted to hire him.

The late Victorian era of Sherlock Holmes was also the time when the study of crime became increasingly professionalized. The unsolved Jack the Ripper murders, which happened a year after the first published Sherlock Holmes novel, birthed our modern ideas of criminal profiling. In France, the "father of sociology," Émile Durkheim, spent the last decade of the nineteenth century writing and popularizing the study of crime as an important element of how societies, not just criminals, worked. Doyle's own mentor, Joseph Bell, had been a pioneer of forensic science and had consulted on several murder investigations while Doyle had been writing the Holmes novels. In 2002, England's Royal Society of Chemistry awarded Sherlock Holmes an honorary fellowship for his contribution to the use of science in criminal investigation. Holmes remains the only fictional character to ever receive this honor.

Arthur Conan Doyle's balance of professional ambition and multiple outside interests seems to have worked for him. By all accounts, he had a happy, rewarding life. But might he have had more peace of mind about Sherlock Holmes if he had been a bit more like Sherlock Holmes, if he had fully embraced his professional gifts as personal destiny? I don't know. But while we have loved and looked on in wonder at Sherlock Holmes for over a century, he strikes me as someone whose obsession with his chosen career is admirable but not likeable, someone to look up to but not befriend. The only friend Holmes needs is Holmes. "He's outside society," said novelist Leslie S. Klinger, who penned a revision of Holmes in which Holmes is a female detective named Mary Russell. "He is driven by a pursuit for justice, but it's his own brand of justice, and I think part of us yearns to be like that: strong, independent, above worries, above how we fit in with society."[4] All of which sounds very heroic but not exactly warm and inviting. Watson and Doyle seem more generous, likeable, and, quite frankly, happier.

It is rare to find people who can focus on only their profession, no matter how much of a calling it may seem, and not sacrifice their own happiness. I marveled when I saw a documentary on the folk singer Pete Seeger, who is ninety-two years old and still playing his banjo for schoolchildren, much as he has done for the past seven decades. Here is an artist who was lucky to locate his life's meaning at a very young age and devote himself to it fully. But Pete Seeger is also a happy and contented man, not because he is a musical legend but because music served as a roadway to meaning elsewhere, in social justice, politics, family and friends, and the beloved Hudson Valley where he lives. Had he just concentrated on being a great folk musician, I wonder whether he would be this happy now. Would he have even lived this long?

It would be wrong to suggest that Sherlock Holmes depends on obsession or single-mindedness. Even his genius would be less interesting if it were not decorated with ornaments—the filthy office, the tobacco inside a slipper, a weary relationship with the London police. A darker Holmes shows up elsewhere in the canon; he is prone to depression, mania, and fits of cocaine use. But Holmes has no wife, no friends, little family to speak of, and none of that gets in his way of being the world's greatest detective. Is Sherlock Holmes happy with Watson and his cases and his genius? Doyle does not answer that but leaves more than a few clues lying around the Holmes stories for the reader to decide.

The character of Sherlock Holmes is as alive now as ever, having never gone out of print and being the subject of a new BBC series, the show "Elementary" on American television, and a film franchise. In the franchise's first film, Watson's prowess as a doctor is of great consequence; the first forty minutes of the film practically hinge on it. This might simply have been the impossibility of casting a star like Jude Law as Watson and having to relegate him to taking orders from Holmes. Or it might have been that a modern audience simply would not understand a character called "Doctor" who never acts as one and whose job seems to matter so little in the face of his outside interests, without having a giant trust fund or living with his mother.

Are you a Holmes or a Watson? Perhaps an Arthur Conan Doyle? When it comes to work, I am mostly a Holmes. When it comes to life, I strive for Watson and Doyle's balance and sense of contentment. What I love about the Sherlock Holmes novels is not just that Mr. Doyle created perhaps the most memorable character in modern literature; he then topped himself by throwing in an equally compelling working partnership. Holmes and Watson are not just colleagues, friends, blood brothers, and bickering siblings. They are also a detective and his agent, a second-career doctor and a new profession taking shape before our eyes.

There are more than two ways of viewing work, to be sure. But the choices Holmes and Watson represent feel as real and compelling to me today as when they took them up and down Baker Street through the fog over a century ago.

23

WORKING AT RELAXING WITH DAVID FOSTER WALLACE

David Foster Wallace did not see himself as a journalist, even though he made a significant part of his living that way. Wallace put together an income as most successful-but-not-Stephen-King-successful novelists do—book sales, magazine and newspaper assignments, teaching gigs, the occasional speaking engagement, grants, and awards. But when asked about the journalism part of that living, he'd answer as though journalism were a weekend hobby, like gardening or building model trains. "I think of myself as a fiction writer," he told Charlie Rose in a 1997 interview.[1] Never mind that Wallace was on Rose's show under professional obligation to promote his first published collection of magazine journalism, *A Supposedly Fun Thing I'll Never Do Again: Essays and Other Arguments*.[2] "If there's a shtick," Wallace told Rose of his magazine work, "the shtick is, Oh gosh, look at me, not a journalist, who's been sent to do all these journalistic things."

The "not a journalist" was underselling on Wallace's part. Nearly every piece in *Fun Thing* required substantial reporting, interviewing, and research, the basic toolset of good journalism wielded with the skill of a master craftsman. Wallace's magazine work received heaps of praise, including a National Magazine Award in 2001. Yet he preferred to call the contents of *Fun Thing* "essays," a literary classification closer to what he saw as his real work at the desk of fiction. Novelists often dip into writing "essays." A journalist writing an "essay" would probably call it "an op-ed" or a "back-page piece." Wallace segregated these two kinds of writing he practiced, using the term *work* as a divider: journalism was "work" that paid the bills. Fiction was "work," as in "an artist's collected creative output."

Following David Foster Wallace's suicide at age forty-six in 2008, there was a bit of debate about whether his true legacy is his five works of fiction or his two collections of essays. I've no idea why it's either/or and not both. In an article written on the eve of Wallace's fiftieth birthday, book critic Daniel B. Roberts reported that in some academic circles the rush is on to steer newcomers to Wallace's singular achievement, the 1,100-page cliff face of a novel, *Infinite Jest*.[3] To begin with the essays, the argument goes, is to take the literary low road and therefore cheat oneself of Wallace's true genius.

Horseshit. Had I listened to this argument, I would have started *Infinite Jest*, given up after a week, and never looked twice at *Fun Thing* or any other book of Wallace's. That the collection's eponymous title essay is ninety-three pages long was intimidating enough. Starting with Wallace's leviathan and then expecting a new reader to wipe their mouth and circle back to the essays is machismo masking wishful thinking, like inviting someone into the White House in hopes they develop an appreciation of attics.

"A Supposedly Fun Thing I'll Never Do Again" (the essay) refers to a report David Foster Wallace filed after seven days aboard a luxury cruise ship. It's relaxation at gunpoint and a barn-sized target for ridicule, and yet Wallace is not cynical or mean, not stoned by the insanity or too precious to enjoy it. Instead he put together one of the greatest pieces of writing about our relationship to work I have ever read. And it works on three levels: as a study of vacationing as the antithesis of working, as a look at how hard we should "work" at happiness and contentment, and as the question of how successful we can be at something we don't really consider our true calling. These are questions everyone who doesn't sleepwalk through a day on the job has on their mind. It's probably entered your thoughts even while you're trying to relax or "get away from it all." Wallace raises these questions in a manner both brilliant and, more important, hilarious.

"Fun Thing" began life as a 1996 article in *Harper's* called "Shipping Out."[4] At ninety-three pages in book form, I can only assume the article must have seemed as gigantic in the magazine as the cruise ship itself or that it had been typeset by a potato bug. The essay also includes 137 footnotes, which can make it seem like the author didn't know when to keep quiet. But Wallace's footnotes are every bit as entertaining as the essay itself, a director's commentary that magically adds to and doesn't get in the way of the movie.

Book critic Laura Miller called David Foster Wallace "a noticing machine," which may be putting it lightly.[5] Not one moment of the sensory supernova that is a luxury cruise escapes him. A note of praise to a "narcoleptically comfortable" deck chair takes twelve lines and builds to the compliment that the chair doesn't "stick and produce farty suction noises whenever you shift your sweaty weight on it."[6] A look around his cabin is a full nine pages with mini-treatises on window glass, hair dryers, shower heads, and a screamingly funny musing on where precisely waste goes when flushed down a shipboard toilet ("less removed than hurled from you").[7] Jet Skis® are labeled "the mosquitoes of the ocean," a perfect characterization I'd never considered.[8] Wallace tosses off a few of those each paragraph. A dozen or so pages in, and you're ready to follow David Foster Wallace through an afternoon of filling out an income tax form.

Wallace also abbreviates like mad, digresses as much as stays on topic, and footnotes as if being held to a quota. All of which could seem like linguistic wankering if "Fun Thing" didn't take full advantage of the cruise ship as thematic framework. David Foster Wallace has been paid to go on vacation, to work at relaxing. He notes repeatedly that the cruise staff is working very, very hard so that you, the passenger, do not exert a second of unnecessary effort. Wallace also spends half a dozen pages trying to sample a day's worth of "relaxing, fun activities" advertised to passengers. He gets to about 10 percent of shipboard offerings and is exhausted by nightfall. I was just as exhausted reading about them, which raises the question: Is it a vacation if, at every turn, someone is in your face trying to make it more relaxing and fun for you? If your experience is as micromanaged and worked-over as that of a hyperactive toddler? On vacation I prefer to be left alone with a book, coffee, and an unmade bed to sit around in. Is being "off work" the power to decide how to spend your time or to have enough distractions so you don't have to think about it?

Wallace took his cruise in March of 1995. To his credit, with the exception of a stray detail (GPS is overexplained, as was necessary for the pre-smartphone reader) and modern omission (no one is scurrying to the business center to check their e-mail), "Fun Thing" could have just as easily been written about the *QE2* in 1968 or any of the four ships in the Disney Cruise fleet right now. The same month Wallace boarded his ship, the Yahoo!® search engine went live. Amazon.com debuted that summer. Wallace wrote this essay only a few moments before a new era dawned, one where the entire world was a few clicks away. "Fun Thing" feels, then, like a sunbaked glimpse into our own reality from nearly twenty years ago. When did we start to feel overwhelmed by the sheer number of ways to busy ourselves? When did normal life begin to feel unsatisfying enough to need this drastic a break from it? Without meaning to, David Foster Wallace might have captured the point in our history when it became ordinary to say, "I need a vacation from my vacation."

It takes tremendous skill to write both funny and perceptive journalism about a ridiculous situation and not have it read like snobbery-for-hire or an acid trip on someone else's dime. Hunter Thompson avoided the latter by assembling his thoughts afterward with a clear head and rigid allegiance to the basics of great storytelling. David Foster Wallace did it with a superhuman eye for detail and linguistic diligence. An "obsessive reviser,"[9] according to practically everyone who knew him, Wallace worked tirelessly for exactly the right phrase that was not only correct but singular: "field-stripping their camcorders"; "an untasteful affair of crepe and horns"; a chambermaid "deslobbing a room."[10] Without these phrases and their hard polish, "Fun Thing" would be a giant bore, an emptied suitcase of tricks and cleverness in serious need of a "deslobbing." David Foster Wallace may have seen journalism as a lesser priority than his fiction. But he worked at it just as hard.

A lot of me wishes I had read "A Supposedly Fun Thing I'll Never Do Again" while I was on vacation so I could snort at the irony. But then I'd just be having a self-satisfied laugh at Wallace's fellow passenger—spending all that money and effort to relax when I can relax by falling off the sofa. I'd have become self-righteous about relaxation, turning Wallace's examination of what it means to be working and "off work" into a hatchet job. I'd have missed the point entirely.

Instead, I'm glad I read it in the thick of writing this book, working within days of my own structure and making. In a minor swirl of contradictions, largely nonexistent a few decades ago and just becoming commonplace when Wallace boarded ship, we can now work in places that used to be just for relaxing, at hours formerly reserved for leisure: on a plane, atop a mountain, or under the sea. The break from our work is no longer physical but mental. In a way he couldn't have predicted, Wallace in "Fun Thing" points to questions we now ask as routinely as "How are you?"—about work/after work balance, about the state of being disconnected or "unplugging," and about what kind of break our hard, necessary work entitles us to.

I've come to David Foster Wallace's writing only recently. He was eleven years older than me, so it would have been impossible to read him in high school. When he became famous, I was a burdened graduate student who had shut leisure reading out entirely. By the time of his death, I had read exactly one of his essays, heard of his novels, and expelled him from my reading agenda like a party guest with body odor. I knew his fiction was long, complicated, writerly, and mostly fawned over by people I didn't like. The essay I'd read was "E Unibus Pluram: Television and U.S. Fiction,"[11] which felt like pedestrian cross-media snobbery, a lazy sucker punch well below the skills of the so-called greatest writer of his/my generation.

It was this caviar spoon of evidence that I used to condemn the man and his output—a writer too clever by about three-quarters, too pleased with his bag of tricks to care about my pleasure as a reader, a tortured rationale to explain why all this trickery was innovative and why legions of readers were dumb enough to fall for it. When an old friend told me that David Foster Wallace gave him a headache, I wore that excuse around my neck on a chain. I'd never read enough Wallace to get a headache. I never read Wallace again until now. I was terribly unfair to him and missed a lot of great writing because of it.

The only positive I can see from the horror that was his suicide is this: perhaps now his work will be seen as contemporary but historic enough to be taught in high schools. I'm sure some schools already do include his works, those in fair-sized coastal cities with the word *progressive* on the brochure's front page and a semester tuition that would buy a pair of Jet Skis. The others may be more open to including Mr. Wallace in a contemporary literature course, despite his tics, wisecracks, lowbrow subject matter, and occasional cursing.

"A Supposedly Fun Thing I'll Never Do Again" should be in every school's career counseling office and available as a free download when booking travel. Whether heading out into the working world or escaping from it, this essay compels you to ask yourself whether you want a job (or a life) where this drastic kind of escape feels necessary, whether you have to leave everything behind in order to "relax." Even if your work is not your calling (as journalism was not for David Foster Wallace), can you find something in it, through effort, an open mind, or plain old artful imagination to make it beautiful? Can you be proud, even relaxed, once the work of it is done?

24
AT THE OFFICE WITH "MASTER HAROLD" . . . AND THE BOYS

"Master Harold" . . . and the Boys is a play of one act, no intermission, and barely sixty script pages in length. It takes place on a single weekday afternoon during the early years of apartheid and has three characters: two middle-aged men and a teenage boy. It is also the twentieth play written by South African Athol Fugard, who was then in his late forties and was considered (as he is now) to be one of his country's most important dramatists and critics of the old regime of formalized racial segregation.

"Master Harold" was first staged at the Yale Repertory Theatre in the spring of 1982 and moved to the Lyceum Theatre on Broadway later that year. Its time on Broadway was followed closely by the revival of David Mamet's play American Buffalo at the Booth Theatre seven blocks uptown. American Buffalo also had a single set and three characters—two men the same age, one much younger. New York Times critic Frank Rich praised both Buffalo and Boys as "one of the great plays of the decade."[1] But American Buffalo also has two act breaks, an intermission, day passing into night, and a burglary as a climactic action. "Master Harold" has, in total, two conversations—a convivial workplace chat between the café's two black waiters and an argument between one waiter and the teenage boy, whose mother owns the café. The climactic action is the last 10 percent of the second conversation and contains two obscene gestures. We don't find out the reason for the play's title (no one is named "Harold" and there is only a singular "boy") until five minutes before the curtain falls.

I've read *"Master Harold"... and the Boys* several times but have not yet seen it performed. As a work of literature, its confined set of resources feels to this reader like Mr. Fugard's choices are as exacting as the movements inside a pocket watch. Themes of racism and intolerance and how they can infect the young like an airborne virus are Fugard's first order of business. But nestled in this compact, deliberate story are the where and how of that intolerance, which makes this a very different kind of drama.

When I read *"Master Harold"* as a teenager, my classmates and I talked almost exclusively about racism and apartheid. It was the late 1980s, and South African politics was a nightly news item. As I read *"Master Harold"* now—postadolescence and postapartheid, I can't help noticing how consequential the setting (a workplace), character relationships (workers and putative boss,) and several spikes in dialogue seem to be. Athol Fugard has written a personal drama about racism that has a second life as a study of workplace relationships, about how meanness and cruelty can be excused as business as usual or even as necessary when it happens on the job.

The "Master Harold" in question is the teenage boy Hally, who at the beginning of the play returns home from school. Sam and Willie, the two waiters, have been cleaning up the café and discussing a ballroom dancing competition Willie has entered. Hally chats with the two men about a school assignment. The conversation turns to the dance competition that evening. A phone call from Hally's mother regarding his absent father turns the boy's mood cold and violent. Sam attempts to return to work when Hally lowers this hammer.

> All that concerns you here, Sam, is to try and do what you get paid for—to keep the place clean and serve the customer. In plain words, just get on with your job. . . . You're only a servant here and don't you forget it. . . . And as far as my father is concerned, all you need to remember is that he is your boss.[2]

When Sam answers that he works for Hally's mother, Hally shouts back,

> He's a white man and that's good enough for you.[3]

The venom of the line hits us first. But, still smarting, we can flip back through script pages and see that Fugard has warned us ahead of time. At least three times prior, Hally senses Sam and Willie getting too comfortable and scolds them to "cut out that nonsense and get on with your work."[4] Race does not enter the dialogue until the play's final moments. Until then, the power structure between Hally and the two men has been a workplace power structure, employees and boss's son. It's impossible to remove race from what makes this workplace unbalanced. But their climactic conflation reminds us that Fugard has locked our gaze on this setting and on these characters for a reason: work here is a kind of stand-in for moments when we delude ourselves into thinking abuses of power are warranted. Hally may be a bratty child who feels entitled, whether by self-pity or privilege, to act as he does. Many of us have had a boss or manager act that way simply because they could.

The dateline of *"Master Harold" . . . and the Boys* is 1950, two years after the establishment of apartheid. South Africa is in the early days of this new system of legal segregation, and the play functions as a look into a single workplace in the midst of that adjustment. When the play was first staged in 1982, a decade had passed since the United Nations had officially declared apartheid a "crime against humanity." The remainder of the decade would be marked by increased economic sanctions against South Africa, activism on college campuses around the world against apartheid, and the 1989 election of South African prime minister F. W. de Klerk. De Klerk would authorize the 1990 release of Nelson Mandela from prison and share the Nobel Peace Prize with Mandela in 1993 for the dismantling of the apartheid system.

Fugard wrote this play about the beginning of apartheid just as the air was beginning to smell of its end. His characters are adjusting to a new reality that the audience of the play would have lived with for that last forty years. In Fugard's native country, a life of apartheid was, perhaps, all some members of that audience ever knew. His American audience was working in and around New York during the recession of 1983, a full decade before workplaces ruled by petty power struggles and colleagues putting each other in their place would be, if not less common then less contemporary, a scar from an earlier, less enlightened time.

"Master Harold" . . . *and the Boys* was a left turn in Athol Fugard's body of work for many reasons. It was his first play that debuted somewhere other than South Africa. It is personal rather than overtly political and is the example he most often cites of his work drawn from his own life. ("Two extraordinary men, Sam and Willie," he told the *Paris Review* in 1985, "who were literally my closest, and virtually my only, friends for a period of my childhood."[5]) The result is a story that feels universal because it is drawn in spare outlines rather than full color relief. Removed from nation and ideology, there's room for our own experience in a story about two older men working for a younger one who abuses the advantage of his position.

"Master Harold" . . . *and the Boys* was nominated for a Tony Award for best play in 1982. That same year it received a Drama Desk Award for Best Play. It was adopted for television in 1985 and for the screen in 2010. That same year, Athol Fugard received a Lifetime Achievement Tony Award.

I've wondered from time to time what kind of conversations an office field trip to see *"Master Harold"* would incite. I'd organize one myself, but (1) my workplace is me, and (2) the first time I see the play performed, I'd like to be by myself. I'd like to think about my own business dealings with others in positions of less power than me. Do I display the contemporary version of Hally's cruelty—impatience, indifference, or condescension? If so, do I blame a "bad day" when that really means "I feel lousy about myself and my inability to handle a bad day"? Do I remember the grace, dignity, and thoughtfulness Athol Fugard showed in writing about this very dynamic from his own youthful past? And then I'd think about the kind of dramatic stage a workplace is everyday, where we have just as much opportunity to be our graceful selves as we do to be little boys and little brats.

25

BURNING BOOKS:
ONE CRAPPY JOB

Ray Bradbury could not have picked a better place to write his second novel, *Fahrenheit 451*. The author had been driven from his writing post in the family garage by his children and their habit of pestering dad during the workday. Bradbury was already a published author with several short stories and a successful first book, *The Martian Chronicles*, behind him. But his family did not have the extra income to rent him an office. So Bradbury took himself and his idea about firemen who set fires to books to the only place he could think of that would let him write in peace—a typewriter room at the UCLA library. For twenty cents an hour, he typed madly, breaking between jammed ribbons and paper refills to wander the stacks as he had done every Monday night as a boy growing up in Waukegan, Illinois.[1]

After two weeks of typing, Bradbury had the first draft of what would become *Fahrenheit 451*, named for the temperature at which a book will burn and perhaps the most widely read American novel about censorship and free expression since its publication in 1953. To this day, it is often cited when books, bookselling, or readers are threatened by cultural barbarity as a prophetic nightmare coming true.

It's a sloppy tribute to Bradbury's vision that the phrase "Fahrenheit 451" gets nailed to all manner of perceived speech suppression and supposed literary crime—e-readers, closing bookstores, reductions in library hours. The author himself told *LA Weekly* in 2009 that the novel has been misinterpreted as a tale of government censorship, despite landing like a Molotov cocktail amid the end of McCarthyism and the Ethel and Julius Rosenberg persecutions.[2] Instead, Bradbury submitted that *Fahrenheit* is a warning against the opiate of easy answers, of information over imagination, of consuming without thinking. Bradbury saw television as the culprit, then the new medium on the scene. A half century later, he could have been speaking of today's hyperconnected world where "catching up on e-mail" at 11:00 p.m. on Sunday is seen as normal, even necessary.

There is no Big Brother in *Fahrenheit 451*, no government body out to burn "impure" ideas as the Nazis did. The evil in this book comes from the foot soldiers, firemen tasked with burning books instead of putting out fires. This evil is far more bland than vitriolic—its purpose is to clean up the "mess" of our active minds. Ideas are not dangerous. They clutter a simple, happy life. "Don't give them any slippery stuff like philosophy or sociology to tie things up with. That way lies melancholy," says the novel's villain, Fire Chief Beatty. "Fire is clean."[3]

The book's protagonist, Guy Montag, is a third-generation fireman asking *why*—not why his job requires destruction and fear in a way it didn't for his father and grandfather, but why burning books leaves him feeling dead inside. He was never a great reader, but if there are people like Mrs. Blake, a woman who died with her books while Montag ignited them, perhaps what books have is very real, tremblingly alive, a way to feel different than the way he feels now.

That Montag reduces Mrs. Blake's suicide to this is half-baked logic to be sure, but it points to the second half of Bradbury's terrifying prescience: work without purpose is not a harmless means to an end. It is a daily dose of battery acid, burning the worker empty from the inside. Bradbury may have reached this conclusion by simply looking around (Sloan Wilson's *Man in the Grey Flannel Suit* was published a short two years after *Fahrenheit*); but his narrator's discontent is hardly a relic of the era. "Why do I give so much to this job that leaves me broken?" may also be the plaintive wail of our time.

Great books hold multiple meanings at multiple points in history. The counterculture of the 1960s held *Fahrenheit* up as the story of an individual knocking down the steep wall of conformity. Guy Montag's teenage neighbor, Clarisse McClellan, was seen as a kind of proto–flower child who gets him to question the choices he's made. Two decades later, as personal computers and video games found their way into the home, *Fahrenheit* again was cited as predicting our dependence on screens and how they aided in what media theorist Neil Postman called "amusing ourselves to death."[4]

Now that we carry a screen in our pocket and can be summoned at any time, I wonder if Ray Bradbury also wrote a great novel about work. He adapted *Fahrenheit* from his own short story "The Fireman," which describes a job, not a concept. In the early 1980s, a Los Angeles theater company asked Bradbury to create a stage version of *Fahrenheit*. He added scenes fleshing out the backstory of the villainous Beatty, who owned a giant library of illegal books he hoarded but did not read. And when Montag asks why, Beatty answers that books are not an adequate defense to the oppressive demands of life.

> Life happened to me, Montag. . . . And nowhere, nowhere the right book for the right time to stuff in the crumbling wall of the breaking dam . . . offering no solace, no harbor, no true love, no light.[5]

Beatty applies for a job with the fire department, presumably to ease the pain of this sad awakening. Montag's own awakening is the adversarial converse: we cannot fill the empty hole in ourselves with work, particularly work that demands we not question it under the mistaken premise that it's easier if we don't.

Fahrenheit 451 remains among the most assigned books in American schools, probably due to its modest length (165 pages), kinetic plot, and seeming focus on thought control—catnip to teenagers. My heart breaks for the adult who calls the novel his favorite book. That reader probably still thinks we live in a dystopia where seditious ideas are set ablaze then stamped out of consciousness. Unless that reader lives someplace where the government actually does such things, this reader is also, most likely, paranoid, miserable, and has never heard of the Internet.

I'd also bet that this person probably hates his job. Work is sadly the place where far too many of us feel like Guy Montag—unheard, pinioned, and avoiding "why" because it feels easier than asking why we feel like we are rotting inside. How many of us feel as though work obligations have the same face of *Fahrenheit*'s Mechanical Hound—relentless, menacing, and impossible to turn off?

Fahrenheit 451 was an instant and lasting success—in print continuously since the Eisenhower administration—and it made Ray Bradbury famous. *Fahrenheit* was made into a 1966 movie by François Truffaut and has been adapted for radio at least four times and as many times for stage. In the 1980s, the novel became a text adventure game. In 2009, Ray Bradbury wrote the introduction to the graphic novel version. Against his wishes, *Fahrenheit 451* was released as an unburnable e-book in 2011.[6]

It's fitting that Ray Bradbury's work on a book about book burning was written in a library, where the author surrounded himself with old friends. It's as fitting that Bradbury chose to complete it in a West Coast version of his childhood dreamland, ensuring he wouldn't feel like Guy Montag after a hard day's work. It's why I like to give *Fahrenheit* to anyone ready to get out of their current job. Guy Montag leaving the fire department meant leaving his whole world behind. Unlike Guy Montag, we all have the option, as Mr. Bradbury did, of finding our own quiet room to work, among friends or at least with duties that do not burn us from the inside.

PART 6
FAMILY

26

WHY *TO KILL A MOCKINGBIRD* MAKES A GREAT FATHER'S DAY GIFT

Harper Lee's original title for *To Kill a Mockingbird* was *Atticus*. At the time of its writing, she was an airline-reservation agent living in New York City and working with an editor to craft a novel from a series of character sketches and scenes from her childhood in Monroeville, Alabama. Atticus Finch, the widowed lawyer and father of the book's narrator, Scout Finch, would become one of the most beloved characters in American literature. His origins can be loosely traced to the author's own father, A. C. Lee, also a respected lawyer, civil rights advocate, and one of the most beloved citizens of Monroeville.

Is Scout Finch Harper Lee? Is Atticus her dad? Questions of how much of *Mockingbird* is autobiography have hung around like heavy summer air since its publication in 1960. "Finch" was in fact the maiden name of Harper Lee's mother, but Lee grew up with both parents and with three siblings instead of one. Surprisingly, by many accounts, A. C. Lee was significantly more accepting of his community's laws of segregation than his heroic avatar, Atticus Finch.

Harper Lee did not care for these inquiries into her own childhood and stopped granting interviews in 1964. And despite her being a whole lot like Scout Finch (willful youngest child, precocious, a tomboy), the 2010 documentary *Hey, Boo: Harper Lee and 'To Kill a Mockingbird'* makes a strong case that Lee the grownup is a lot more like Boo Radley, Scout Finch's shadowy neighbor.[1] That Lee has not written another novel nor spoken publicly about *Mockingbird* in a half century is very Boo Radley: Radley's desire in Depression-era Maycomb would convict his creator of a crime new to America in the twenty-first century—the desire to be invisible and left alone.

Harper Lee hasn't told us much about what we are supposed to get out of *To Kill a Mockingbird*, so we've filled in the blanks on our own. It is at once a novel about racism, the American South, growing up, the criminal justice system, family, a small-town girlhood, and moral conviction in the sneering face of intolerance. It may be too easy to explain success—a Pulitzer Prize, Oscar®-winning film adaptation, a half century in print, and still the most assigned book in American high schools—this way, but *To Kill a Mockingbird* may be that rare novel with something for everyone.

I've never quite understood, then, why we often abandon it to the backcountry of childhood, as if we "outgrow" the book when we get closer to Atticus's age and farther from Scout's. This leaves a whole trove of the book's riches wilting in the old tree hole: *To Kill a Mockingbird* is told in flashback from the point of view of a child but in the voice of a grownup. Of course, we can imagine a seven-year-old Scout saying or hearing the book's most famous lines—"Hey, Boo" or "Miss Jean Louise, stand up. Your father's passin'."[2] But a second-grader can't follow up "Hey, Boo" ten pages later with "I never saw him again" unless many years have passed between the story and the adult Scout's telling of it.[3]

Harper Lee was about Scout Finch's age when her father gave her a typewriter and encouraged her writing. She was in her early thirties during the difficult two years she wrestled *Atticus* into *Mockingbird*, far from home, intimidated, and scared. Her mother had passed away nearly a decade before. We know Lee planted a lot of nostalgia and tributes throughout the novel—to siblings, a faraway hometown, a time several decades ago—but filling its center row seems to be a thanks to the author's still-living parent who had believed in her talent and dreams, especially at that time in her life when she needed that faith so much.

Looked at this way, *Mockingbird* is as much a book about parenthood as about it is about childhood, a tribute to a father who confronted—not flawlessly but admirably—the most difficult challenge of having children: that a parent's decisions affect the life of a developing person and that children are learning not just from the decisions you make but from the reasons you had in making them.

It's a kind of heroism we've brushed over in our fifty-year canonization of Atticus Finch. In 2003, the American Film Institute named the character the greatest hero in American Film.[4] The role would be Gregory Peck's signature. Brock Peters, the actor who played Tom Robinson, would deliver the eulogy at Peck's funeral. Supreme Court justice Sandra Day O'Connor and lawyer/novelist Scott Turow have both credited the character with bringing nobility and honor to the American legal profession.[5]

But Atticus Finch is no knight in a white suit. The genius of Lee's invention was to house his heroism in fatherhood as much as in lawyering. We're eighty pages into *Mockingbird* before there is mention of Tom Robinson, and the novel is half-over before his trial commences. *Mockingbird* also begins and ends with Boo Radley, a plot thread that allows Atticus to play the supporting role of both protective father and single parent who knows when to give his children room to fail, to learn, to grow into their own people. His final line to Boo Radley, "Thank you for my children, Arthur," contains both gratitude and sadness, gratitude that his family is safe despite living in a world of cruelty and misunderstanding, and sad resignation that he cannot protect them forever.[6] One day Atticus Finch's greatest act as a parent will be admitting he has raised them as best he can, then letting them go. The adult Scout Finch has written this story, not just to show what a noble thing Atticus Finch did as Tom Robinson's lawyer, but also to show how well she turned out thanks to who he was as her dad.

Mockingbird captures Atticus's second chapter of parenthood. The first may have taken place when his wife was still alive. The third is wherever the adult Scout is now. In the middle, we have a parent who may be the best shot in the county but who is too old to play football with his son (screenwriter Horton Foote, who adapted *Mockingbird*, mentions this in the film's opening scene) and too creaky to get into a fist fight with Bob Ewell.[7] Atticus's power comes not from feats of physicality but from reason: from a steady moral view of a world that makes little sense to his children, even though they've never known another one. Telling them that "courage isn't a man with a gun in his hand" and that you "never really know a man until you walk a mile in his shoes" is his great lesson.[8] It's a lesson not so much of fortitude but of maturity.

It is easy to call an attorney on a moral crusade a hero. It is much harder to see the heroism of Atticus as a widower. He is not poor or ignorant like Bob Ewell, nor is he ostracized and absent like Boo Radley's father. But he understands as no other character does the bargain you make with the universe when you become a parent, that it provides you hundreds of opportunities, mostly in the name of fear and cowardice, to "do as I say, not as I do," to do the easy thing instead of the right one. If as Atticus says, "It's a sin to kill a mockingbird" because "mockingbirds don't do one thing but sing their hearts out and make everyone feel good," he means it for everyone, even those like him who are single parents; sole providers; tired, worn-down people with children who depend on them for a future that makes sense.[9] It's a sin to kill not just a mockingbird but innocence, to take advantage of another's goodwill, to be a bully, to do what is right for you and to speed past how wrong it might be for someone else.

It's why I like to remind parents I know, particularly fathers, of *To Kill a Mockingbird*. I like to imagine Harper Lee on those long days and nights in that little room in New York, thousands of miles from home and neck deep in the largest, most difficult project of her life. I like to imagine her looking down at her typewriter, remembering the one her father had given her as a child as an act of trust and of pride. And I imagine her saying when her book was done:

"Look what you made me into. Look what I wrote. Thank you for showing me who I could be. You had to make hard decisions. And I was watching."

27
THE AMBIVALENT FAMILY OF TONI MORRISON

Toni Morrison was thirty-nine when she published her first novel, *The Bluest Eye*, in 1970. She was divorced, raising two sons, living in Queens, and working in publishing as an editor at Random House. Her closest friends were women in the same position, single mothers working day jobs and stealing time to write fiction. When one had to finish a chapter, the others would babysit. They'd cook for each others' families and loan each other money. Among the group were poet Sonia Sanchez and novelist Toni Cade Bambara. They even had a joke of sending each other money with a note indicating the receiver had won an award given by their friends.[1]

Toni Morrison was far from her birthplace of Lorain, Ohio, newly transferred from her last job in upstate New York. What she did to make room for herself as an artist is something I see over and over in her books, and it is why *Sula* (1974), her second novel, is my favorite: She saw the idea of "family" as much bigger, vaguer, and more deliberate than blood. Family is something we both create, as Morrison and her friends did, and inherit from being born into a certain race, gender, place, and time in history. *The Bluest Eye* is a novel about standards of beauty, violence, and abuses of power. But it is fundamentally a book about individuals, about one family and their terrible secrets. *Sula* is the beginning of Morrison's idea that we are all connected and belong to many families.

Critic Adam Begley called the "skinny 174-page" *Sula* Morrison's "masterpiece."[2] This is a minority opinion. *Beloved*, Morrison's fifth book, remains her best known. Her third, *Song of Solomon* (1977), was the novel that won her the 1993 Nobel Prize in Literature.[3] *The Bluest Eye* and *Paradise* (1997) were both Oprah's Book Club selections. When the *Paris Review* interviewed Toni Morrison in 1993, she mentioned *Sula*, in passing, only once.[4]

Masterpieces can take many shapes, and "grand," "complicated," and "career-defining" are three of my least favorite. *Sula* is the shortest of Morrison's books and perhaps her most accessible. I love it for that. It was also my introduction to Toni Morrison, via an excerpt in some early 1990s *Norton Anthology*. Without *Sula*'s relaxed invitation, I may have never gotten interested in Morrison at all.

I finished high school in 1991 and didn't catch up with Toni Morrison's work until graduate school almost a decade later. By then, following coronations by both Oprah and the Nobel Prize Committee, Morrison was already considered a legend. For reasons I still don't know, I didn't pick up *Sula* where I'd left off but tried to scale *Beloved* and *Jazz* (1992) and failed at finishing both. Both these novels are epic, ingenious, and at the time, way over my head. If getting to know the work of Toni Morrison was like learning to drive, I had hopped into the cab of an eighteen-wheeler holding only a learner's permit and was now too intimidated to get back on the road again.

Toni Morrison is intimidating. At eighty-one, she looks every bit a legend or even a head of some imaginary state called Literatudamus—broad shouldered, silver dreadlocked, a gaze that seeks but does not move. She has won every award there is for a writer to win; has a two-decade-old society established to study and honor her work; and is, according to the Modern Language Association, the eighth most studied writer in American educational institutions, ahead of Mark Twain, Henry David Thoreau, and F. Scott Fitzgerald.[5] Her books will be pored over long after she is gone. Reading most volumes of her bibliography feels like attending a five-act opera. You could come back a dozen times and still feel as though you missed something. Nine pages into just about any Morrison novel, and you already feel like you've missed something.

There are two approaches when getting to know the work of a great artist like Toni Morrison. The first I call the Cannonball: take that artist's most acclaimed, often challenging work and plunge in as deeply and as quickly as you can. The second is the Doggy Paddle, where you begin with the artist's most accessible, often most popular volumes and work your way toward the opuses. Which approach you prefer is a question of style. I get intimidated and scared off easily. I Doggy Paddle.

Sula is a great Doggy Paddle when entering the ocean of Toni Morrison. The novel's language is jeweled yet direct; effortless metaphors add to its sentences but do not hide their objectives (my favorite is a description early on of an army helmet as "an inverted soup bowl").[6] Different characters are the star performers of their own chapters, but they don't stand in the way of the novel's primary story—a friendship between two women over forty years, the different life paths they choose, and how those choices affect the community they inhabit.

Those women, Nel and Sula, and their respective choices (for Nel, to marry and raise children; for Sula, to leave her small town of Medallion, Ohio), plus the book's publication in the midst of the women's movement of the 1970s, have given the novel life as a staple of feminist literature. Some scholars have argued that *Sula* is a lesbian novel, not because Sula and Nel become lovers, but because Morrison uses their story to turn over heterosexual notions of women's friendships.[7] In a 2003 *New Yorker* profile of Morrison, writer Hilton Als submits that one cannot separate Morrison's work from its locations in small-town middle America, which was Morrison's preferred setting, as opposed to the urban flavor of the African American fiction (James Baldwin, Ralph Ellison) that immediately preceded it.[8] In her *Paris Review* interview, Morrison said she had the inherent value of female friendships in mind.

When I was writing Sula, I was under the impression that for a large part of the female population a woman friend was considered a secondary relationship. A man and a woman's relationship was primary. Because of this, there's that whole cadre of women who don't like women and prefer men. We had to be taught to like one another.[9]

For me, the metaphor that gathers all this together is the idea of family as a kind of red thread that leads us via geography, gender, race, circumstance, and time to the people we share our lives with. "Family" takes a gothic turn in *Beloved* when a child slain by her mother returns as a ghost. Many of the characters in *Song of Solomon* have adopted names, a common occurrence in African American history that's also a reaction to being given a name, life's first familial act. The idea of family hits its summit in *Paradise* (1997), a historical tale of an all-black town in Oklahoma and its color- and gender-coded struggle over who belongs and who doesn't. This idea of belonging and the way that shapes our lives begins with *Sula*, a novel as much about family as it is about the way its two central characters and their relationship shape how a town relates to itself.

The subject of Toni Morrison's 1993 Nobel lecture was language—its power and how easy it is to abuse and waste that power.

> Underneath the eloquence, the glamor [*sic*], the scholarly associations, however stirring or seductive, the heart of such language is languishing, or perhaps not beating at all. . . .
>
> The conventional wisdom of the Tower of Babel story is that the collapse was a misfortune. That it was the distraction, or the weight of many languages that precipitated the tower's failed architecture. That one monolithic language would have expedited the building and heaven would have been reached. Whose heaven, she wonders? And what kind? Perhaps the achievement of Paradise was premature, a little hasty if no one could take the time to understand other languages, other views, other narratives period.[10]

Morrison's words are as firm as steel beams, but she concludes not with a shout but a whisper, a simple call for an understanding of our common spirit.

Tell us what it is to be a woman so that we may know what it is to be a man. What moves at the margin. What it is to have no home in this place. To be set adrift from the one you knew. What it is to live at the edge of towns that cannot bear your company.[11]

She ends as she begins, with the image of a wise old woman holding a bird. The bird is language.

"Finally," [the old woman] says, "I trust you now. I trust you with the bird that is not in your hands because you have truly caught it. Look. How lovely it is, this thing we have done—together."[12]

Our family is our first notion of "together." Many of Toni Morrison's books take place in the past. Nearly all transgress reality and have elements of magic, phantasms, and living dreams. But I can't get over how relevant this chord of family she keeps playing is to our lives now. Our family is our first bond as people to someone else, as old an idea as we are. But in our era of social media, "friends" and communication across the world in an instant is most defined not by how isolated we are but by what we have in common. Look at our behavior on such sites as Facebook®, Instagram®, and Pinterest®. It is only half "This is me. These are my interests." The other half is "Are you like this too? Do we have this in common?" Without "What do we have in common?" the great rumbling of our interconnected world is silent.

I'm not going to argue that Toni Morrison and her novels are a prophecy for the early twenty-first century. But they are far less affixed to a past of slavery and African American folktales than they seem. And the rope that pulls them into the present is this idea of family, what we belong to, for better and certainly for worse, and how that tells us who we are.

28

OF WONTONS, MAH-JONGG, AND TIME

There's an old story that author Amy Tan started bringing her dog to book signings in order to avoid this conversation:

> *Fan:* "Ms. Tan, I loved *The Joy Luck Club*."
> *Amy Tan:* "Thank you."
> *Fan:* "But I need to tell you something. You don't make wonton soup that way. The way my family makes wonton soup is . . ."

After about nine thousand of these conversations, Amy Tan had an idea. As soon as a reader would start in on the wonton soup, the author would hand the reader her dog. Oohing and ahhing ensued. Tan discovered the dog interaction cut down significantly on the number of times she had to hear how the families in her novels did things differently (and therefore incorrectly) compared to the families of her readers.

The idea of family as both permanent and always in the process of changing is at the center of *The Joy Luck Club* (1989), Amy Tan's first novel and still her most famous.[1] The club is a gathering of four Chinese women living in San Francisco who have met once a week for the past forty years to play mah-jongg. The friends are immigrants from China who came to the United States in the early 1950s. Their children, now grown and with spouses and families of their own, were born in America. The novel opens with the first meeting of the club following the death of one of its members, with her daughter taking the place of her mother at the mah-jongg table.

After those opening pages, almost none of the remainder of *The Joy Luck Club* takes place in the present. Tan has divided the novel into four sections, two for the mothers and two for the daughters, with each character getting her own chapter to tell her story. The mothers' stories revolve around their childhoods in China and the circumstances of their journey to America. The daughters tell of growing up Chinese American in the San Francisco Bay Area as not only members of an immigrant community but also as first-generation Americans whose parents do not want to completely leave behind the country or culture of their birth.

More than one critic has cited the perfect four-by-four symmetry of the book as resembling a mah-jongg board. I think this symmetry also serves as one of many examples of how readily the pleasures of *Joy Luck* leap into view. Amy Tan's sentences can be read quickly, but they leave an impression like departed waves on sand. Myth and fable stand alongside food prep and bill paying without tripping over each other—which means that *Joy Luck* avoids the pitfall of feeling like two kinds of conventions by leaping silently between them.

Other pleasures: If you want great stories about mothers and daughters, there's more than enough. If you relate to tales of generational conflict, particularly between immigrant parents and native-born children, it's here in barrels. The number of readers—women, Chinese Americans, first-generation immigrants—who feel *Joy Luck* speaks to their experience is vast. That Amy Tan speaks to them in a story with both emotional heft and narrative lightness, digestible without feeling pre-chewed, is one of the book's more admirable achievements. "Complicated" or "challenging" is an easier trick than it seems. Seducing the reader and leaving them rewarded, instead of either with a toothache or in need of a drink, are major accomplishments.

The Joy Luck Club was a bestseller almost immediately, was a finalist for both the National Book Award and the National Book Critics Circle Award, was adapted for the screen in 1993, and has been translated into thirty-five languages. It is also required reading at many a high school and has become an assigned text as both beneficiary and punching bag of circumstance. *The Joy Luck Club* was published at precisely the moment high schools and university English departments were suggesting that perhaps reading lists should include authors and perspectives beyond those of dead white European and American men. *Joy Luck* was often cited as the leading example of an Asian American story told in an Asian American voice, and it was credited with raising recognition of Asian American literature and then derided for being an easy-to-swallow introductory course with white readers in mind. "A rare mesmerizing novel. . . . A pure joy to read," said the *Chicago Tribune*.[2] *Joy Luck* succeeds only by "faking all of Asian-American history" in service of a "pure white racist fantasy," wrote novelist Frank Chin in a now-famous 1991 essay bearing the sneering title "Come All Ye Asian American Writers of the Real and the Fake."[3]

Let us make the terribly boring suggestion that there may be something more to *The Joy Luck Club* than its intended reader. I do not need to tell you that Amy Tan has done a great job of plumbing mother/daughter relationships (*The Simpsons* has already made the best joke about how obvious this is when Lisa suggests how much she loves the mother/daughter dynamic of *Joy Luck* to Amy Tan, and Ms. Tan scolds her by saying, "No, that's not what I meant at all. Sit down. This conversation shames us both."[4]) while also nailing the dynamics of immigrant families, in which children have opportunities parents could only dream of, and yet both have their own immovable thoughts on how those opportunities should be used.

Easy pickings. Instead, let's take a step back from the mah-jongg table because Amy Tan is at work in other rooms, in the garden, out in the world. Her take on "family" centers not just on generations or members of the same gender but also on the nature of time itself. Family is the place where we expect much to stay the same. That sameness is the basis of ritual, of tradition, of continuity, and of cultural inheritance. But family is also the place where everything changes, where children grow up, where parents get older, where members move away, where loved ones die, and where time will have

its way with all of us. What is a family photo album if not both a preservation of memory and the inevitability of change? Family is both
the place where we fume against this change and where we learn to
accept it with patience, struggle, and time.

Reading or rereading *Joy Luck*, you'll be surprised how fast your
loyalties will shift. As a child, Waverly Jong (one of the daughters)
is a plucky neighborhood heroine as Chinatown's chess champion.
In later chapters, Waverly is a divorced tax attorney and mother of a
four-year-old. She's a bit of a snob, a little too eager to show off how
smart she is, as if she never got over the recognition of being a childhood prodigy.

We love and admire the mothers for their struggle, their courage,
and their hard work at providing a better life for their children. But
they are hardly sweet old grandmas; they can be judgmental busy-
bodies or just plain nasty. As a young woman, Suyuan Woo (the
deceased member of the club) walked miles across war-torn China to
escape an abusive marriage and had to leave her two infant daughters by the roadside so that they might be rescued if she doesn't
survive. (This is the only part of the novel that is directly autobiographical and is taken from Tan's mother's own story.) But Suyuan
as an old woman and an apartment-building owner in San Francisco
is the kind of landlady who throws boiling water on a tenant's cat
and attempts to have renters evicted by lying about relatives from
China relocating to town. I've had landlords like this. No matter
their reasons or backstory, it takes a certain heartlessness and cruelty
to abuse an animal and boot people out of their home just so you can
earn more money from it.

If you have not read *The Joy Luck Club* already, I can understand
why you might find my endorsement rather obvious. It is well inten-
tioned, sweet, noble, "good for you," and about as threatening as a
hug. I like to think that its power comes from its lashing together of a
very specific story to a very general theme that keeps showing up like
an old relative who forgot his way home. By dealing with multiple
generations, *Joy Luck* is sitting at a narrative workbench of memory

and time. But by also staying fixed on immediate families (there are assorted spouses, friends, and neighbors, but they do not figure much into the story), Amy Tan insists we consider these two themes together—family as something that we think we will always have, and time, which changes everything like an earthquake knocking dishes off a table.

Even if *The Joy Luck Club* does not speak to you in the obvious ways (I am not Chinese, a first-generation immigrant, female, or from California), allow it to work its magic in this way: read it immediately after a family or high school reunion, after a kid has left for college or a loved one has died. And by "immediately," I mean on the plane home or the next day you're not at work. Let it sink into you. And think about time, about how we are all really at its mercy, and about how we may be petty or mean in contending with that fear. That fear is part of what makes us human. Even something as silly as scolding an author for not describing the recipe for wonton soup the way your family makes it is an attempt to say that time should matter less and not change certain things. Distracting the asker with a dog is really just saying, "We all do family in our own way, with our own traditions, our own methods of—even for a second—stopping time."

29

A FAMILY OF GIANT INSECTS

If you ask someone what Franz Kafka's novella *The Metamorphosis* is about, you'll probably hear "It's about a guy who wakes up one morning as a giant insect." Which is exactly what the excerpt I read in an eighth-grade anthology was about. So I was floored when, this spring, I read *all* of *The Metamorphosis* and discovered that, yes, it is about a guy who turns into a giant insect, but it's just as much about what a family does when one of their own becomes a giant insect. Mr. Kafka, who was terribly neurotic and tortured about his relationships with others, remarked near the end of his life, "All is imaginary—family, office, friends, the street, all imaginary, far away or close at hand, the woman; the truth that lies closest, however, is only this: that you are beating your head against the wall of a windowless and doorless cell."[1] But he leveraged that angst to say a whole lot about family in *The Metamorphosis*, arguably his most famous piece of fiction.[2] It is something of an understatement to say that he took the concept of family in directions that most of us don't, asking if it's just as bizarre to wake up in the body of a giant insect as it is to wake up a member of a familial group you didn't sign up for and don't really understand.

Prague. 1912. Morning. A traveling fabric salesman named Gregor Samsa wakes up in his bed to find he is now a giant insect. Gregor lives at home with his parents and younger sister. His salesman gig is the family's sole means of support, and he's apparently rather good at it, as the family has a cook, a chambermaid, and comfortable quarters. Although Kafka never specifies, we assume Gregor is probably in his early to midtwenties (he's on his way up the ladder at work and has a younger sister who is an adult, but barely), which makes his position as this middle-class family's breadwinner a little odd. In a famous lecture on *The Metamorphosis*, Vladimir Nabokov submits that, some five years before the story began, Gregor's father lost all the family's money and Gregor had to take the salesman job with one of the family's creditors to get them out of debt. This very well might be in the text of the story, but somehow I missed it.[3]

Kafka positions the ordinary facts of Gregor's job and standing with the Samsa family as the story's outboard motor that drives the action forward. Gregor's insect form is discovered when his office sends a clerk over to see why their top salesman has not yet arrived at the office. His family then has a series of reactions, not only to what has become of Gregor but, just as important, to what will become of their economic standing. Their reactions include fear (his father pushes Gregor back into the young man's room with the clerk's walking stick); compassion (sister Grete gives Gregor a bowl of sweet milk that night); facing up to change (the family moves the furniture out of Gregor's room so he may crawl around the walls; they then all find jobs, as Gregor can no longer support them); anger (in a particularly confusing episode, Gregor's father assaults him with apples, one of which remains lodged in Gregor's back and becomes infected); and resignation (despite their efforts, the family cannot support Gregor as an insect nor can they continue in their present condition without his income). Near the conclusion, the family has taken in lodgers to keep creditors at bay, but one lodger spots the insect and terminates his rental agreement immediately. The family decides that the insect is no longer Gregor but a weight on the family's future. They decide to get rid of him, but Gregor dies from the infection in his back before they can do so.

Kafka wrote *The Metamorphosis* in the third person, but he never releases us from Gregor's point of view. The Samsas live in a small enough flat that every conversation the family has is within earshot of the insect, and though his family cannot understand Gregor, he can hear and understand them—only there's very little for him to hear or understand. Kafka gives us no scenes of the Samsas discussing what has happened to Gregor and how they feel about it, of them debating what to do about the challenge of living with a giant insect, or of them saying a version of "times are tough and Gregor is now a bug, so we need to get back to work to keep the lights on." The family is almost entirely defined by their actions toward their now-helpless breadwinner, who, before the story opens, was the most needed member of the family. Gregor Samsa waking up as an insect is only the second-biggest transformation that determines his fate. The first was his transformation from family breadwinner to a ward of the Samsa State—from the head of his family to a hole at its center, from being necessary to being a stranger who cannot leave the one entity of which, by birth, none of us are strangers.

Imagine, then, what *The Metamorphosis* would look like if Gregor Samsa were a single man living with his buddies. Or a widower. Or a bachelor with a girlfriend. Or if some other Samsa brought home the bacon. Keep all the insect business the same. *The Metamorphosis* is now an entirely different tale. We can try to separate Gregor's transformation and its literary and biographical source material (*Jekyll and Hyde*, the outsider Kafka felt as a Czech in Germany, as a Jew, and of course the simple alienation of being trapped in a tale of absurdity) from the family arena where it happens. But then it's not *The Metamorphosis.*

I've mainly heard the world *metamorphosis* used to describe insect transformation, of, say, a caterpillar becoming a butterfly, and metaphorically as the journey from plainness to beauty (ugly duckling to swan is a kind of metamorphosis), or the act of growing up (puberty can also be described as a metamorphosis). In all cases, a metamorphosis is never a freak accident but a natural process. This adds a note of menace to Kafka's story. Was this hideous transformation supposed to happen to Gregor Samsa? Did he do something to deserve it?

But Kafka doesn't do a whole lot of asking why, and his tone here, as in nearly all his work, doesn't invite much asking either. His sentences are flat, literal, unquestioning, binding us to events, reactions, and outcomes. "At its most metaphysical, the novel might go as far as to investigate how selves are made," novelist Zadie Smith remarked in a 2003 essay about Kafka.[4] Smith then argues that that simply isn't the business Kafka is in. He doesn't care why we do what we do or even why things happen to us that we can't control. He's fascinated by "the impossibility of being alive," in other words, how we end up in these roles and relationships we take on without questioning in the first place.

Metamorphosis has a kind of tilted-head lack of understanding of this thing called "family." Kafka has made Gregor Samsa's plight as important as the place it happens and the reaction of his family to it. We've no idea what Gregor was like as a son, a brother, or a provider before he was a helpless insect. None of the story's action takes place outside the family home until the very end, after Gregor has died. Kafka has trapped Gregor, his story, and us in this strange little place called "family," in their ecosystem called "home." We then hold his plight and his family's as uneasy equals, as if waking up an insect is just as strange as belonging to a group you didn't volunteer for but are still expected to feel bonded to.

Bonding with other people was not Franz Kafka's strength. He was the oldest of six children; he hated his father; and he had many friends, a few admirers, and a handful of unsuccessful love affairs. But he did not understand basic human priorities at all—the need for self-definition, to relate to others, and to have both commonalities and differences as the basis of connection. He wasn't arrogant in thinking he couldn't be bothered. It was a shortcoming of his personality he knew he had, and it tortured him. Walter Benjamin put it very well when he said it was as if Kafka "had spent his entire life wondering what he looked like, without ever discovering there are such things as mirrors."[5] Kafka died of tuberculosis in 1924 at age forty without gaining a whole lot of clarity as to why people, the most social of animals, do the things they do.

The bulk of Kafka's output and recognition came after he died. *The Metamorphosis* was the longest piece of fiction he published in his lifetime. His three novels—*The Trial, The Castle,* and *Amerika*—were all published posthumously and became the basis for much of the critical study of Kafka today. *The Metamorphosis* still gets plenty of knocking around, but I think its place as a standard item on high school reading lists (and its easy parallels to puberty and to feeling like an alien in one's own house) has probably dampened that a bit.

Look at a picture of Kafka. He has a stub nose, pointed ears, and deeply sunken eyes. He usually appears to be looking past you, far away and somewhere else. If he were drawn as a comic book super-hero, I could imagine him leaving his body and transforming into a giant insect, as he already seems halfway between this world and a dream of himself as a creature from elsewhere. In photographs, he looks like someone very preoccupied with his own thoughts, who probably wouldn't quite know what you meant if you said, "Hey, Franz, look over here. We're in the middle of a conversation."

It doesn't surprise me, then, that in *The Metamorphosis* Kafka seems puzzled, even tortured, by this most basic of human connections, the family. He views the family as a strange country we arrive at the day we are born. Waking up in it as a giant insect is a grotesque reframing of the same question: Who are these villagers, and how am I supposed to relate to them? It was probably a difficulty Kafka felt more acutely than most of us, even though we've all thought siblings and parents and children we thought we knew at times resembled hideous creatures or mysteries that arrived one morning without notice. Kafka seems to be saying that if a family member wakes up one morning as a giant insect, don't be surprised. That enormous bug is just an understudy for the mystery that is family itself.

30

MAUS: A COMIC BOOK ABOUT FATHERS, SONS, AND GENOCIDE

Meet *Maus*, by Art Spiegelman: the most awarded and studied work of its kind, and, inescapably, a comic book about genocide.[1] *Maus* did for the graphic novel what *The Birth of a Nation* did for cinema. It didn't invent the form, but gave it a hard shove into maturity and therefore represented the next milepost of its evolution. Like *The Birth of a Nation*, *Maus* uses a mass-entertainment medium to tell a story about racism, war, and mass murder.

Do we belittle horror when we examine it with the instruments of escapism? Or does *Maus* act as all great cultural leaps do, shaking its reader, using both excitement and violence, from his previously held ideas? A dozen pages in will answer that. Told as a blend of reportage and memoir captured in the firm, frightened black-and-white pen strokes of an old newspaper strip, *Maus* is the "bridge book" between the first and second generations of writing about the Holocaust, when its horrors moved from survivors to their children, from testimonial to legacy. Between its slim red covers resides the literary embodiment of a stage of grief—the attempt to move from "this is my story" to "this is the next chapter of my story."

Cartoonist Art Spiegelman's life changed forever when he decided to draw a long narrative of his father's escape from and survival of the Nazi death camps. In his early thirties and newly married, Spiegelman was casting around for a new project after his first comics anthology, *Breakdowns*, had been published to what he called "resounding indifference."[2] In the summer of 1979, he began tape-recording his father's memories of life as a young Polish Jew during the rise of Nazism. The name *Maus*, the German word for *mouse*, came from Spiegelman's decision to depict Jews as mice, Germans as cats, Americans as dogs, and Poles as pigs. His author "photo" on the inside back cover shows a man sitting at a drawing table wearing a mouse mask.

First serialized in the underground comics magazine *Raw* (which Spiegelman edited) and then collected as books in 1986 and 1991, the two-volume project marked the arrival of the graphic novel as a mainstream literary genre and crowned Spiegelman as one of its great practitioners. In 1992, *Maus* won the Pulitzer Prize. It is now required Holocaust reading in schools and universities around the world, alongside *The Diary of Anne Frank* and Elie Wiesel's *Night.*

Maus tells two concentric stories: the life of Spiegelman's father, Vladek, in occupied Poland and his deportation to Auschwitz, and the author's recollection of the story told in the present day. Spiegelman the elder is no sweet old man. He's selfish, intolerant, and a royal pain to have around. He tells Art that he wants to forget the horrible things that happened to him, and yet he lives as if anti-Semitic persecution is alive and well on the streets of Rego Park, Queens, where he still lives, forty years after the fact.

Art Spiegelman's equal treatment of his own story in *Maus* proved revolutionary—both for comics and for Holocaust literature. Comic books had long used an omniscient voice ("Meanwhile, at the Hall of Justice!") or a first-person protagonist, but rarely did artists draw themselves or their creative process as part of the plot. This kind of self-inclusion—of characters bearing visual and psychic resemblance to the author—would become increasingly common during the "alternative comics" boom of the late 1980s and '90s, a window *Maus* is often given credit for opening (Adrian Tomine's *Optic Nerve*; the Hernandez brothers' *Love and Rockets*; and, later, Daniel Clowes's novels like *Ghost World* and *Art School Confidential* all have narrator stand-ins). The unsentimental manner in which Spiegelman portrays his father also meant that, in literature and public perception, Holocaust survivors were no longer heroic ideals but human beings living frightened, scarred lives. First-person memoirs like Elie Wiesel's *Night* and Primo Levi's *Survival in Auschwitz* are the sacred tests of early Holocaust literature and have made moral giants of their authors. Vladek Spiegelman survived the same horrors, but he is the kind of broken man who makes racist remarks to store clerks and mistakenly calls his son by the name of his dead brother.

Maus had more than its share of critics, including guardians of Holocaust and comics orthodoxies who didn't think words and pictures laid out in panels and strips held the moral authority to take on this subject. Fellow comics artists Harvey Pekar and Robert Crumb both derided *Maus*'s animal metaphor as amateurish and crude, and Pekar judged Spiegelman's treatment of his father as an opportunistic hatchet job.[3] Writer Adam Gopnik loved the book but concluded, in a long review for the *New Republic*, that Spiegelman had simply done better drawing in his earlier work and that the figures of *Maus* were "deliberately folklike, stiff and unvaried," a work of courage rendered in fear.[4] Was it necessary for Spiegelman to work below his talents to make a larger point? Did the enormity of the subject demand it of him?

Maus not only elected Art Spiegelman the class president of a new generation of cartoonists who worked both as artists and entertainers (Alan Moore, Dan Clowes, and Spiegelman were drawn as a muscled band of superheroes in an episode of *The Simpsons*); it also made him America's graphic poet of mass tragedy. His September 11 cover of the *New Yorker* magazine—an all-black field with barely visible etchings of the World Trade Center—is considered one of the premier visual renderings of the attacks. His 2004 graphic novel *In the Shadow of No Towers* uses the same image and earned Spiegelman a designation as one of *Time* magazine's one hundred most influential people of 2005.[5]

It was George Bernard Shaw who said, "All great truths begin as blasphemies." It was my own father who, after I giggled during my grandmother's funeral, smiled and said, "There is no right way to grieve. Everyone picks the one that works for them." *Maus* is a story about unspeakable horror and the anger at not being able to escape its shadow. It began with someone's definition of *blasphemy*—comics, animals, a Holocaust survivor deeply flawed—but has become a book about openness. It gives us permission to be human in grief— creative; resentful; but, most importantly, real—in order to finally awaken into acceptance. I've actually given the book to loved ones in the late stages of mourning. It may seem like an odd gift, but I always attach the following note: "This is how a man named Art Spiegelman told his father's story of never-ending grief. In here is permission, when you are ready, to draw a map out of yours."

PART 7

IDEAS AND LEARNING

31

THE RENAISSANCE NERDS
OF *THE PHANTOM TOLLBOOTH*

You probably did not read *The Phantom Tollbooth* in high school. A well-meaning parent or librarian most likely suggested it in mid-October of grade five, at which point you devoured it and have had pleasant if infrequent memories of it since. Or you call yourself a nerd without shame, reread it annually, and dressed as the Mathemagician for Halloween last year. In either case, calling Norton Juster's classic "a children's book" is like calling the Washington Monument "a pointy thing." *The Phantom Tollbooth* has earned a rightful place on everyone's reading list, fifth-grader or grown person, nerd or not.

Let us begin with nerds, as I am one. *The Phantom Tollbooth* is a dyed-in-the-wool book for nerds. It's filled with broad, silly puns, surreal pirouettes in logic, and a wonderful, loud message about the value of knowledge. It's a fantasy/fable that never violates its own wacky system of rules. The hero is a bored, gentle boy named Milo who becomes a hero by becoming smarter. In a *New Yorker* profile honoring the book's fiftieth anniversary in 2011, writer Adam Gopnik called it "the American *Alice in Wonderland*."[1]

I can't remember the last prom king who identified with Alice in Wonderland. If he existed, his name was probably Milo. If you've met him, I've a purple tollbooth and an electric car to sell you.

Yet to say *Tollbooth* has something for only fellow Milos—the pale, the awkward, the slow of foot—is to miss something. I'm sure there are *Tollbooth* readers like this who may feel the same bond with

Norton Juster's creation as they do with *Alice* or *The Lord of the Rings*. They are the *Tollbooth* faithful. There's also a whole other kind of *Tollbooth* reader, who I think will get more out of rereading it now than when they first read it as a kid.

The Phantom Tollbooth remains, over fifty years after its publication, an argument for brain over brawn, for Seas of Knowledge engulfing Mountains of Ignorance. But Juster and his illustrator Jules Feiffer had a different braininess in mind, one that was practically in the water supply in 1961—the year of the book's publication—but that is in short supply half a century later. *Tollbooth* prizes the renaissance nerd instead of its neoclassical cousin, the naval officer/architect/author/professor, as Norton Juster was, or instead of the single-minded software engineer.

The story of *The Phantom Tollbooth* is well known: Milo is a teenage boy resigned to what he perceives as a pointless existence. "Wherever he was, he wished he was somewhere else and when he got there, he wondered why he bothered."[2] One lonely afternoon, he receives a mysterious gift of a toy-sized tollbooth. With nothing better to do, he sets it up, deposits a coin in its coin box, and drives through it in a toy electric car.

He immediately finds himself in Lands Beyond, a kingdom divided in two by the great empires of Dictionopolis (whose citizens worship words) and Digitopolis (where the only value is numbers). The split occurred when the sisters Rhyme and Reason were banished to the Castle in the Air by two warring brothers, King Azaz the Unabridged (Dictionopolis) and the Mathemagician. After several encounters in the outer boroughs of Lands Beyond (the neighborhood of Expectations is represented by the Whether Man, who asks questions and gives no answers; the district of the Doldrums is gray and soporific), Milo and a watchdog named Tock and a giant insect named the Humbug (Juster's version of the Scarecrow and Tin Man) must take the electric car across the kingdom to free Rhyme and Reason. The princesses have been imprisoned in the Mountains of Ignorance and are guarded by Demons (like the Horrible Hopping

Hindsight and the Gorgons of Hate and Malice), who have also befouled the spirit of Wisdom, the first great city of Lands Beyonds.

The Phantom Tollbooth came about through stalling and distraction. Juster was in his early thirties, unmarried, childless, and he had a Ford Foundation grant to create a children's book about cities. Amid a fit of procrastination, he amused himself with wacky little scenes of a young boy untangling the mysteries of language and numbers. Jules Feiffer, his upstairs neighbor, offered to illustrate the story, and a friend of a friend, the legendary editor Jason Epstein, got it published in 1961—a difficult task. At the time, conventional wisdom for children's books followed three rules: don't confuse kids with words they don't know, don't have a hero who seems depressed or angst-ridden, and don't hang out too long in the realm of fantasy because kids get confused.

Juster and Feiffer violated all three. The puns (Chroma, the great conductor of color; the wagon that requires silence because it "goes without saying") blew over my head in grammar school. Feiffer's illustrations, while twitchy, antic fun, resemble more the black-and-white etchings of newspaper and editorial cartoons than the arboreal renderings of a Grimm's fairy tale. "I get a lot of 'Oh, I get it now!' letters from teenagers," Juster told an interviewer in 2011, evidence that *Tollbooth* is a book to be reread at the very least until freshman year at university.[3]

Milo is probably about fourteen and a product of late-Eisenhower America. His flat affect, Sunday-best haircut, and preoccupation with too-much-to-do-none-of-it-interesting is a junior version of the airless men of *Revolutionary Road* boarding the train to work. Milo seems to want very little except to understand the point of it all, and as a school-aged boy, "it all" is learning and education, which takes up two-thirds of our day at that age. His adventures beyond the toll-booth suggest that learning and adventure are the same, that education and experience cannot be separated, and that we become bigger people not by hiding out in the library but by driving headlong in our electric cars into an undiscovered country. This idea was all over 1961, from President John F. Kennedy's "New Frontier" to several of the era's cultural icons—Pan Am airline stewardesses, Apollo astro-nauts, dancers on *American Bandstand*.

The same idea was also the implied motto of the American edu-cational system at the time, the envy of the world still in the after-glow of the GI Bill and the postwar explosion of spending on public libraries. Clifton Fadiman had published the bestselling *Lifetime Reading Plan* the year before, a populist argument for great works of literature and their enduring gifts to each of us. Fadiman, like Juster and Feiffer, belonged to the Jewish working class from New York's outer boroughs, and his American dream hinged on easy, affordable access to the great conversation of the world's great minds.

Fifty years later, this kind of liberal arts boosterism seems both necessary and ridiculous. The Internet has lowered the drawbridge to the greatest march of wisdom and knowledge the world has ever known, wisdom all the more necessary as the world becomes bigger and more connected. At the same time, the cost of a college edu-cation is rapidly climbing out of reach of most people, and para-lyzing student loan debt compels those who do attend and graduate to focus on "practical" majors leading to remunerative careers. Even now, the overspecialized myopia that plagues the demons of Lands Beyond may not be anyone's idea of wisdom and well-roundedness, but it's sure an easier way to pay for it.

However naïve it seems now, *The Phantom Tollbooth* reminds us that learning isn't just medicine to be downed, that it doesn't need to be calibrated like a scale or put to use like a C-clamp. Learning can be silly or ridiculous, scary or beautiful. And it can and prob-ably should happen out in the world instead of hidden away from it. A trip to the science museum or concert hall should have the same antic spirit as a visit to the Forest of Sight or the Valley of Sound.

High school, when learning is vitally necessary to oncoming adulthood yet marginalized by the very real demands of fitting in, is exactly the time we need to hear this message. But since *The Phantom Tollbooth* has pictures and imaginary animals, it probably will remain an elementary school staple for now.

No big whoop. *Tollbooth* is as important to the nerd adult as to the prom king, to all of us in the data blizzard of the twenty-first century who do a whole lot of learning with very little time for experiencing. Though it is clearly the product of a dead-and-gone time in American history, *The Phantom Tollbooth* is that rare miracle of a book that argues that learning more by reading and learning more by getting out and doing stuff are just as valuable.

Use it for both, nerds and prom kings. Read it again, then do as Milo did. Remember: "books to read" but also "songs to sing, places to go," that "everything looked new—and worth trying."[4]

32

CAMPING IT UP
WITH SUSAN SONTAG

1. **"Notes on 'Camp'" is an essay of 6,049 words (about seventeen book-length pages) published in 1964.** It contains two pages of introduction, then fifty-eight paragraph-long "jottings" that attempt to decipher and decode what the author calls "the sensibility—unmistakably modern, a variant of sophistication but hardly identical to it—that goes by the cult name of camp."[1]

2. *The Partisan Review* **(1934–2003) was the essay's first home.** A left-leaning political and cultural quarterly, it was also the Emerald City for the young author of "Notes on 'Camp.'" Susan Sontag once remarked that her desire was to "write for the *Partisan Review* and be read by 5,000 subscribers."[2]

The essay next appeared in the collection *Against Interpretation*, published in 1966. *Against Interpretation* has been in print for forty-five years, largely because it contains "Notes on 'Camp,'" which is now widely considered one of the most important essays of the twentieth century and which announced its author as an important American intellectual. Sontag would never be read only by *Partisan Review* subscribers again.

3. Susan Sontag published "Notes on 'Camp'" in 1964. She was thirty-one and had only the year before exited academia to write full time. She was a young, divorced mother with a single novel, *The Benefactor*, on her bibliography. In its lukewarm review, the *New York Times* called *The Benefactor* "an unfortunate exchange" between "insight and trickery."[3]

"Notes on 'Camp'" made Susan Sontag into a celebrity. "The dark lady of American letters" would have a four-decade career as America's most public intellectual.[4] When she died in 2004, she had written four novels, six collections of essays, and four additional nonfiction monographs. She wrote and directed in both the cinema and the theater and was awarded the National Book Award, the National Book Critics Circle Award, and the Jerusalem Prize for literature. Though she has been gone less than a generation, there are already a half dozen retrospectives of her life's work in print.

The larger world knows her best—often only—for "Notes on 'Camp.'"

4. "Notes on 'Camp'" is not high school reading. Unless you went to a much fancier high school than I did, you probably didn't encounter the essay until college or graduate school, perhaps in the back of a dusty bookstore on a Sunday afternoon or from a know-it-all friend who used it as ammunition when labeling something "campy." They may have even used the phrase "In the Sontagian sense of 'camp,'" but let us hope they didn't. Or, if they did, let's hope that you followed it up with a punch in the mouth.

5. The essay should be high school reading, as it remains even more relevant and useful now than in its own time, an asymmetrical achievement on par with Philip Roth besting *Portnoy's Complaint* and *Goodbye, Columbus* with the novels of his golden years.

Sontag's prose is lean and direct, making "Notes on 'Camp'" a short, brisk read, but her reasoning, like that of an illusionist ("look this way, no this way, perhaps over here"), will leave a high school reader both perplexed and itching for the clarity of discussion.

If I had read "Camp" in high school, I would have been baffled but not frustrated enough to run away. Instead, I'd have wanted answers to "Why read it?" "How does this camp idea apply to my own life?" and, finally, "Has Sontag created a decoder ring I can use to explain the styles—'indie,' 'hip-hop,' 'glam,' 'mod'—taped inside my locker door?"

6. Camp is now everywhere. Remove camp and there would be no Lady Gaga or celebrity designer collections at Target, a lot less reality television, and no one getting famous off an Internet meme.

Any teenager trying to understand the age they live in will need to contend with camp. This essay is their microscope. A skilled teacher will demonstrate how to use it well.

7. "Notes on 'Camp'" is a phrase now part of everyday speech. A Google® search reveals a number of straightforward references to the essay, as well as critical examinations of the author herself ("Notes on Notes on 'Camp,'" "Notes on Sontag"); the phrase's influence on gay culture (a policy report on the subject titled "Sour 'Notes on Camp'"); knowing winks at the phrase's ubiquity (a public-radio documentary on summer camp, which borrows the phrase); and disappointment with linguistic ubiquity itself (journalist Ron Rosenbaum posted an article on Slate about hackneyed catchphrases, called "Notes on Catch"). If this kind of digital annotation and borrowing is a twenty-first-century indicator of influence, the nearly fifty-year-old "Notes on 'Camp'" is showing few signs of middle age.

8. The grand achievement of "Notes on 'Camp'" was detonating the wall between high and low culture, or, as Sontag argued, camp itself "turned its back on the good-bad axis of ordinary aesthetic judgment."[5] Sontag's effortless knowledge of great writers, painters, and philosophers, coupled with her own credentials (Harvard, Oxford, University of Chicago), rendered her intellectual chops unquestionable. She then used them in the service of understanding why both Camus and Flash Gordon comics deserved our consideration.

Before "Notes on 'Camp,'" midcentury American intellectuals had seen much of their job as deciphering which aspects of culture were worthy of their time, of championing present and future canonical art, and of avoiding "low culture" as one would an open sewer. Sontag gave us an entirely new set of tools. What mattered now, she argued, was *how* one focused on the intellect, not *on what*. The intellectual's job was to wield their minds as a laser, not an air filter.

9. The second grand achievement of "Notes on 'Camp'" was its intellectual rigor and moral neutrality toward gay culture. "Camp" came out five years before the Stonewall riots and a decade before the American Psychiatric Association stopped labeling homosexuality a mental illness. Sontag devotes notes 51 through 53 on "the particular relation between camp taste and homosexuality," on how gay culture uses camp as theater, as aesthetics, as a social battering ram.[6] She says nothing about whether gayness is right or wrong, or whether it is worthy of her attention. Its inclusion in the essay answers that question on its own.

10. To know of Susan Sontag means having an opinion on her politics and viewing her politics with one eye closed. Sontag's *New York Times* obituary noted that

> She was described, variously, as explosive, anticlimactic, original, derivative, naive, sophisticated, approachable, aloof, condescending, populist, puritanical, sybaritic, sincere, posturing, ascetic, voluptuary, right-wing, left-wing, profound, superficial, ardent, bloodless, dogmatic, ambivalent, lucid, inscrutable, visceral, reasoned, chilly, effusive, relevant, passé, tenacious, ecstatic, melancholic, humorous, humorless, deadpan, rhapsodic, cantankerous, and clever.[7]

All of which were true. Susan Sontag may be one of the few public intellectuals who didn't view consistency as part of her job description. She redacted positions and critiqued her older writings in hindsight. Her prose's sparse clarity made her assertions feel as inarguable as chemical formulas, and she wasn't polite toward those who disagreed with her. And yet when being interviewed or lecturing, Sontag's voice would quiver and her eyes would tear when she spoke of her most beloved writers, filmmakers, and ideas. Her serious mind left plenty of room for emotion, including both rapture and doubt.

11. It also left room for fun. Susan Sontag's body of work is substantial, but she often joked of chronic battles with procrastination. She loved parties and socializing, was photogenic and knew it, and enjoyed showing up in profiles in *Rolling Stone* and *People* magazine. She mentored many younger writers. She laughed easily. And though

Sontag once told an interviewer "All I am really defending is an idea of serious, a true seriousness,"[8] her life outside her work reveals that she did not equate seriousness with fear of having a good time.

12. Susan Sontag hated writing essays. The form she is most famous for gave her fits. The metallic smoothness of her prose came from many months of revising.

13. Hard work is Sontag's great lesson. We know she thought of herself as a novelist first and as an essayist a distant second. She became a legendary essayist through great struggle and hard work (to "essay" means "to attempt"). Her point of view slithered away from easy characterization, then doubled back, leaving us with the phrase "have an active mind" as a consistent thread. And though her alliances were clearly with what we now call "high culture," she found it stultifying to keep herself there and argued in the title essay of *Against Interpretation* for "an erotics of art," for a marriage of the mind and the gut, of passion and intellect, of approaching an idea as an athlete might, with thought soaked in sweat.[9]

14. "Notes on 'Camp'" is not a Rosetta Stone but a pair of pliers. We're missing the point if we read the essay and think it holds some kind of answer for what camp is or what it has become. Instead, we should view "Camp" as a tool for prying open confusion, for taking an equally complicated topic ("class warfare," "liberalism," "indie rock") and running it through the same obstacle course of the mind, as Sontag did with the concept of camp. Weigh it against what you already know, seek out and study what you don't, ask questions, and don't be afraid to change your mind as circumstances change and as you become wiser.

It may seem impossible to find the time at first, but like any muscle, the mind, argues Sontag, becomes limber only with use.

15. The Ultimate Sontag Statement. We do not read "Notes on 'Camp'" or any Susan Sontag piece for answers; we read in order to learn how to ask good questions, how to think in a fighting stance rather than in a slouch, and how the rewards for the effort are thoughts clean and clear rather than cracked and fogged.

This isn't always true and is certainly not true for every word Sontag ever committed to paper. It is the case only under certain conditions and with certain reading experiences, like the one I've tried to outline in these notes.

33

"THE WORK OF ART IN THE AGE OF MECHANICAL REPRODUCTION"
BY WALTER BENJAMIN,
NOTES BY KEVIN SMOKLER

Walter Benjamin's 1936 essay "The Work of Art in the Age of Mechanical Reproduction" has been ubiquitous and influential since the day it was published. If you've ever had a spirited conversation about what is and isn't considered art and culture since graduating from college, this essay might have come up. If not, it would certainly have contributed to the discussion in an elemental, omnipresent fashion, the way sunlight contributes to the red in the petals of a rose.

Benjamin's writing is brilliant, overstuffed with ideas—and maddening for both those reasons. Susan Sontag described his sentences as "having to say everything, before the inward gaze of total concentration dissolved the subject before his eyes"; needing to finish "just before they self-destruct."[1] Personally, I think that's being a little romantic. My experience of reading "Mechanical Reproduction" was a nineteen-page bout of bipolar disorder: I was alternately lifted off the ground at the sheer genius of Benjamin's ideas, then infuriated by the muck in which he drowns them. A great Benjamin thought (and there are several dozen here) is a treasure wrapped in rubber bands. The untangling comes with the joy.

Let us untangle. Below are my own notes to the essay, advising you on how to quickly cut through the rubber bands to get at the treasure.[2] I'll discuss how to make deft use of the essay in your next debate over the relative worth of modern art or video games or tweets as haiku. The idea here is to underline what is useful as well as astounding about Benjamin's ideas. Benjamin's gold can be used for both brooches and electric wire.

OPENING QUOTE

Benjamin leads off with a quote from Paul Valery, the French poet and philosopher of the generation before Benjamin's. The two most important lines:

> Profound changes are impending in the ancient craft of *The Beautiful.*

and

> We must expect great innovations to transform the entire technique of the arts, thereby affecting artistic invention itself and perhaps even bringing about an amazing change in our very notion of art.

This is the opening bell of Benjamin's argument. He is clearer here than he will be for the majority of his essay.

PREFACE

Benjamin has two paragraphs about how Marx's theories of capitalism influence his own ideas about the role of politics in art. The role of politics in art is, at best, a minor component of the rest of the essay. If Marx is a bone you like to gnaw on, go right ahead. Otherwise, skip ahead without guilt.

SECTION I

Benjamin leaves the runway and starts lining up insights in brilliant succession:

- **Art has always been reproducible.** The Greeks used bronze molds for vessels and statuary, metal sheets to stamp out coins and amulets. The Middle Ages gave us the woodcut and printing. The modern era invented lithography and photography. "Art" as unique and singular is under suspicion right away.
- **Photography and its descendant, motion pictures, change the speed at which art captures the world.** The measurement of that speed is now how fast the eye can see rather than how fast the hand can draw or paint.
- **As indoor plumbing and electricity grab something far away and bring it effortlessly into our home, the ability to reproduce sound and images will also bring them into our lives at the flick of a switch.** Art therefore has an identical historical trajectory to what we now call "utilities."

The first argument contextualizes everything from Andy Warhol silk screens to hip-hop sampling to mash-up entertainment. Before we dismiss culture because it copies and riffs, we must bear in mind that "uniqueness" is a shaky platform from which to mount definitions of art. The third argument points the way to television, the Internet, and the smartphone, and reminds us of the premium our actions place on information/culture/entertainment without even acknowledging it. Access to images and information is not a luxury but a utility on par with electric light and flushing toilets.

SECTION II

Nuggets

- **Reproductions lack the original, unique context in which something is created.** Yes. Yes, they do.
- **Artwork can be reproduced in different ways to achieve different results.** A copied painting feels like a cheaper version of the original, whereas it feels silly to fetishize the "original" print of a photograph. Something in the DNA of photography dictates that it is meant to be copied.
- **Reproduction allows an artwork to come to the viewer when a viewer cannot come to it.** Yep. By reproducing a work, however, it is removed from its original context. The Taj Mahal isn't a giant marble building when you see it on TV. It's at the very least a digital copy of a giant marble building.

Benjamin then runs all over creation explaining this removal from context, leaning on terms of abstraction like "object authority" and "domain of tradition," none of which he explains. He goes so far as to call reproduction a kind of "liquidation," which seems like a thoughtlessly used word for a writer as careful as he is. Maybe these are old favorites he's used before.

Takeaway

Reproduction changes how and why we regard an art object, even if it's meant to be reproduced.

Moving on . . .

SECTION III

Here Benjamin explains his idea of "the aura" (the term nearly everyone who read this essay in eleventh-grade history class, as I did, remembers). He defines the aura as the singular uniqueness of an object, which it both contains and emits at a distance. Our desire to possess the uniqueness of an object explains our desire to reproduce it, as we simply can't get physically close enough to everything that turns us on. The problem with this desire is that reproducing it is to "pry an object from its shell, to destroy its aura."

There are then a few sentences about the relationships of "the masses" and "reality" and "perception," which make no sense at all. Skip them and return to this "aura" idea. Interrogate the issue of reproduction and specialness. Are you the sort who can listen to music in MP3 format but likes to watch movies only on a big screen? Would you be satisfied seeing Rembrandt's *The Night Watch* as a color plate in a book, or would you prefer to book a plane ticket to Amsterdam to see the real thing?

SECTION IV

According to Mr. B, the history of art goes a little something like this:

- **In the beginning.** Art is magic. Primitive man painting a buffalo on his cave wall is asking the gods to make something magical happen. The communication is from earth to the heavens.
- **With the coming of religion, art becomes ritualized.** Art is still the nexus between humanity and the eternal, but the art object itself is also venerated publicly (see the stained-glass window).
- **After the Renaissance, art is still venerated but for aesthetic rather than religious reasons.** Art is now beautiful all on its own, right here on earth.
- **With reproduction, art is in many places at once, in many ver-**

sions at once, so it can no longer be at the center of worship. Benjamin says art then "begins to be based on another practice—politics," which will make sense when and if Benjamin explains. He doesn't here.

SECTION V

A rehash of IV. Onward.

SECTION VI

A quick diversion into the early history of photography in which Benjamin explains that portrait photography (a direct descendant of painting) is photography gradually giving up the mantle of ritual and worship and becoming a reproducible art form. There are also a few lines on how a photo caption inherently politicizes a photograph by recontextualizing it forcefully for the viewer.

All great stuff if you are a big nerd about shutter speeds and lens gels. Otherwise, proceed directly to the following.

SECTION VII

Benjamin turns his attention to film and the early debates over whether the moving image is art and how its early proponents first described it in the language of ritual, even though film is the lead blocker in this new arena of art meant to be reproduced.

I suppose you can ask the question "Does a new medium first need to be argued for as ritual before we can label it as art?" Or "Is object of ritual to object of beauty the life path of all new art forms?" But that's all there is here. It's essentially throat clearing for what is to come.

SECTION VIII

Benjamin will be staying with film for a while. In this single-paragraph section, he submits the following:

- **As opposed to actors in the theater, actors in a movie are directing their performances at a camera.** The camera has taken over the position of the theater audience.
- **An actor's performance is not a unified whole but an edited sequence of "best takes," which Benjamin equates with "optic tests."** This metaphor makes sense only if you have never been on a film shoot.
- **Since actors do not present their performances to the audience in person and since the audience is watching an edited sequence of the actors' best work, the audience assumes the role of the critic.** Which makes sense. I just wouldn't have argued it that way.

The idea that the very nature of a movie is the act of an actor auditioning for the audience is a compelling one and goes a long way toward explaining (a) the behavior of many audiences in movie theaters and (b) why everyone on earth has an opinion about the movies. The way Benjamin gets to this point is like using a bulldozer to fill a flowerpot.

SECTION IX

Benjamin gets stupid brilliant here and submits that an actor in the theater is a venerated art object (like a painting or a Grecian urn) with its own aura. An actor on film has been separated from his or her aura. Benjamin doesn't say this specifically, but he implies: in order for an art object to have an aura, it must have an audience to feel it.

Whoa. We've just thrown into the air the question that pervades nearly every discussion of the worthiness of art. Does the audience matter? Is something "art" all on its own or must it be engaged with by someone who didn't create it? If art falls in the woods . . .

We can stop now. There's enough to chew on here for the next several cocktail parties and college reunions. But he isn't quite done yet.

SECTION X

There's way too much about Marxism gumming up the works here, but Benjamin blows more fire into two points from the last section.

> It is inherent in the technique of the film as well as that of sports that everybody who witnesses its accomplishments is somewhat of an expert.
> At any moment, the reader is ready to turn into a writer.

I'm getting the vapors. Does "Mechanical Reproduction" point to our contemporary culture where production of art is democratized; where the din of opinion is deafening; and, by extension, where the manner in which we select what culture to consume becomes a kind of expertise all its own? Was he talking about social media, the democratization of creativity, and content curating seventy-five years before such things existed?

I don't know. But the possibility is making me weak in the knees.

SECTION XI

Oy vey, Walter. You've got some great insights here about the artistic role of a motion-picture cameraman and how the job resembles the art of a surgeon: cutting into something (in the case of the cameraman, a spool of film) to create a new whole. But the argument is quickly lost under a pile of undefined terms and incomplete conclusions. The last paragraph is all you need. And then . . .

SECTION XII

Three knockout punches here.

> The conventional is uncritically enjoyed, and the truly new is criticized with aversion.

Probably the most (over)quoted line in the essay. I prefer the simpler "All great truths begin as blasphemies" from George Bernard Shaw, but it is still an unassailable truth elegantly stated.

> Individual reactions are predetermined by the mass audience response they are about to produce, and this is nowhere more pronounced than in the film.

Read: Reactions to art have a momentum of their own, like an avalanche. Film is, traditionally at least, watched in a group setting, with your reactions influenced by those sitting near you.

Older art forms like painting are not as easy to observe in a group setting, at least not on the same scale as reproducible arts like film. Benjamin submits that this lack of collective harmed the acceptance of certain movements in painting, like surrealism. I'm not so sure. But tucked in there is an equally interesting question. Do we first think "painting" when we hear the word *art* precisely because we are more likely to view a painting by ourselves, in a rarified location?

SECTION XIII

A long windup leading up to this: A film allows us to see things in ways our eyes cannot ordinarily perceive (from above, from very close up, from underwater). In doing so, it parallels the unconsciousness, a record of emotions, memories, and utterances that we cannot perceive but that are quite present.

I dig that.

SECTION XIV

Another brilliant double shot. First paragraph:

> One of the foremost tasks of art has always been the creation of a
> demand which could be fully satisfied only later.

WB then explains that when art becomes grotesque and exaggerated,
it is not a vulgarity or the end of days; art is effectively crying out
for the next wave of innovation to take it forward. This signifies an
optimism we almost never get from the melancholy Benjamin that I
now want to slap on the back and buy a drink.

The last paragraph has some gorgeous stuff about the shock
of art mentioned in the first paragraph. Does the pulverization of
shocking images deaden us or make us hyper-aware as we would be
if the images were, say, bullets flying at our head? A thought for our
hyperkinetic age.

SECTION XV

> Panel Painting is a creation of the Middle Ages, and nothing guar-
> antees its uninterrupted existence.

Preach! Take that, O cynic of modernity, O handwringer, O "it was
better when." All art movements are here at our pleasure as a species,
not by the mandate of heaven.

Benjamin complicates this, saying that there is some art we must
take time to notice (like a painting) and that other art becomes successful when we relate to it less consciously, out of habit (like archi-
tecture). He concludes with "The public is an examiner, but an
absent-minded one," an odd, cryptic phrasing that leaves open wide
thoroughfares of inquiry: How does art become ubiquitous in this
way? How long must we wait for it to happen? And the wondrous

possibility I'm stuck on: if art is to become so ubiquitous as to be ordinary, (a) is this a good thing? and (b) if so, how long must we wait and how much do we need to trust each other for it to happen?

EPILOGUE

Ignore it. Benjamin tries to come back around to art and politics and fascism and communism, but it's too late. The best stuff has already been said.

Takeaways

- Reproducibility does not determine if something is art or not. Art has always been reproducible. Consider this the next time you're at a museum and say, "I could paint that."
- Our relationship with the arts has traveled the same path as our relationship with electricity and indoor plumbing, a resource produced far away that we wish to have effortlessly brought to us, a utility we take for granted. Consider this the next time your local school sees art programs as a budget surplus to be trimmed.
- When art is grotesque or weird or disturbing, it is pushing its own boundaries, trying to evolve into the next version of itself; it does not exist just to give you nightmares. Consider this the next time you take offense to anything created by those younger than you. As we grow older, even wiser, we may understand less.

34

HELLO, I'M WILLIAM SHAKESPEARE

This essay is about the work of William Shakespeare. If Mr. Shakespeare is already a vital part of your reading life, skip ahead. You don't need to hear what I'm about to say. But if you read the title of this essay and thought "I had more than enough Shakespeare in high school, thank you very much!" read on. I have you in mind.

I've yet to hear an argument for reading Shakespeare after high school that doesn't sound like an endorsement of leafy green vegetables—inarguably good advice, obvious, a little scolding. Yes, yes, the man is a genius/the greatest dramatist ever/an all-star contributor to the English language/make impatient hand circles now. We all sat through this sermon well before our eighteenth birthday. We know the clichés of balconies and Poor Yoricks, of comparing our beloved to a summer's day and "Once more unto the breach." We've sat through a few movie adaptations and stage performances. In adulthood, we probably have an annoying blowhard of a friend who thinks saying "I love Shakespeare" means "therefore I'm a better person than you." We should all then be forgiven, even sympathized with, for waving at Shakespeare sitting back in high school English class from our vantage point here in the present, then turning around and leaving him there.

But as someone who loves books and the gifts they give, I feel like I'd be missing something—well, a lot of something—just to say "no, thanks" to Mr. Shakespeare, with his silly accents, his preposterous plots, and greatness as thrilling as gravity. And I don't submit that because any one writer is indispensable. None of them are. I think I should not leave Shakespeare behind based solely on the crude democracies of time and influence.

You may think "YMCA" by the Village People is an awful song. As of this writing, "YMCA" is thirty-four years old and is still more beloved than hundreds of songs by Sonic Youth or Miles Davis or many other artists who have achieved greater cultural respect. And to say that's just the lowest common denominator at work is to be intentionally myopic. At some point, "good" or "bad" recedes before "remembered." Longevity is the great judge, not awards conjured up by great minds now fertilizing tulip beds.

Arguments based on Shakespeare's technical wizardry do not sway me either. He had his failings as a craftsman, and there are plenty of acclaimed writers to fill the rest of one's reading hours if Elizabethan-era stage drama isn't your bag. Instead, I am persuaded by the degree to which Shakespeare's work has shaped our language and stuck around for remixing. The list of phrases he invented—"in the blink of an eye," "forgone conclusion," "heart of gold"— now spoken as easily as our own names, is simply staggering. And how many other playwrights can you name who are not just performed everywhere all the time but performed everywhere all the time in different settings, set to music, in prison, and in drag?

Shakespeare seems to never be unnecessary; he has graduated out of the canon and has become an element on the cultural periodic table. If I were a chemist, I'd like to be familiar with nitrogen. I like books and stories. So I'd like to be familiar with Shakespeare.

I've returned to Shakespeare recently, and at times, I still feel the shiver of cultural coercion I remember from high school. "Shakespeare" is practically synonymous with "genius" or, more specifically, synonymous with "Kneel before Zod!" At precisely the moment we are exposed to his work, the time in life of rebellion and uncomfortable change, we're ordered to have only one opinion about Shakespeare's place in the world. Does a high school sophomore feel at liberty to say that Shakespeare's plots can feel contrived, that he borrowed too liberally from his contemporaries, or that his work can feel hurried and sloppy at the edges because he had funders and theatrical audiences waiting for him to finish it? That the man might be great but not great every single time? I hope so, because in the tenth grade I sure didn't feel comfortable saying this. And if adulthood means not having to return to what was force-fed to you as a young person, Shakespeare might be the least deserving yet most understandable example.

I'm older now. If you're at the same place with Shakespeare— possibly interested but uncertain—the first step is to listen to that sense of caution. It is way too easy to always feel that your Shakespeare efforts are inadequate because you haven't read all thirty-seven plays, you haven't memorized a dozen sonnets, you don't know which character uttered the phrase "the game is up," and you feel bullied by the last "Shakespeare fan" you ran into who wanted to lock horns on the matter of Olivier's Hamlet versus Gielgud's Prospero; so reintroducing yourself to Shakespeare isn't worth the bother.

Now go for it anyway. As Clifton Fadiman said so well, "Shakespeare was a man, not a demigod. . . . He is meant to be read and enjoyed as much as admired."[1] I'm with him. Shakespeare is a vast body of water. Splashing around doing handstands is just as rewarding as deep-sea diving.

A few tips on how to do this.

1. Start with the plays and sonnets you already know. Could be those you read in high school or just know as the clichés of the Shakespeare library. Doesn't matter. Rereading gives you the advantage of not having to go in cold with plot and character. The outlines of the stories will be familiar enough to focus on the good stuff: great lines, turns of phrases, and then radical ideas of storytelling that have become tried-and-true since.

2. Cheat. No one's giving you a grade. So if you don't remember who Dogberry is or would like a quick introduction to a play before diving in, use CliffsNotes® or Wikipedia or the shortcut of your choice. No one will slap your hand with a ruler, and you won't spend the first forty pages trying to keep all the characters straight. You lose nothing except perhaps the surprise. You gain focus and time.

3. Cheat elaborately. Shakespeare wrote for the stage. He intended the work to be seen, not read, usually in front of a raucous crowd that hurled things at the actors and shouted suggestions when they didn't like where a play was going. If you can find a duplicate of that experience, lucky you. But if you'd rather see a play than read it, do so. Ask around for a respectable theater company nearby, read some entries on Wikipedia or check out other online sources to get the basic outline of the play, then go see how Local Theater Company X is interpreting it, as Shakespeare is remixed as often as played straight. I like to go to the theater on weekend afternoons when I can eat lunch beforehand, don't have to rush over from work, and can finish the day with coffee and dessert. I usually have to drink a diet soda beforehand or I'll fall asleep. Whatever you need to do to make a visit to the theater pleasant, do it. Treat it like an obligation, and it'll feel like one.

4. Grab sonnets at random. There are 154 of them. I'm sure some are better than others, but I really don't know. Many are pretty dang romantic if love poetry is your sort of thing. Regardless, a sonnet is fourteen measly lines, and the language is uniformly beautiful. Think of them as exquisite mints to top off a day of reading or a visit to the theater, or to redeem a day of doing nothing that feels wasted.

5. Enlist friends. You want to read Shakespeare alone? I don't. Why not be the one to make a group game out of it, lubricated by alcohol and rich pastries?

6. Be selfish. There's so much great stuff in Shakespeare, you can't possibly appreciate it all the same way. So figure out what itch he scratches for you and keep coming back to it (for me, it's the origins of popular expressions and new ways of saying simple things). Once that itch has gone away, find another. But don't think for a second there's something you're supposed to be "getting" out of reading Shakespeare and that

you're the slow-wit for not knowing what it is. Whatever you get—even if it's a great Falstaffian word for bodily fluids—is up to you. It should bring you joy first and foremost.

One of my favorite things about no longer being in high school is not having to rebel for its own sake, being comfortable with what I like to read, watch, and listen to without having to explain it as oppositional. Saying, "I'd never read/listen to/watch this! How dare you! Can't you see I'm plainly in the anti-this camp?" gives you an electric charge of self-righteousness when you're sixteen. Now it feels like defensive nonsense, responding to a judgment no one has passed. Be happy with what you like. No explanations or apologies necessary. Nap afterward with impunity.

A quick story: two decades after graduation, I'm still known at Greenhills School as the asshole who once declared Shakespeare's plays to be "trite." Actually, that's an exaggeration. As I remember, we were reading *As You Like It* in junior year and thought it was an idiotic plot device that Rosalind disguised herself as a boy named Ganymede. I might have called it "trite." But I was talking about a cross-dressing gimmick I'd seen on two dozen sitcoms, not the bibliography of the Bard of Avon/Greatest Playwright Ever/That Guy whom I had spent the last three years writing papers about and resenting. The following year I recited the St. Crispin's Day speech from *Henry V* at graduation and was introduced as "the student who once declared Shakespeare trite." It got a long and knowing laugh.

35

UNDERSTANDING MARSHALL McLUHAN

Marshall McLuhan does not make it easy. Even if his name isn't familiar to you, his ideas and their snappy formulations are—"the medium is the message," "the global village," "the age of information," and "we shape our tools, and then our tools shape us." The fact that McLuhan first brought these ideas into our consciousness with the publication of his third book, *Understanding Media*, in 1964 (when the personal computer was still exotic enough to be introduced at a World's Fair) and not, say, last Thursday is mind-blowing. We now refer to "the global village" as easily as we do popular songs and lines of poetry. But actually *reading* McLuhan's explanation of the term is a hot mess akin to being trapped in an exploded crate of Silly String®. This is a big reason why the man and his genius drive us crazy.

An English professor at the University of Toronto when he became famous, McLuhan was a master at catchphrases and was terrible at explaining them. His interviews (and he gave a ton of them during the four to six years of white-hot media attention following the publication of *Understanding Media*) were long, digressive walks of the mind during which McLuhan would change subjects midthought, throwing off literary and historical references without explanation like produce spilling from a flatbed truck. He rarely let facts get in the way of a good argument. "I don't believe half of what I say" and "You don't like those ideas? I got others!" are two consistently beloved and cited "McLuhanisms."[1] A 1996 *Wired* magazine profile called "The Wisdom of Saint Marshall, the Holy Fool" notes that McLuhan was an engaging but exhausting companion. Management theorist and old friend Peter Drucker recalled opening his front door one rainy morning to find a soaked, unannounced Marshall McLuhan standing there. McLuhan "just wanted to talk."[2]

Here's McLuhan "just talking" in a section of *Understanding Media* that I found by throwing the book, spine up, on the living room floor:

> The massive theme of the press can be managed only by direct contact with the formal pattern of the medium in question. It is thus necessary to state that "human interest" is a technical term meaning that which happens when multiple book pages or multiple information items are arranged in mosaic form on a one-sheet. The book is a private confessional form that provides "point of view." The press is a group confessional form that provides communal participation.[3]

Eh, maybe?

To me, the effect of listening to and reading McLuhan (there really isn't much difference) was to be fascinated and annoyed simultaneously, then jumping ship about three-quarters in (as I did several times with McLuhan's 1969 *Playboy* interview, *Understanding Media*, and sections of his other books). I needed time to both process what I had heard and take a nap with a hand towel over my head.

Explaining, debunking, and praising McLuhan (who died of a stroke on New Year's Eve, 1980) is now a cottage industry several times bigger than the collected work of the man himself (Remember the joke in *Annie Hall* where Woody Allen refutes a guy bloviating about McLuhan by pulling the real McLuhan out of a movie line? Imagine several dozen of those guys arguing with each other). McLuhan was pretty much over by the time of his death. Much of *Understanding Media* focuses on the great change television would bring, and, by the Reagan era, nobody questioned that. Media and its author were, as Lewis Lapham put it in his introduction to the 1994 reissue of the book, "sent to the attic with the rest of the sensibility (go-go boots,

Sgt. Pepper, Woodstock, the Vietnam War) that embodied the failed hopes of a discredited decade."[4]

And then came the Internet. Suddenly McLuhan seemed not like a footnote but a prophet. *Wired* magazine named him "their patron saint" in the magazine's very first issue.[5] New biographies were written. For McLuhan's centenary in 2011, nearly eighty official events were planned worldwide.

McLuhan remains vitally important and terribly unpleasant to read. I've no idea if today's high school students are assigned *Understanding Media* in its entirety, as an excerpt tucked into a photocopied course pack as I did, or not at all. He is difficult to place— History? Sociology? Politics?—and how many high schools actually do media studies in any formal way? I certainly hope it's only a few, as the last statistic I saw on media studies mentioned that people under twenty-five spend half their waking hours interacting with various forms of media.

Marshall McLuhan may be one of the few great minds best approached through interviews, documentaries, and writings *about* him rather than through the work itself. From the outside in, you can taste the greatest hits like "the medium is the message," and then dig into the liner notes, the B-sides, and the documentaries on the making of, if you want. If you choose to delve into his books, it might be difficult hiking, but it certainly won't feel like brain masturbation. McLuhan's ideas might be hard to sort out. But they are the farthest thing from impractical.

Let us take a clutch of McLuhan's best, explain them as cleanly as one can, then include the possible relevance of these ideas for the century McLuhan didn't live to see but predicted better than anyone else.

THE MEDIUM IS THE MESSAGE

McLuhan's most-repeated and least-understood phrase. He meant a couple of things by it.

1. **The package content comes in is as important as content itself.** A Shakespearean sonnet contains the exact same fourteen lines whether they are printed in a book, read on the radio, or decorated on a giant sheet cake. But our relationship to that sonnet changes based on how we receive it. Example: the 1960 Kennedy-Nixon presidential debate. Few of us remember exactly what was said. We remember instead that it was the first televised debate, that Kennedy looked relaxed and handsome, that Nixon looked sweaty and nervous, and that those listening on the radio thought Nixon (not Kennedy) had won. The exact same debate, watched or listened to, takes on an entirely different meaning.

2. **Content is still important, but it is not the only thing that's important.** Focusing only on that Shakespearean sonnet and not on how it is presented blinds us to several things: (a) that someone is probably looking to make money off that sonnet and will present it any way we want, even on a sheet cake; (b) that same person will put "happy birthday" or "congratulations" on that sheet cake (instead of the sonnet) if we decide we want that; and (c) biggest of all, "media" is creator, object, medium, and audience all awkwardly holding hands in a line. McLuhan saw the audience (us) at the end of that line and thus

3. **He saw "the medium is the message" as a warning.** "All media exist to invest our lives with artificial perception and arbitrary values," McLuhan wrote.[6] And since he considered tools and technology like the lightbulb to be as much a part of the delivery of "media" as the television set, the television set will tell us how to interact with it much as a canoe would. At its worst, thought McLuhan, we become slaves to our own messengers.

Takeaway

Fear not. Despite the protests of parents of teenagers and how we feel when we lose our cell phones, we are not slaves to the media windows in our lives. McLuhan didn't think the answer was to reject technology but to think ahead of it, how we use it, what it means when we do, what purpose it serves, and where it falls short. "Resenting a technology does not halt its progress," he told *Playboy* in a 1969 interview, but he argued in that same interview that we bend and change media when we become cognizant of its limitations.[7] The $99 reading device represents both a business opportunity and us wanting an affordable, electronic, connected book. It's an idea Walter Benjamin played around with thirty years before in his essay "The Work of Art in the Age of Mechanical Reproduction"—and it's a fundamentally optimistic one. Media ultimately makes great changes only when we decide it has done all it can for us now. We are in control.

Try it sometime. Go a week without your cell phone or declare "e-mail bankruptcy" and delete everything in your inbox. It will not only be less tragic than you think; it will be liberating.

WE SHAPE OUR TOOLS, AND THEN OUR TOOLS SHAPE US

Our behavior, thought, and actions change based on the media in our lives, often imperceptibly. The presence of media is not value neutral. Twenty years ago, nobody checked their Facebook® six times a day. That may seem like a harmless example, but it isn't without consequence. As Brooke Gladstone, host of the NPR show "On the Media," wrote, "We get the media we deserve," meaning that if we are distracted, fragmented, and unaware, we can't complain that the media ecosystem feels that way too.[8]

Takeaway

Recent arguments about "media diets" (i.e., what we put into our heads being as consequential as the food we put into our bodies) point to this idea. Now list the last five books you read, movies you watched, musicians you listened to. How many of those did you consume "to escape," "to forget," "to not think," to, in other words, treat as junk food? We do not consume junk, at least not regularly, without participating in an ecosystem built around making junk.

THE GLOBAL VILLAGE

Not complicated. McLuhan thought the television screen would connect us all by electronic-screen-based communication. The Internet did it instead.

Takeaway

Not everyone in the village is at the same place or point in their evolution with media. Much of sub-Saharan Africa skipped over landlines and went straight to mobile phones. Those are the same mobile phones you might think your kid spends too much time with, texting. The same tools used to post status updates of cookies being baked are also used to foment political revolution.

We may all have the same tools of connection, but we use them for as many different reasons as there are people. In the end, we are ourselves, whether the village is micro or global.

AT THE POINT MEDIA BECOMES ALL PERVASIVE, IT BECOMES INVISIBLE

A couple of years ago, I was asked to talk about the future of books and writing with a group of high school students. Somehow the conversation wound its way around to the future of music, of movies, of video games, and of media itself. And at some point in that hour, I realized that this group of high school students saw the production of media much as I had twenty years earlier: Music was paid for by record labels and sold in record stores. Movies were made in Los Angeles, featured well-dressed famous people, and sent out from there to the rest of the world. Books were sired by institutions called "publishers." To them, the term *published* meant the same as *well written*. Even though these kids were living in the time of the $100 movie camera, GarageBand® software, iTunes®, and the Internet, to them "media" was made by someone else far away, which they then consumed at the end of a long chain of events.

I don't think these kids were dumb. I've met hundreds just like them who also see media as something they create. But I wonder whether those kids—remixing the news, uploading YouTube® videos of their own animations, and e-mailing web comics they create to their friends—are the stylish minority. For most, thinking about media is like thinking about metabolism. It happens; we don't notice its beginnings or endings. It just is.

Takeaway

Not every kid growing up wants to be a media maker. That's fine. But every one of us is a media consumer. And having ideas about media three decades out of date—that media simply rolls downhill from Olympus and we collect it in a wheelbarrow—is not just inaccurate; it is dangerous. It's the intellectual equivalent of thinking all food is the same, simply because it's all edible. It also makes the audience a receptacle when almost fifty years ago McLuhan argued that the audience is as vital to the media ecosystem as are both media and message.

Television is not just a box or a program but content, a method of delivery, and a viewer's relationship to it. They all affect one other. The relationship is not top-down but push-me–pull-you. Even if we create nothing and only consume, we matter. And we will realize that only through self-education and thoughtfulness, which McLuhan argued is the only optimistic way forward.

Start there with McLuhan. Wade in slowly. It's up to you if you'd like to know more—and there is a ton more to know. You just don't need to hear it from him first.

PART 8

VIOLENCE AND LOSS

36

HOLDEN CAULFIELD, THAT LITTLE BRAT

You're rolling your eyes right now, aren't you?

The Catcher in the Rye? *Are you nuts? Who would read that book again? Who would want to feel like their angry ninth-grade self again? Do I need to remember when I actually wore a trench coat and red hunting hat for about eight days? Maybe glance at a few pages before loaning it to my high-school-aged niece. But read it myself as an adult? Again? Only the sad and crazy do that.* The Catcher in the Rye *belongs to your alienated youth. If you need it later on, it's time to grow up and stop fantasizing about killing celebrities.*

Now unscowl your faces, good people. Objections noted. In fact, I had more trouble deciding if *Catcher in the Rye* belonged in *Practical Classics* than any other book. *Catcher*, it seems, belongs to a small group of classics with a built-in self-destruct button. No one reads *Atlas Shrugged* past age twenty-five unless they voted for the Objectivist candidate in the last election. No one pores over Kahlil Gibran's *The Prophet* once they can legally pour a glass of whiskey. And everybody reads *The Catcher in the Rye* in high school, but no one sees reason to afterward. I decided early on that both boxes had to be checked for the book to qualify as not just a classic but as a "Practical Classic."

Hell, even a nostalgic fool like me hasn't read the novel since high school. I've grown up, but since 1951, Holden Caulfield has not.

Now I'm scowling.

In 2010, its author, J. D. Salinger, died at age ninety-one. Those are the times that try a nostalgic fool's soul. I could not find the old edition of the book my mother gave me (with a Norman Rockwell–style cover showing Holden Caulfield at Grand Central Station) when I was fourteen, so on a Sunday afternoon, I went to my neighborhood bookstore, picked up a six-dollar mass-market paperback (with the line drawings of carousel horses on the cover), and read it over two and a half cups of coffee and a second scone I should have avoided.

There are reasons to give *Catcher in the Rye* another go—even if you are now the person who worries about having a Holden Caulfield who asks to borrow the car. Scan this list and see if any of the sentences in bold speak to you. Focus on those and do what you like with the rest. I will not give you a "crumby" scowl or call you a "phony."

I recommend you give *The Catcher in the Rye* another look if

. . . you are presently the parent, older sibling/aunt/uncle/mentor/ friend to a teenager.

Catcher has over three hundred one-star reviews on Amazon, most of which are by teenagers who had to read it for school. The book still sells 250,000 copies a year. I'm sure most are to teenagers or to adults buying them for teenagers. The likelihood the adolescent in your life will run into *Catcher* is high. There's a decent chance they will hate it.

These kids on Amazon don't hate the book because it's been forced on them. Their reasons sound more like this:

Hi, I'm Holden Caulfield . . . I get kicked out of school because I'm a rich preppy spoiled brat, and I lose all my money as I hide out in a hotel, chicken out with a hooker, and get beat up by her pimp. Who can blame him? I'm a total loser, I really am.

Their reviews have titles like this:

Extremely Dated and Overrated!

Wanna know who the phony is? HOLDEN CAUFIELD!

I'm sure it was great in 1951[1]

In 1951, *Catcher*'s publication year, Holden Caulfield—white, upper class, handsome, prep-school educated, drinking and smoking and hanging out at a hotel in New York City—probably seemed pretty damn glamorous, a kind of Eisenhower-era *Risky Business*. The WASP ideal that fantasy borrows from is long gone, and the teenager who reads *Catcher* now is more than likely to be poorer, browner, more hardworking, and more ambitious than Holden Caulfield. So whether they like the book or not, we must first accept that teenagers now could understandably view Holden Caulfield's story as a cave painting from a distant ancestor, if they can relate to it at all.

Catcher arrived at the very beginning of the cultural recognition of adolescence. A few short years later would bring the labeling of "juvenile delinquency," the movie *Rebel without a Cause*, and the early days of rock 'n' roll. Now youth culture is a multibillion-dollar omnipresence and the world where teenagers live. Any discussion should first begin by addressing this radical change in only a half century's time. Holden may have played hooky in New York without a cell phone, credit card, or access to an ATM. But today, a hotel clerk would be fired for checking in a teenage boy in the middle of the night and not alerting the police. Times aren't better or worse—just really, really different.

. . . you find those differences interesting instead of frustrating.

Someone needs to rewrite *The Catcher in the Rye* set in the present. Imagine if Holden could text Jane Gallagher to see if she actually wanted to talk. He'd use Bing® to find out if the ducks in Central Park have a place to stay in the winter when their lagoon freezes. He could book lodgings online at AirBnB.

Catcher does not make me long for my own adolescence. But it does make me ache just a little for how slow time seems to go by in this book, how much of it Holden has to kill, and how he ultimately fails to spend just four days alone in New York without going home. I read this book in 1987, and even with Nintendo® and cable TV and

American Top 40 on Sunday mornings, I remember how often I felt bored, like the world had its own business to tend to and wasn't there to entertain me.

Nowadays, I could kill four days stranded at sea if I had an iPhone®. When I visit New York now, every day feels too short. I'd rather have that than boredom. But I've lost much of my capacity for patience and humility. Now I think the world really is there to entertain me.

Teenagers who read this book will never know this slower world. Use this book as a way to talk about this with them. Focus on change, not better-then, worse-now. If you weren't interested in hearing about the good old days when you were sixteen, neither are they.

. . . you'd like an unconventional tour of New York.

Visiting Holden Caulfield's New York, particularly around Christmas like he did, will give you a daguerreotype of the city you probably haven't seen. Your tour will include places that no longer exist (the Grand Central Station where Holden stored his suitcases was torn down in 1963; the Biltmore Hotel where he met Sally Hayes for their date fell in 1981); some that never did (the Edmont Hotel where Holden meets a prostitute is made up and so is the Wicker Bar where he meets Carl Luce, his old schoolmate); and some that remain unchanged (the Radio City ice rink, the Museum of Natural History). You'll want to find substitutes for the missing pieces (the clock in front of the Sherry Netherland Hotel is as good a meeting place as the clock at the Biltmore) and get at least some of the novel's great questions answered. Late December is a great time to visit the Central Park lagoon, where you'll no doubt see that the ducks have probably moved in closer to the center of the lagoon, which freezes last. According to parks department officials, fifty years later they still receive several calls a year asking where the ducks go when the lagoon freezes over. In Holden's time, the answer was to the East River or the Hudson. Now the lagoon almost never freezes over. "It's a lot easier to be a duck now than in 1951," said one official in a 2010 *New York Times* article.[2]

Procedural note: A *Catcher in the Rye* tour of Midtown and around Central Park can largely be accomplished by walking east–west on the numbered streets. This will be much easier in Midtown than walking north–south on the congested-with-holiday-shoppers avenues.

. . . you are fascinated by the criminal mind.

Do you watch crime shows on TV, not so much to solve a mystery but to study why criminals do criminal things? Have you read more than a few books about serial killers? If I told you Stephen Sondheim wrote a musical about presidential assassins, have you just stopped listening to me because you're looking for tickets?

The Catcher in the Rye has played a role in at least two high-profile murders and one presidential assassination attempt. On December 8, 1980, Beatle John Lennon was shot and killed outside the Dakota apartment building in New York City, where he lived with his family. The murderer was a twenty-five-year-old security guard named Mark David Chapman, who, immediately following the shooting, sat on the sidewalk and began to read from a paperback copy of *The Catcher in the Rye*. Inscribed in his copy was the sentence "To Holden Caulfield, from Holden Caulfield. This is my statement."[3] Four months later, on March 30, 1981, President Ronald Reagan was exiting the Hilton Hotel in Washington, DC, when twenty-five-year-old John Hinckley Jr. fired six shots at him. No one was killed during the incident. Hinckley later said that *The Catcher in the Rye* was his favorite book, and it was among the six found in his apartment. And finally, on July 18, 1989, actress Rebecca Schaeffer answered the door of her apartment to find obsessed fan Robert John Bardo standing there. Bardo shot her at close range in the chest and was carrying a copy of *The Catcher in the Rye* at the time of the killing.[4]

The answer to why certain works of art motivate crime is too often dismissed as simple copycatting and misinterpretation. Holden

Caulfield is a young man, angry at the world and convinced of its betrayal. Chapman, Hinckley, and Bardo contorted Salinger's creation into a rationale for murder. The larger, more interesting questions are why and how we use art for our own purposes, and what the resulting power dynamic is between audience, artist, and artwork. *The Catcher in the Rye* is an iris opening onto the richness of those questions.

. . . you love a good monologue.

Does Aaron Sorkin make your kind of TV? Does Eve Ensler or Eric Bogosian or Anna Deavere Smith make your kind of theater? If so, you are probably as smitten with monologues as I am.

The Catcher in the Rye is the subject of one of the greatest monologues of the modern era. Around minute twenty-three of John Guare's 1990 play *Six Degrees of Separation* (adapted as a 1993 film), the character of Paul (a con man posing as a graduate student and as actor Sidney Poitier's son) explains that he is writing his thesis on *The Catcher in the Rye*. The five and a half minutes that follow, during which Paul ties together Holden Caulfield's reliance on the word *phony* and the character's fear of intimacy and human connection, murder, the modern death of the imagination, Beckett, Jung, fashion, and *Star Wars*, are among the most spellbinding I've ever seen. The three characters listening to the speech are starstruck. When Paul is done, all his listeners can say is "Indeed" and "I'm going to pick up that book as soon as I get to the airport."

Don't take my word for it. Watch the 1993 film, in which Will Smith, in his first dramatic role, the one that gave him a career beyond *The Fresh Prince of Bel-Air*, delivers the monologue.[5] Or find a community theater production of same. The speech and its use of *Catcher* as source material is dramatic writing of such effortless genius, it would take a drunk armadillo in the role to foul it up. But Will Smith really nails it.

. . . you have a healthy perspective about your own adolescence.

J. D. Salinger did not have teenagers in mind when he wrote *The Catcher in the Rye*; he was writing more for the adult readers of magazines like the *New Yorker*. The character of Holden Caulfield had been appearing in Salinger's fiction for a decade before *Catcher*'s publication. Stories written for both *Collier's* magazine and the *New Yorker* would later become chunks of *The Catcher in the Rye*. As an army sergeant during World War II, Salinger carried pages of the unfinished novel on his person. Holden Caulfield was with him as his regiment advanced on the beaches of Normandy and later liberated the death camps at Dachau.[6]

The images of slaughter and the death of comrades would haunt Salinger for years afterward. According to biographer Kenneth Slawenski, the author poured those feelings of loss into Holden's pain over his dead younger brother, Allie.[7] At a key moment in the novel, just before Holden meets Phoebe at the carousel—the redemptive climax we all remember and the first time Holden uses the words "so damn happy"—he walks in misery a block at a time uptown, at each crosswalk saying, "Allie, don't let me disappear."[8]

I have read *The Catcher in the Rye* at least six times and never remembered that Holden Caulfield had a dead brother and how important this is to his story. And I have no idea why I didn't remember.

Yes, Holden is lonesome and sad because it is winter and he has failed again at school and he thinks the world is full of phonies and he can't trust anybody and it isn't worth trying. This is being a bratty teenager. This is also exactly how we all feel when we are grieving.

That Salinger's book has become "the handbook of the adolescent heart" is neither a mistake nor anyone's fault.[9] It just is. But far more ageless is its near-perfect capture of the numbing frostbite of loss, of how the world feels like a lie, and how it is pointless to trust or remember anything. We feel this way because the world has taken something from us, punished us even though we are innocent. We may feel this more acutely as teenagers, but Mr. Salinger wasn't writing this book for teenagers. He was after something bigger: a story about a young man whom he used to capture the pain he felt from the battlefield and that actually nailed the ageless, universal heart in mourning.[10]

With any hope, we're more familiar with loss and better at grieving as we get older. Even if it hurts no less, we've been there and know what to do. We don't have to hide out, rage at the world, or pretend nobody cares.

We might think that Holden Caulfield is a spoiled brat and hate the fact that exactly the wrong kinds of people have idolized him for it. Or, with enough distance and regard, we can think that maybe Holden Caulfield is just a kid in pain who misses his brother.

37

ALBERT CAMUS,
THE UNSEXY *STRANGER*

For a certain breed of teenager, *The Stranger* by Albert Camus contains some terribly sexy ideas: life is ridiculous, one bad deed is the same as the next, no one person counts more than anyone else, and only the persecuted and misunderstood are wise to it all. The plot lays the alienated glamour on even thicker: protagonist Meursault is young and aimless; he has a pretty girlfriend who loves him, but he won't commit to her; he smokes and drinks too much coffee, he murders a member of a group that bullied his friend; and he mouths off to a priest who tries to get him to repent for his crime. "Absurdism," "existentialism," and "nihilism" are the philosophical headers we give this sort of thing. They feel exactly right when you must have the car home by midnight, when your potential date to the prom doesn't "like you in that way," and when nobody understands that the prom is stupid anyway.

The Stranger came out in 1942. Its 120 sinewy pages became both a manual and a pile of red meat for high school students of the next three generations who rolled their eyes at student council elections. I am out on no limb when I suppose that young admirers of this book might also be fans of the work of Charles Bukowski, William S. Burroughs, and Kathy Acker. Might they also prefer to spend Saturday nights at repertory screenings of the early David Lynch filmography? Or taking black-and-white photos of empty chairs and tables? Might I be throwing crab apples at the broad side of a bus? That I read *The Stranger* after finding out it was the inspiration for the

Cure song "Killing an Arab" makes me only slightly less a cliché than a tipsy Red Sox fan on St. Patrick's Day.

But the pointlessness of existence and of unexplainable shit "just happening" are only sexy for so long. At seventeen, you've got little influence on your own life, so of course whatever you say or do doesn't seem to matter. Putting words to that helplessness feels like being in on the truth. But once you've got a job and a family, a house, a lawn mower, and framed artwork, you've got skin in the game. You're now banking on random shit not happening, on being able to spend a day at the beach, and on not having an argument with a young man holding a gun. When you have something to lose, chaos and absurdity aren't glamorous anymore. They're terrifying.

Here in Grownupland, *The Stranger* has to spin our propellers for some other reason. I found mine when I went looking for the kind of person who would write such a haunting, hopeless little book. Someone heavy-eyed and wounded, no doubt, a Diane Arbus of French literature who probably used dead birds as home decor.

Wrong, wrong, and wrong. Albert Camus was athletic, gregarious, and as handsome as a movie star. He was embraced not only as an artist but as a national icon. *The Stranger* was his first novel; beyond that lay twenty more years of fiction, essays, journalism, and a Nobel Prize in Literature in 1957. And though he maintained his contention that life was a kind of cruel game in which no one informs us of the rules, his attitude was not despair or self-righteousness but caution, rectitude, and thoughtfulness. *New Yorker* writer Adam Gopnik, in a 2012 profile, described the Camus outlook as holding to "short term commitment to the best possible course of action."[1] Which sounds like advice you get from Miss Manners. It doesn't sound dark or glamorous or sexy at all.

Born in Algeria, Camus lived only forty-six years before dying in an auto accident in the winter of 1960. His passing was mourned by his entire adopted home of France, many of whom considered him a kind of national conscience in print. Camus's passing, remarked Susan Sontag in an early essay, was "felt as a personal loss by the whole literate world."[2]

It is within the sentences of *The Stranger* and the music they make that we can hear and find reason to come back to this book later. *The Stanger* is a story about a single violent act. Camus abhorred all violence, but he particularly hated the kind born of a rotting intellect. "Arrogant certainty" (Meursault's rebuke to the priest sent to comfort him in prison), a point of view defaulted to instead of considered, leads to arrogant, intolerant acts.[3] Violence was the sad outcome of lazy minds and convenient convictions to fill them. The tone Camus took in both fiction and in his ample editorial writing for newspapers done after *The Stranger* was measured, reasonable, and elegiac, sad at trying to be thoughtful in a world mad with thoughtless, highhanded certainty.

For the first half of *The Stranger*, beginning with the death of Meursault's mother and ending with his murder of a young Arab man on the beach, Camus's sentences are as flat and blunt as the head of a hammer. "Just then the nurse came in." "Night had fallen suddenly." "I drank the coffee. Then I had a smoke."[4] This is the voice of someone who doesn't care what is happening and probably hasn't stopped to think about it either, someone dictating, not processing, life as it happens. It belongs to a mind not at apathetic rest but in a tight, thoughtless march from one event to the next.

Part 1 of *The Stranger* ends with the killing and a weird poetic note. The flat, literal Meursault says this:

> Then I fired four more times at the motionless body where the bullets lodged without leaving a trace. And it was like knocking four quick times on the door of unhappiness.[5]

That last phrase—metaphoric and trafficking in emotion instead of incident—is different from what we've heard before. It also seems to be looking at the murder from a step removed. Meursault is no longer simply recording the story as it happens. We now sense that he is telling us something that has already happened.

The second half of *The Stranger* alternates between the two voices. When the focus is on Meursault's trial and legal proceedings, sentences are hurried, functional, and inevitable, as if this part of the story has already been determined and Camus is just catching us up. When Meursault is alone and thinking, we get lines like this:

> Throughout the whole absurd life I'd lived, a dark wind had been rising towards me from somewhere deep in my future, across years that were still to come.[6]

We know that Meursault has been sentenced to die. We now know that *The Stranger* is a story told in reverse, narrated by a man awaiting his own death. It is not a confession but rather a 120-page consideration of the violent act that got him here. Whether or not he learned something is hardly the point. Meursault is also hardly a reliable narrator, so we might not believe him if he said he had.

Instead, if we pair what Camus has done in prose with the leading priorities of the remainder of his writing life, we've got ourselves a pretty good reason to give *The Stranger* another look. *The Stranger* uses a murder as a kind of roleplay for what can happen to us around trauma: nearly all acts of trauma are momentary compared to the aftermath. And though it would be better if awful things never happened at all, they will, Camus seems to say. If there is nothing else to be derived from them happening, they at least compel us to slow our minds, to think, to understand, and to go forward as our best selves, with care, calm, and responsibility.

That may be fool's thinking on both Camus's part and mine. I'm not so sure I would road-test this theory on someone who has just lost a loved one or been injured in an accident. *The Stranger* is not the novel for right after the terrible shit happens. Instead, it's a great read for considering that random horrors happen all the time and that we're going to need some kind of working strategy when they do. That realization is one of maturity, and, in the face of darkness, we have the opportunity to be small and thoughtless and violent or to take a moment, probably many of them, and be sober, unsexy, and thoughtful.

It won't make random awful shit not happen. Camus wrote *The*

Stranger in Nazi-occupied France, where awful shit probably felt as unending as the sky. But it will make us feel like empowered adults and not like wounded, helpless, teenagers when it does happen.

38

SHIRLEY JACKSON'S RITUALS OF VIOLENCE

Shirley Jackson's short story "The Lottery" has been adapted for the movies, television, radio, and ballet. It inspired an episode of the cult TV series *Dark Shadows* and a B-plus joke on *The Simpsons*. I haven't partaken of any of its alternate versions yet, even though I love "The Lottery," have read it a few dozen times, and would like to see what becomes of it in someone else's hands.

I'm also a big, fat scaredy-cat. Ritual murder is an experience I'd rather avoid. My adult imagination, thanks to Shirley Jackson, has already visited this place once and still shudders every time I reread "The Lottery"—really every time someone even speaks its name.

"The Lottery" is like an insult that haunts you months after hearing it—simple, blunt, and cruel. The story is a little over ten pages with prose as plain and ordinary as breakfast. It also contains exactly one plot twist, when the nature of the lottery is revealed. The rest is lead-up: a summer day, a small town, the annual ritual of neighbors drawing slips of paper from a box and selecting an unlucky soul among them—then stoning that person to death.

The stoning occupies only the final three paragraphs of the story, a hundred words at the most. Beyond the first rock thrown and a few screams from the victim, we see nothing. Or rather Jackson gives us nothing. She ends the story abruptly with the line "and then they were upon her" and lets us sit there, terrified, with our imagination barking, "Well, then what happened?"[1]

Our imagination, prowling and scared, is a powerful thing. When the *New Yorker* published "The Lottery" in the summer of 1948, thousands of readers wrote in demanding Jackson tell them how the story really ended and what she meant. Others canceled their subscriptions. More than a few wanted to know where this lottery actually took place so they could attend and watch. Those last readers are a reminder why the relationship I have with "The Lottery" in print is more than enough.

It also makes me relieved that I didn't first encounter the story in high school, where ritual meanness can be practiced at the level of professional sport. "The Lottery" is now among the most-assigned stories in American secondary schools, but I hadn't heard of it until my first job out of college, where I shared a desk row with, of all people, Shirley Jackson's biographer.

I can imagine, however, liking it as a tenth-grader. Read alongside *The Diary of Anne Frank* and Arthur Miller's *The Crucible*, I'd have taken its modest length and easy prose at a gulp, then dribbled at the mouth about its condemnation of conformity and mob thinking, the favored literary explanation of a teenager on the wrong side of conformity and mob thinking.

My own school was small, bookish, and light on bullies, at least of the psychopathic kind. I still worry, the baseless worry of a near-forty adult, that "The Lottery" both warns against bullying and could give a potential bully funny ideas.

Shirley Jackson, who didn't care much for explaining her work or herself, would, when asked, say that "The Lottery" was about anti-Semitism. I'm convinced she both believed that and crafted this explanation to shut up whoever was asking. Given that the Nazis had been defeated only a few years before and that her family had been targets of anti-Semitic harassment in Bennington, Vermont (the basis for the story's nameless town), few were inclined to argue with her. An urban myth even sprouted up that Jackson had thought up the idea for "The Lottery" after local children had thrown stones at her and her baby daughter while they were out shopping.

It didn't happen that way. Jackson had been out running morning errands with her daughter and passed by Bennington's central square. She'd had tribal rituals on the brain (her husband was an anthropology professor), and her mind flashed to an image of her neighbors engaged in an ancient sacrifice of one of their own. She hurried home, put the baby in her playpen, wrote the story in two hours, and claimed later to have barely changed a word. I believe her.

"The Lottery" as parable about the horrors of bigotry and violence is a fine place to start, but it isn't the whole story. Societal bigotry is intentional. A lottery by nature is random. There is no preselected target in Jackson's story, no ancient grudge waiting to be acted on or disguised retribution between neighbors, as in, say, the Salem witch trials. No citizen is singled out because of who they are, what they believe, or the deeds they've done. The murdered are simply the unlucky.

Within the story, Jackson sneaks in only a slight but horrifying explanation as to why the lottery happens at all—because it is tradition. We learn by the second page that "the lottery's original paraphernalia had been lost long ago"; by the fourth page that much of the ritual itself had been "forgotten or discarded"; and by midstory we overhear two townspeople arguing that "there have always been lotteries" but that some neighboring villages have stopped doing them.[2]

The lottery has always been. It happens the same day each year (June 27, says Jackson in the story's opening line; the *New Yorker* published it on June 28), so it feels as regular and ordinary as Christmas. Every participant will be either killer or slain, so the system seems barbaric but fair. It happens at the beginning of summer, which positions it as the opening act of a season of freedom and celebration. The author even slams the door before anyone dies.

Right there is where Shirley Jackson leaves us. By providing just enough cover for the ritual to seem common rather than sinister, she deceives us not into sympathizing with the victim but understanding the perpetrators. "The Lottery" isn't a condemnation of violence or mob rule. Rather, it feels like a cold stare you know is mean but correct. That stare says we are in fact worse than brutes. We are the enablers who set the table for brutality and who have convinced ourselves that it's normal to have a murderer over for dinner. The murderer in these circumstances is always someone we recognize: a friend, a neighbor, even ourselves.

We are all guilty of this kind of violence, says Jackson—the violence of collusion and rationalized inaction. Jackson, a great talker and intellectual combatant, seems also to be implying that a lazy, unquestioning mind is the first step toward the mass thoughtlessness that can produce a tradition like the lottery. And, not letting the reader off the hook for a second, she ends the story abruptly, as if to ask, "Why do you need an explanation of your own behavior? Somewhere in your life, at an enemy or a neighbor or even a loved one, you've gone along and thrown a stone."

Instinctively I think of "The Lottery" in a bundle with other pocket-sized case studies of groups gone terribly wrong. Robert Cormier's young-adult novel *The Chocolate War* (1974) is the story of an exclusive boys' school that uses a chocolate sales competition to punish the school's misfits. Stephen King, who cites Shirley Jackson as an influence, spent much of his early career depicting small-town cruelty, perhaps most effectively in *'Salem's Lot* (1975), where a plague of vampires is an excuse for citizens to wage micro-wars on their neighbors. The 1981 film *The Wave* (which I did see in high school) is based on an actual experiment in a Palo Alto high school where an English teacher convinced his students they were part of a mass youth movement called "The Wave" and asked them to spy on and report nonbelievers. At the end of the experiment, he called them to an assembly to receive a special broadcast from the movement's national leader. The broadcast was a newsreel of Adolf Hitler.

It's easy, then, to look to each of these examples and say, "Yes, of course Shirley Jackson was talking about Nazism in 'The Lottery.'" But I think that lets us off too easy. "The Lottery" is intentionally small in scale, not only because it was Jackson's area of interest but also because she didn't want the crime to be so big we couldn't recognize ourselves in it. With an engineered system of mass murder like Nazi Germany, an argument can be made that even good people must participate out of fear and that such a thing is a wild, historical aberration; people are basically good otherwise.

Jackson gives us no "otherwise." In "The Lottery," there is no coercion or indication that the citizens live in times of upheaval. No one is fleeing town. No one except the victim raises an objection. The victim no doubt participated as murderer the year before.

"The Lottery" is a great story to dig up and talk about with one's children, particularly if that child is a teenager. Odds are they have read it already. Read it yourself without saying anything (telling your kid might embarrass them; I immediately shut down when embarrassed as a teenager). Then keep it in mind when you must have that conversation about bullying, whichever side your kid lands on. If yours is a bully (and at some point, we all are), tell them, as "The Lottery" sternly reminds us, that bullying is the product of small minds and small people, and that they are neither. If your kid is the victim, remind them, as Shirley Jackson did, that "The Lottery" is the result of people believing there is no other way. Tell them there is always another way, and that the rituals considered inevitable in both the story and in high school don't apply here and don't follow them home.

39

THE STONE-FACED TRIP OF *SLAUGHTERHOUSE-FIVE*

Kurt Vonnegut's *Slaughterhouse-Five* contains several scenes of horrific violence and suffering amid its modest 215 pages, and I remember exactly none of them. They didn't register when I first read the novel at seventeen, nor did they stick out much after rereading it last week. Now, I'm a wuss and normally have a hard time with such things. I've teared up reading passages about summer becoming fall and had a couple of sleepless nights after a single Mary Gaitskill story. But Billy Pilgrim listening to his fellow soldiers delight in torturing animals or being forced as prisoners of war to stack piles of corpses didn't make me stop and swallow. Those scenes didn't trip me up any more than the passages of Billy Pilgrim making love to an old movie star while his alien captors watched. I just stayed stuck in Mr. Vonnegut's time and read on.

Kurt Vonnegut wasn't telling his readers to "pay no mind to my narrator watching dead bodies incinerated with flame throwers!" Vonnegut himself was a POW during the 1945 Allied bombing of Dresden. This novel was the end result of a multiyear attempt to capture the central horror of his life in literature. Its first chapter is a kind of disclaimer/apology from the author ("I have told my sons that they are not under any circumstances to take part in massacres.") and followed by resolution ("People aren't supposed to look back. I'm not going to look back any more. I've finished my war book now. The next one I write is going to be fun.").[1]

Vonnegut's voice will stay exactly this plain even in scenes where it feels wildly out of place, like an auctioneer reciting a sonnet. If Joseph Heller's *Catch-22* saw war as an absurd prank, *Slaughterhouse-Five* captures it like an acid trip narrated by your high school math teacher. The reality of the novel is on a tilt that sends the reader rolling downhill toward this question: If life's greatest horrors are captured in the same tone as driving to work, paying bills, and unclogging a drain, what's going on? Denial? Coping? Artistry? Maybe all three?

Since *Slaughterhouse-Five* reads like a nutty dream, the plot seems easier to remember in small chunks. I recalled a main character named Billy Pilgrim who had "come unstuck in time" and spends the story leaping between moments of his life.[2] He grows up in Illium, New York, marries the daughter of the town's best optometrist, inherits the business, serves in World War II during the bombing of Dresden, survives a horrific plane crash back home, and is kidnapped by aliens. I also remembered that Vonnegut tells Billy Pilgrim's story out of order and that, whenever death is mentioned, Vonnegut's next sentence is the phrase "So it goes." I didn't remember that Vonnegut used that phrase 106 times, to follow everything from the death of a soldier to the flattening of champagne. I didn't know that the phrase became a slogan for opponents of the Vietnam War or that *Slaughterhouse-Five*, Vonnegut's sixth, was the book that made him famous, made him a hero of counterculture America, and sent him into suicidal depression.[3]

Here's Billy Pilgrim landing in a mental institution:

Billy uncovered his head. The windows of the ward were open. Birds were twittering outside.

And one page later, what got him there:

Billy had seen the greatest massacre in European history, which was the firebombing of Dresden. So it goes.

And five pages later, at the next scene change:

Billy traveled in time back to the veterans' hospital again. The blanket was over his head. It was quiet outside the blanket.[4]

The unshakeable calmness of Vonnegut's prose and the intoning phrase "So it goes" speaks for the novel's gifts but against my enjoyment of said gifts. The uniform sound of passages about wildly different subjects flattens them like a rolling pin over dough but also opens a dozen tantalizing doors: Is the novel a work of art on coping with tragedy? Does style distance us from the impact of violence or illustrate violence's lack of control over us? Does slapping "So it goes" after every death—humans, bacteria, champagne—remind us that death is everywhere and that's awful or that it isn't as awful as we think? That violence and horror at their worst are utterly unreal or that their unreality is the stuff of art?

Twisty passages like these are one of the central joys of reading. They can also give you a headache. *Slaughterhouse-Five*'s weird trip could not hold me the way it did at seventeen. Perhaps it felt cute instead of necessary. Perhaps it felt like listening to someone else's tales of a stoned weekend about twenty minutes past caring.

I wonder if today's teenager would be shaken by any of the violence here. One as fragile as I was back then might be. But even though the American Library Association cites *Slaughterhouse-Five* as one of the books most frequently challenged by local censorship efforts, the evidence suggests that's got little to do with the horror of war and more with harsh language and the seemingly antiwar message.

Today's tenth-grader would probably say, "Hey, cool!" to that. But measured in spilled blood, they'd hold up Vonnegut's tilted phantasm of a war story next to *Saw III* and *Call of Duty*® and YouTube® snuff videos and shrug.

Half a century on, *Slaughterhouse-Five* reads as a kind of sad, demented fable spun by a crazy uncle, brilliant in its commitment to its own weirdness and disturbing for exactly that reason. It's the kind of story that makes you want to sit far from that uncle at Thanksgiving dinner but tell all your friends about him the next day and for weeks afterward. The part of you it moves most is your curiosity.

I'm sure hordes of *Slaughterhouse-Five* readers older and younger have covered up whatever discomfort it created by saying something like "This book makes me want to get high!" (I'm convinced all the surviving copies of the novel's original print run smell like Cheech and Chong's garage). But whatever is disturbing about the novel (mostly its motionless tone of an impending nervous breakdown) feels like uneasy befuddlement, a scraping noise in the other room rather than the feeling of having your wind knocked out. Kurt Vonnegut doesn't put us in the action with Billy Pilgrim and his story of growing up; marriage; infidelity; war service; and, yes, communion with aliens from the planet Tralfamadore. Rather, he puts us inside the cracked hall of mirrors that is the author's own imagination. We're not on this novel's battlefield. We're inside the mind that created it. And that mind is tantalizing even if the story it tells doesn't hold up as well.

Slaughterhouse-Five was published in the spring of 1969, almost exactly a year after the My Lai Massacre and the murder of Martin Luther King Jr. The tide of popular opinion was turning against the Vietnam War, and the previous summer had seen the assassination of Robert Kennedy and rioting in major American cities. Just ahead lay the Manson Family murders and Altamont—a violent, unreal end to a decade whose spirit *Slaughterhouse-Five* captured under glass.

Both *Time* magazine and the Modern Library rank *Slaughterhouse-Five* as one of the twentieth century's great novels. It's been adapted for the stage by Chicago's Steppenwolf Theatre Company, as a radio drama by the BBC, and for the screen in 1972. Director Guillermo del Toro has optioned it for a remake, which feels just right to me: Del Toro is an artist who, in films such as *Cronos, Pan's Labyrinth*, and *Hellboy*, uses high style as a prism to peer into the many sides of monsters and their place in our dreams.

While writing this essay in a café, I set my old copy of *Slaughterhouse-Five* with its torn back cover on the table next to me. A stranger walked up to it and asked me, "Have you read *Deadeye Dick*?" (Vonnegut's tenth novel, published in 1982). I had not, and the stranger asked if I knew whether *Deadeye Dick* was the source of Vonnegut's quote about "a little peephole of life opening quite suddenly"—that you must "watch out for life" and be ready when "light and sound poured in."

I didn't know. But now I had to. Where did that line come from, and who said it? Why? What twisty passage would I be sent down in finding out? Even if I didn't care for *Slaughterhouse-Five*, there had to be somewhere else I could meet Kurt Vonnegut and his frustrating, brilliant mind. Eight novels and nearly forty years of life remained for him, space wide enough to confound me again with his topsy-turvy view of family, mortality, creation, and violence. I may have missed what he wanted to understand about Dresden and about horror, but I was ready and eager to read on, to know what else he had in mind, had done with his life outside its central tragedy, before and beyond the great horizon, long after Billy Pilgrim had touched down in time.

40

AN ACT OF VIOLENCE,
A BOOK OF FORGIVENESS

I've seen Dorothy Allison speak at a midsize bookstore, and I've been in the audience as she addressed a crowd of hundreds. She is funny and self-deprecating, but she is also direct and has what you'd call presence, which arrives in the room a moment before she does. She seems to know that you probably first heard of her because of her first novel, *Bastard Out of Carolina*. She knows the book is technically labeled fiction, but it is her story, and you've guessed that already: her story of growing up poor in South Carolina, of suffering physical and sexual abuse at the hands of her stepfather. She does not ask you to feel sorry for her. She is not angry, bitter, or haunted. Nor is she some kind of superhero, her youthful suffering a requirement for her later greatness. Her achievement is more basic, more human, and greater than any of that.

In *Bastard Out of Carolina*, Allison has written her own story of violence as an act of forgiveness, a book brimming with something unmistakably called love. She has no judgment, no blame, no prescription for how you should feel on her behalf. She has already made up her mind. The people she writes about are her family. She loves them, has forgiven them, and has continued to live. And standing before you, it is obvious that she will continue to do so, remarkably.

Bastard Out of Carolina was published in 1992, the year after I graduated high school. But had I been a decade younger, I don't think even the high-minded Michiganders who taught my contemporary literature courses would have assigned it. Though the novel was a bestseller, a finalist for the National Book Award, compared in its *New York Times* review to *The Catcher in the Rye* and *To Kill a Mockingbird*, its central subject is the violation of a child.[1] The horror of that subject led to the book being rejected by school boards in both California and Maine, and to the 1996 film adaptation being granted an X instead of an R rating. In wide circles, *Bastard* is considered a go-to text for survivors of sexual violence. All of which I think gives it the unintended reputation as a book that is scary, depressing, cathartic, and mostly for readers who have been victims of something.

I have reread *Bastard* twice, and each time I believe a little bit more that this is a book about forgiveness. And that Allison conveys this in tone rather than through the actions of her alter ego, Ruth Anne "Bone" Boatwright. There is no conclusion where Bone's abusive stepfather apologizes. Her mother ends up returning to the abuser and then disappears. We are not granted a flash-forward of Bone (Allison) as the successful academic, feminist activist, and mother of a teenage son she would become. The novel ends as it started in sentences as clear as ice water that seem to nod shortly after they finish. They read as though they know they will be heard.

When Bone is born to a young woman named Anney, she is mistakenly declared illegitimate. Anney's second husband, Glen, is the son of a prosperous dairy owner, but he loses his job and begins molesting and physically abusing Bone. Anney leaves Glen, and her brothers assault him as retribution.

In a showdown, Bone tells her mother she will not go back to living with Glen, but she will forgive her mother if she must return to her marriage. Her mother agrees not to return to Glen, and when Glen hears of it, he corners Bone at her aunt's house and is in the midst of raping her when Anney interrupts and fights him off. The two end up reconciling, and while Bone heals with her aunt, Anney returns, asking for Bone's forgiveness.

In the novel's most important scene, Bone does not let her off the hook. She expresses that she is not angry but sad—not because she has made a mistake in forgiving her mother but because love means you forgive even when people let you down.

Bone:

> I wanted to tell her lies, tell her that I had never doubted her, that nothing could make any difference in my love for her but I couldn't.
>
>   Maybe it wasn't her fault. It wasn't mine. Maybe it wasn't a matter of anyone's fault. Maybe it was just like [Aunt] Raylene said, the way the world goes, the way hearts get broken all the time.[2]

There is no apology here. But there is an understanding of how Anney failed her daughter, and how her daughter loved her anyway. It's a forgiveness that Bone seems able to extend to her mother, who cannot extend it to herself.

It took Allison nearly ten years to write *Bastard Out of Carolina*, her first novel after publishing a book of poetry and a short-story collection called *Trash*. By that time, she was living in New York City, the first person in her family to graduate from high school. She had a master's degree, several teaching positions, and bylines with publications like the *Village Voice*. She was a long way from Greenville, South Carolina, yet reconciling the seemingly irreconcilable forces of distance and intimacy is what gives *Bastard* its unique point of view. Allison is no longer the little girl who could not defend herself against a violent man. She is also mature enough to be proud of where she came from; to not need to run from it; to see her family as her own, failings, wrong turns, and all.

Allison opens the novel with my favorite quote from James Baldwin's *Go Tell It on the Mountain*, also a debut novel, also fictionalized autobiography.

> People pay for what they do, and still more for what they have allowed themselves to become. And they pay for it very simply; by the lives they lead.

We don't realize it, but the author has put forth her plan right away. With the benefit of understanding and time, we don't have to be angry at those who disappoint us. Their lives will be a reflection of how they have lived, and so will ours. If we remain unforgiving of what happened to us then, we will never have a "now." The violence of the past becomes a kind of death-by-a-thousand-cuts that we inflict on our own future.

The forgiveness in *Bastard Out of Carolina* comes when you can both imagine a future but also know your time is not unlimited. Forgiveness of this kind is a long, hard time in coming and is as great a feat as the novel that surrounds it.

In his book *The Sunflower: On the Possibilities and Limits of Forgiveness*, Nazi hunter Simon Wiesenthal tells a story of being brought to the deathbed of a German soldier while Wiesenthal was a prisoner at the Lemberg concentration camp. The soldier wishes to speak to a Jew and ask forgiveness for his crimes. Wiesenthal decides he cannot forgive the man and remains silent.[3]

In 1981, the son of Florida businessman John Walsh was kidnapped from a Sears department store and found murdered two weeks later. Walsh has since become America's most public anti-crime activist, hosting the television program *America's Most Wanted* and penning four books with titles such as *Tears of Rage* and *No Mercy*. Though Walsh stated in a 2009 interview with Oprah Winfrey that he no longer feels any bitterness, his life's work has been fueled by the burning fury over his son's murder. John Walsh with forgiveness is someone else entirely.

In 2009, Nobel Peace Prize laureate Desmond Tutu released a book titled *No Future without Forgiveness*. It details his work as the chairman of South Africa's Truth and Reconciliation Commission, where both victims and henchmen of the nation's former apartheid regime face each other in an attempt at forgiveness and mutual understanding. Though the process had significant critics and detractors, it is largely credited with enabling South Africa to become a modern nation.[4]

Which of these is the correct approach to forgiveness? I cannot say. Nearly all the world's spiritual practices advocate forgiveness in the face of violence and suffering. I happen to agree. But I have never suffered the way John Walsh or Simon Wiesenthal or Desmond Tutu has. I have never been placed in the situation Dorothy Allison was as a young child. If it were me, I can't say what I would do. And I don't feel I could blame anyone in that situation for their anger even if it burned long past the point of usefulness.

Forgiveness allowed Dorothy Allison to become the writer she is today. *Bastard Out of Carolina*, with its warm, solid three hundred pages, is a brisk read that remains instead of dissipates. My life as a reader is better for it. But it's fair to ask if this act requires a presence and person as strong as Dorothy Allison. Can only the strong forgive, or does forgiving make us strong? *Bastard Out of Carolina* doesn't answer that for us. It only shows us what we are and how we will speak when we do.

41

THE SHAMELESS CASE
OF WALT WHITMAN

My copy of Walt Whitman's *Leaves of Grass* has what looks like a charcoal sketch of the poet as a young man on the front cover. He's bearded, strapping, and assured, hat tilted slightly, one hand in his pocket and the other rather defiantly balled on his hip.[1] A little research informed me that this was the graphic from the frontispiece of the first edition of *Leaves of Grass*, published when Whitman was thirty-six. At that point I realized I'd never seen a picture of a young Walt Whitman before. In my imagination, he was always a white-bearded old man, frail, with kind eyes—but still wearing a hat.

I knew Whitman revised *Leaves of Grass* continuously (as few as six editions, as many as twelve, depending on whom you ask) throughout his life until his death in 1892. The last edition, published two months before, is jokingly referred to as "the deathbed edition." For Whitman, revising meant that poems were added and taken away, portrait photos at various stages of his life were included, and even negative reviews were reprinted. It's fair to say that each revision was not only a reexamination of the text but also a repackaging of its author's public image. The voice of the poems—grand, triumphant, heroic, and generous—was reshaped by a man whose body probably felt very different. Picture a seventy-year-old Walt Whitman reading the collection's centerpiece, *Song of Myself*, when the "myself" was in his early thirties.

It's part of what makes *Leaves of Grass* and *Song of Myself* a little maddening. Before I started reading this time around, I kept mixing up the two. Then I had to decide on an edition from the five available at the library. Finally, as I read, I had to continually ask myself, "Which Walt Whitman is this?" All of which is funny, because not only does *Song of Myself* spell out its intentions in the title (the title, by the way, came with the book's final edition; before that, the poem was either nameless or just called "Walt Whitman"), but Whitman's language is pitched at the level of pronouncements from heaven. It's hard to be in the figuring-out business when you feel like the author is shouting his intentions at you from across the fruited plain.

You remember high school English conversations about this poem, right? Who is "myself"? Is it Walt Whitman, voice of the everyday American, or Walt Whitman, the big-hearted narcissist who cannot imagine a leaf falling anywhere without his soul being imbued in it? Is *Song of Myself* an intimate testimonial or the kind of self-invention that John Updike called "The poet as bard, the writer as egotist, the writer as celebrity, the poem as confession, the poem as reality itself"?[2]

It only complicates things that during his life, Walt Whitman could not shut up about Walt Whitman and was a shameless hustler for his own work. Maybe it feels a little dirty that America's greatest poet was also one of American literature's hardest-working self-promoters. Or maybe that sounds just about right for a country that enthroned Benjamin Franklin, who, as a young man, used to drag a completely unnecessary wheelbarrow to work so the good citizens of Philadelphia would think him hardworking and industrious.

For those of us who find heroes in our favorite writers, artists, filmmakers, and musicians, Walt Whitman is a tough case. He is undoubtedly one of the greatest poets America has ever produced—the Mark Twain of verse, just as committed to capturing his nation, his first true love, in its own voice. Robert Frost may have given us miles to go before we sleep and a road not taken; Wallace Stevens, a baker's dozen ways of looking at a blackbird; and Emily Dickinson, a sad biography that overshadows her most brilliant sentences. But without Walt Whitman, we have no "O Captain! My Captain!" no "I Sing the Body Electric," no "Pioneers! O Pioneers!" and no sounding of a barbaric yawp over the roofs of the world. Without Walt Whitman, we have no *Dead Poets Society,* no finale from *Fame,* no title for Willa Cather's best novel, and no hundreds of open-mic poetry nights. And I haven't even gotten to the ready-packaged high school yearbook salutations of "Do I contradict myself? Very well, then I contradict myself" and "I am large, I contain multitudes." Walt Whitman may have proclaimed, "I hear America singing," but his poetry became the preeminent example of nineteenth-century America singing. The line from *Song of Myself* to "God Bless America" to Aaron Copeland to *On the Road* to Bruce Springsteen is not a very crooked one.

That causes a few problems. One: Whitman's verse cannot help but sound anthemic, every line swelling with awe and glory. But that also makes it a little too perfect for when *we'd* like to be swelling with awe and glory—at high school debate competitions, during university commencement exercises, on congratulatory greeting cards, and on plaques hung in dens. Whitman can seem too obvious, too arms-outstretched naïve, too inarguable. To refuse to be taken in by his passion feels like sitting during the national anthem. Adding him to your own canon of heroes can resemble idolizing the Beatles or Stephen Spielberg, a safe choice for someone who hasn't looked very hard and doesn't know any better.

Whitman was a man of humble background and poor education—and he was deeply ashamed of it. He saw becoming his country's voice in poetry as his calling and his escape, and he poured everything into it. His hard work and desperation is palpable everywhere from the soaring yet too-often hollow ring of his verse to his repeated revising of *Leaves of Grass* to his continual scramble to self-mythologize. He was even known to fabricate glowing reviews of his work, as if he did not trust his own talent or the existing system to recognize it.

When we look to our creative heroes, we don't want them to be pleading for our approval or screaming too loud for our attention.

The latter alone is fine: "I'm the greatest and don't care what you think" is an old standby of artists (think hip-hop, fashion designers, and anybody called "the bad boy/bad girl of"). So is "effortlessly likeable" (think Tom Hanks, Dick Clark, any artist who doesn't court controversy and you prefer it that way). But "love me!" and self-promotion (another way of saying, "Here's why you should love me!") are a tough pair. We'd like our artist heroes to be working on making great stuff and then be comfortable with us calling it great. Demanding we notice upsets the dynamic between admiring and admired and is a little embarrassing to both.

Maybe it shouldn't be. The debate over how much artists should promote their own work (and by extension themselves) and how much they should remain hidden in their studios creating has burned on since at least the advent of mass media over a century ago. Even today, ask ten authors how much hustling they feel they should do for their books, and at least five will say it should be someone else's job. Of ten visual artists, maybe three would say that it's someone else's job. Filmmakers, actors, and musicians seem to have given themselves over to "doing press" long ago. Today any responsible person giving those same artists career guidance would say that, in our contemporary media landscape, where the art admirer has thousands of words, sounds, and images to pay attention to at any one time, "hustling" is the only way artists and their work get noticed.

Walt Whitman had much more critical than financial success in his lifetime, and biographers have argued how his poetry would have endured if he had not shouted about it endlessly. The issue isn't made any easier by Whitman's masterpiece being a seventy-one-page poem about the poet. It makes the questions of ego and artistry, of creation and promotion as inseparable from Whitman as being rich is from Edith Wharton.

To me, it doesn't matter. I really don't care how great literature, music, and film come into my life—only that they do so at a rate I can swallow and not gag on. But do I want the artists I admire to be aloof and unknowable or to be singing for their supper? Do I want them to be heroes or my best friend? Depends on the work, depends on the artist, depends on the day of the week. Walt Whitman's life and *Song of Myself* are a place where we wrestle, like Jacob versus the Angel, with those questions. Like all good debates, *Song of Myself* gives us several selves and therefore several answers.

42

EMILY DICKINSON'S LESSONS FOR SUCCESS

I've heard more than once that Walt Whitman and Emily Dickinson are the father and mother of American poetry. That probably makes T. S. Eliot the snotty eldest son, Robert Frost the brooding middle child, and Nikki Giovanni the artsy youngest who graduated high school early so she could do summer stock theater in another state. I'm not the first to have this fantasy, nor am I the twentieth to speculate that in this scenario, Mom and Dad would not have gotten along.

Whitman and Dickinson were contemporaries but never met. Whitman didn't know of Dickinson because almost no one did during her lifetime. We have a little evidence that Dickinson had heard of Whitman's opus *Leaves of Grass* ("I never read his Book—but was told that he was disgraceful," she wrote in a letter), but that's about it.[1] What we do know is that their personalities, as revealed in their poetry, were as different as two could be.

Whitman was a nomad who, as a young man, read Ralph Waldo Emerson's essay "The Poet" and its call for a great American poet. Whitman then devoted the rest of his life to being that guy. His voice was loud, declamatory, without armor, and in love with everything his country held, including himself. Emily Dickinson's poetry is quiet, thoughtful, and intimate, with a slight smirk at its own cleverness. Dickinson never left Amherst, Massachusetts, the town of her birth, and during her most productive years during the American Civil War, barely left the house. Whitman saw every man, woman, and creature as his friend. Dickinson had siblings, mentors, an unknown lover she called "master," and her garden. It shouldn't surprise us at all that we have dozens of portraits of Whitman throughout his adult life (he helpfully included one with nearly every new edition of *Leaves of Grass*) and exactly one authenticated daguerreotype of Dickinson at age seventeen (she lived to be fifty-five). In this little family tree of American poetry, we know perhaps too much about Dad and tantalizingly too little about Mom.

We'd be missing something, though, to view Walt Whitman as Mr. Barbaric Yawp and Emily Dickinson as the fragile shut-in of American literature—oil-and-water contemporaries who meet only in our imagination. For anyone in love with the creative act, Whitman and Dickinson are two different but complementary visions of artistry. The aspiring poet (or actor, filmmaker, musician, video-game designer) has as much to learn from Whitman if they are quiet and retiring as they do from Dickinson if they are boisterous and self-promotional. There are many reasons to see both as heroes and role models, even if you feel more like one than the other.

For now, let us set aside what we already know about Ms. Dickinson, because it's less helpful than we think. Yes, Emily Dickinson, middle daughter to a prosperous Massachusetts attorney, published few poems in her lifetime and spent the last two decades effectively hiding from the world in her family's home. In her forties, she took to dressing entirely in white, and after she died of kidney failure in 1886, her younger sister Lavinia discovered nearly 1,800 poems in Emily's room, mostly contained in hand-sewn albums. According to Dickinson scholar Christopher Benfey, we know so little about Emily Dickinson (she kept no diary, had few friends, and referenced a lover in her correspondence she never identified) that "it has been easy for her many and diverse admirers to invent their own private Emily: Emily the fierce feminist; Emily the pliant lover; Emily the 'voice of war'; Emily the prophet of modernism; Emily the guardian of old New England; and so on."[2] I'm afraid we can add to that "Emily the shy genius." It was John Barr, president of the Poetry Foundation, who called Emily Dickinson "the matron saint of all yet-to-be-published poets" and "the special friend to all poets who write privately and have an aversion to self promotion" (as Dickinson knew her poems had something, wanted an audience for them, yet struggled with the act of presenting them to one).[3] It's a morbidly romantic image—Dickinson as pale, fragile, deadly serious, and unrecognized in her day and for most anyone who has had artistic ambitions, an awfully seductive idea to turn to on bad days. It makes lines from one of her most famous poems—

> I'm nobody! Who are you?
> Are you nobody, too?
> Then there's a pair of us—don't tell!
> They'd banish us, you know.
>
> How dreary to be somebody!

—sing with both pride and smug camaraderie.[4] It's just fine to be unrecognized. A genius like Emily Dickinson was unrecognized too!

That attitude is pretty useless here in the real world. Voluntary years of isolation and discovery after death are not conditions most aspiring artists will ever experience. And when looking for heroes and role models, something we can emulate rather than admire in the abstract makes a lot more sense.

Emily Dickinson also had much more to teach us than her weird behavior. My favorite of her lessons makes Dickinson sound much more like a go-getter, an entrepreneur of her own soul, than a delicate Miss Havisham to be pitied and taken care of.

Maybe I'm being silly, but I bet the life of Emily Dickinson would make for a damn-fine business book or at least a volume to hand to young artists early in their careers. I'm going to call her most valuable lessons "The Dickinson Principles." I've mapped them out as I understand them here.

1. WORK YOUR ASS OFF

Numbers. Emily Dickinson wrote 1,789 poems. That's nearly fifty poems a year or almost one a week for every single year of her adult life. During her most fertile period in her early thirties, she was known to write a poem a day. Some became legendary, many did not. "For every great poem Dickinson wrote, she wrote ten that were imperfect or flawed," wrote literary scholar Elaine Showalter. "Like all great artists, she left sketches, drafts, fragments and experiments."[5]

Emily Dickinson completed this giant body of work while making almost no attempt at public recognition. She wasn't after fame or money. She chose her readers and mentors carefully (more on that later). And there is a compelling argument to be made that she was not agoraphobic or psychologically maladjusted but that her isolation was part of what Joyce Carol Oates calls "guerrilla warfare against the confines of her daughterly life amid a conventional Protestant small-town society."[6]

Emily, like many unmarried women of her day, was responsible for the domestic duties of her household, obligations she resented and gradually avoided. Before her most productive period in her early thirties, she was known to snatch time to write immediately after putting away the dishes or right before hanging out the laundry to dry. It's quite possible her isolation in adulthood was as much about creating conditions where she could write the poetry she had inside her as it was about any abnormality she might have had.

In 1862, at age twenty-nine, Dickinson famously wrote to Thomas Wentworth Higginson, a well-known literary critic: "Mr Higginson, Are you too deeply occupied to say if my Verse is alive?"[7] Note she says "alive," not "publishable," "award winning," or even "any good." "Alive," meaning "Where am I toward becoming the best I can be?" "Alive" also implies "How can I get better?" This is Dickinson, who had already been writing for over a decade, effectively asking for more work if mastering her craft required it. As any writing instructor will tell you, these are exactly the right questions for a young artist to be asking. Higginson and Dickinson would remain correspondents until her death.

There is a well-known story that when playwright David Mamet was in college, a class of his required each student to write three plays before semester's end. Mamet wrote many more than that. Most of those plays, he later said, were complete garbage. The three best were instrumental in launching his career.

Moral: The greatest joy of an artist is in the work itself. If you wouldn't do the work anyway, whether or not anyone stood up and applauded, you are becoming an artist for the wrong reasons.

How true it was for Emily Dickinson.

2. KNOW YOUR STUFF WELL ENOUGH TO INNOVATE IT

Beethoven played scales long after he became famous. Michael Jordan shot free throws on his day off. Essential to their mastery was never forgetting the fundamentals.

Clifton Fadiman once said of Dickinson, "Her language is so original we can't fit her in. She is the despair of critics. What are we to do with lines such as these?

> And then, in Sovereign Barns to dwell—
> And dream the Days away
> The Grass so little has to do
> I wish I were a Hay."[8]

He's not alone. Dickinson scholars and fans have tied themselves in knots with how mysterious and singular her poems are. None are titled, most are short, and she never explained herself. Yet Emily Dickinson's uniqueness did not fall from the sky and land in Amherst. Dickinson knew her fundamentals. She had read William Wordsworth and the Brontë sisters and Shakespeare as a young person. Her poems often fell in traditional English rhyme and meter and would take odd turns in the middle lines. Her vocabulary was simple, relatable, and common—describing plants from her garden, furniture from her home, birds, food, nature, and books. And yet her presentation is something we've never seen before. How about "a Soul selects her own Society" or "there is no Frigate like a Book" or the inscrutable yet fascinating deployment of capital letters and only occasional punctuation?[9]

Dickinson's uniqueness comes from a baseline of relatable material and elemental poetic tools. She then takes those ordinary objects and, in her own words, "dares to do strange things, bold things."[10] Dickinson's methods are both an argument for innovation and for being educated enough in the basics to know from where and with what to innovate. Or, as she put it: "Never try to lift the words which I cannot hold."[11]

3. SEEK OUT MENTORS

Dickinson was no misanthrope. Throughout her life, she reached out to people she could trust, those who knew more than she did and who she guessed could make her poetry better—family friend Benjamin Franklin Newton, her sister-in-law Susan Gilbert, newspaper editor Samuel Bowles, and Thomas Wentworth Higginson. She asked questions, she listened, she pushed herself to be better while still remaining true to her own vision and sensibilities.

What I like about Dickinson's example is how much weight it puts on the latter parts of mentorship. Mentorship isn't just about finding someone smarter or more accomplished than you. It's about knowing what to ask, when to question, how to create a relationship that you know is both challenging your work and leading you toward making it better. I doubt there is an Emily Dickinson the great poet without Emily Dickinson the great student.

It's harder to say if just reading Dickinson can give you the kind of heroic guidance that knowing a bit about her methods and life can. Clifton Fadiman suggests you grab twenty of her poems at random, read them, and see how you feel.[12] He also admits that not everyone will be satisfied with this method. I'd go a step further and say that, while this is a way to get a sense of the kind of writer Dickinson was, it is not the most direct course to being inspired by her. I think it's fine to start with her greatest hits, the poems that history has found most accessible or understandable, then poke around with how she put even the easier ones together, to learn a bit about the artist behind the image and the superstitions.

I love the quote from the second *Spider-Man* movie where Peter Parker's Aunt May says simply, "I believe there's a hero in all of us, that keeps us honest, gives us strength, makes us noble."[13] She's talking about the inspiring nature of sacrifice. The cousins of sacrifice are conviction, effort, and belief that we can take another crack at creating tomorrow. We can glean all this from the work of Emily Dickinson, if we look past stale clichés of how she lived her life.

In Dickinson's own words:

> Hope is the thing with feathers
> That perches in the soul,
> And sings the tune without the words,
> And never stops at all.[14]

43

LITTLE HEROES AND *LOCUST*

*T*he Day of the Locust *by Nathanael West is one of those books that
raises questions a teenager will solve with pat answers and will tie
an adult in knots. It's about Hollywood, which means any kid who saw
a bad movie last weekend could argue it's also about moral depravity
and broken dreams. The title and the bulk of the novel also contain
biblical allusions. I fear this means that right now a poor teacher
somewhere is grading forty-five identical essays about the "plague of
fame" and its sufferers.

You can read *Locust* now and make the same judgments, but
I'm going to suggest something else. Let *The Day of the Locust* and
its 126 smooth, brutal pages roll over you. Its principal characters
are Hollywood extras, has-beens, and minor studio employees trying
to make it in the movies. Much of their time is spent committing
small acts of cruelty and violence upon each other, mostly to remind
themselves they are still alive and that their resentments have someplace to go. "They've come to California to die," intones West on the
novel's second page, introducing a sad, operatic cast of freaks, raging
against a mirage and unable to make themselves happy.[1]

Now pack this cast together like a snowball and roll them forward
in time. Watch *The Day of the Locust* gather up Diane Arbus's photographs of twins and giants. Watch it roll along Oedipa Maas's phan-
tasmagoric road trip in Thomas Pynchon's *The Crying of Lot 49*, then
Tom Waits's band of outcasts on the albums *Swordfishtrombones* and
Rain Dogs. The *Locust* snowball could easily sweep in Hubert Selby
Jr.'s novel *Last Exit to Brooklyn* and the early films of Errol Morris
and Larry Clark. It wasn't as ordinary to populate the canvases of

American art with the disposed *and* monstrous in 1939 as it is now. Nathanael West came early to the idea.

West's band of dwarves and dumb starlets of *Locust* aren't there for our pity or our understanding, or even for us to relate to. In fact, they seem to be doing nothing but telling us their own sad story, one without heroes, redemption, or anything learned. It's fair to ask why. If Nathanael West saw *The Day of the Locust* as a sunburned fable of misery, designed only to make his readers miserable, I doubt we'd still be reading it.

West instead keeps his reasons to himself. He seems to like his characters without wishing them well. He looks at their deluded, self-annihilating ways and says, "Few things are sadder than the truly monstrous," which sounds both kind and horrified in the same breath.[2]

But we are busy people here, and that won't do. *The Day of the Locust* is short enough to be read in an afternoon. But if it's just weird for the sake of weird, what to *do* with it other than say, "How sad. How strange" and rush on?

It's a question that has been batted around for the last seventy years as the work of Nathanael West has been unearthed, canonized, then returned to fandom and high school classrooms since his death in 1940. West was only thirty-seven when he and his wife were killed in an auto accident. *The Day of the Locust*, his fourth and final novel, had been published a year before and hadn't sold very well. His second novel, *Miss Lonelyhearts* (poet Elizabeth Hardwick called it "West's other masterpiece"), was his only success and brought him to Hollywood, where he wrote a dozen screenplays for movies you've never heard of.[3] And though he had many friends and admirers in high places (F. Scott Fitzgerald, Edmund Wilson, Lillian Hellman), it would be only after death that West's compact bibliography would get a long look—and be seen as both a perfect snapshot of its time and the beginning of a whole lot more.

West died the year Hollywood began to exit its Golden Age. Earlier that year, *Gone with the Wind* had won the Best Picture Oscar®, beating out *The Wizard of Oz*; *Goodbye, Mr. Chips*; and *Mr. Smith Goes to Washington*. A decade into the Great Depression, Americans still went to the movies in record numbers. Studios were fat and happy, and stars were as glamorous and big as the movie palaces that housed them. The year 1939 is widely considered the most successful year in American film history.

The publication of *Locust* in May of that year now resembles the era's photo negative, capturing both its essence and opposite. Almost a decade into the Depression, *Locust* features no breadlines, unemployment offices, or WPA projects. Although 1939 was the grandest year for Hollywood, West's novel leaves out movie stars, studio chiefs, and Duesenbergs. There is only one mansion, belonging to a "successful screenwriter" named Claude, who is mostly around to enjoy the human comedy of the other characters' failings. This is the Depression, LA style, where the town's biggest factories hum merrily along but lock the book's characters outside the gates.

History tells us that the factories were about to sputter. In the 1940s, Hollywood was hit by the jab-cross-hook of antitrust lawsuits, HUAC investigations, and the coming of television. Movie studios would never again have the same hold on the country's imagination, and the genre that seemed to represent this anxiety best was film noir, a composite of hard-boiled detectives, femmes fatales, rain-soaked streets, and flawed people who try to do the right thing but who trip over their own shortcomings. Film noir was a cinema of anxiety, reflecting not just an industry in transition but a nation confronting the horrors of World War II, the atom bomb, and America's uneasy place as the world's great power. *Stranger on the Third Floor*, considered the first Hollywood example of the genre, was released the year of Nathanael West's death. Film noir captures, as Roger Ebert once said, a time of "no more heroes."[4]

Or perhaps it captures heroes of a different kind. Film noir movies and the novels by Raymond Chandler, Dashiell Hammett, and Patricia Highsmith that inspired them resemble classic heroes' journeys. The consequences are often tragic, the decisions characters make are morally hazy, but the "hero" faces adversity, recovers from setback, tries again, and recognizes error, even when it's too late. The stops on the hero's journey are all there.

The Day of the Locust has left these things out entirely. Novelist Jonathan Lethem argued that "making a hero's progress through a typical plot even if it's a tragic one. . . . It's just not West's way."[5] Tod Hackett, Faye Greener, Homer Simpson, the vivid, unforgettable crew of this novel are all incomplete, fragmented souls with characteristics left out like redacted passages of a government document. "If West's characters are human, they are only unfortunately so" (Lethem again) in how they fall short by what they lack— self-awareness, reserves of strength, and the ability to distinguish immature dreams from attainable realities.[6] "In West's cosmology, exaggeration rules," said critic Virginia Heffernan of *Locust*, "a moment of self-doubt becomes profound self-loathing; fleeting hostility becomes a blow to the head."[7]

None of these traits are the romantic parts of a hero's journey. We remember dragons being slain, not the hero's ability to avoid freaking out at the coming of the dragon. But by leaving them out so completely, Nathanael West has shown us something very real via that same photo negative—what is there by what is not.

Heroes comic, romantic, or tragic have obvious visible parts: conviction, selflessness, the ability to marshal themselves after defeat. *Locust* highlights the unglamorous, invisible parts by omission. Heroes, even of the simple, contented kind, do not yell "favoritism," as a stage-mom neighbor of Tod Hackett's does. They do not pick a fight with anyone who disagrees with them, as the dwarf Abe Kusich does. And they do not death-grip their own ideas of success and happiness when those ideas produce neither success nor happiness, as Faye Greener does. True heroes take responsibility for their own happiness. West's characters in *Locust* cannot make themselves happy. They are convinced that, like what they see in the movies, the answers to their dreams lie elsewhere, outside themselves. Someone else must let them in.

The author feels for their efforts. "It is hard to laugh at the need for beauty and romance no matter how tasteless, even horrible the results of that are," he says in the novel's opening pages.[8] But he also handicaps them by leaving these tools out of their toolboxes. They can't be heroes even to themselves.

West doesn't tell us if we can draw the same conclusions about ourselves. He doesn't think he can. In a letter to his friend Edmund Wilson, he remarked, "I forget the broad sweep, the big canvas, the shot-gun adjectives, the important people, the significant ideas, the lessons to be taught. . . . There is nothing to root for in my books and what is even worse, no rooters."[9]

The novel's most famous scene is its finale, a movie premiere where the waiting crowd whips itself into a violent mob. This is the swarm of locusts we've been waiting for. Tod Hackett, who throughout the novel has been working on a painting called "The Burning of Los Angeles," wherein the characters of the book torch the city in a mayhem of violence and fury, is caught up in the madness. Injured, he is scooped up by an ambulance and begins to laugh along with its siren, a gesture both lunatic and utterly mysterious.

There's nothing else. But West has drawn us into this sad world to the point that our imaginations can go on, perhaps another few pages. It's night, the crowd has been dispersed, and the streets are empty. We are confronted with that emptiness; the characters we've known are missing, unable to make their own lives better. Nothing stares back at us; West leaves us alone with ourselves. He doesn't ask us if we could do it better, but the emptiness forces us to see there's no one else there. You only have you. What do you do about it?

Somewhere through the hopelessness of *The Day of the Locust*, I emerge with this: We cannot say this is just a novel about sad, hobbled people. We have to ask, "What are they missing that made them sad and hobbled?" And if those things could have made them the little heroes of their little lives, if we have them, could they do the same for us?

44

VISIT *TINKER CREEK*.
THEN KEEP GOING.

I n 1975, Annie Dillard won the Pulitzer Prize with her first book. She was twenty-nine years old, and two years earlier, she had spent a cycle of seasons living by Tinker Creek in the Shenandoah Mountains outside Roanoke, Virginia. Her book about the experience, *Pilgrim at Tinker Creek*, was an immediate success and was named by Edward Abbey as the rightful heir to Thoreau's *Walden*. On its twenty-fifth anniversary, the Modern Library named *Tinker Creek* to its list of the 100 Best Nonfiction books. The reader's list, where the first two spots are occupied by Ayn Rand and L. Ron Hubbard, placed *Tinker Creek* even higher than the MLA board.[1]

The attention did not interest Annie Dillard. On the heels of *Tinker Creek*, she was asked to model for *Vogue*, to write for Hollywood, even to host her own talk show. She refused to go on a book tour and has stuck to this policy eleven books and nearly forty years later. Her website's home page reads:

> I'm sorry. I've never promoted myself or my books, but I used to give two public readings a year.
>
> Now I can no longer travel, can't meet with strangers, can't sign books but will sign labels with SASE, can't write by request, and can't answer letters. I've got to read and concentrate. Why? Beats me.[2]

Her photo is right next to this disclaimer. Annie Dillard has a healthy smile and sparkling blue eyes. She looks like a neighbor who would help you haul something heavy up the stairs. I doubt she's unfriendly or misanthropic. I think she's got a head so full of ideas and plans that it keeps her busy pretty much all the time.

You'd be right, then, to wonder why I've included Annie Dillard and her best-known book in this section about heroes. It's probably the last thing the author would call herself, and she didn't spend a year in the woods even as a younger person as proof of her mettle or on a quest to unlock nature's secrets. Annie Dillard likes to create her own adventures. (*Tinker Creek*'s most famous passage comes early when the unnamed narrator finds a frog that has been eaten by a water bug: the dead frog doesn't move when the woman tries to scare it, a favorite game of hers) Dillard begins by defining her goal with a quote from Thoreau: "a meteorological journal of the mind."[3] Looking inside, we see what I'd call the heroic place where the creative act and the spiritual quest meet: the attempt to make real what is elusive, difficult, or unknowable. That *Tinker Creek* acknowledges that this is ultimately futile but worth doing anyway is a different sort of heroism, one where we acknowledge the limits of our passions, no matter how brightly they burn, but march into the darkness still.

The word Annie Dillard uses to describe *Tinker Creek* is *theodicy*, an inquiry into the effect of the divine on our path through this world. Dillard calls it "tranquility and trembling," an attempt at reconciling the holiness of nature's beauty and its violence, loss, impermanence, and fear—all of which are part of that beauty as well.[4] Understanding our place in the world is the oldest heroic quest we have. But *Tinker Creek* refracts it: Dillard alternates her chapters between names of seasons ("Winter," "Spring") and her method of processing distinct slices of them ("seeing," "stalking," "nightwatch"). Her sense of wonder is everywhere, but Dillard is too well read, too subtle in her reasoning, and frankly too mature, even at twenty-eight, to just gape at the beauty of it all. Wonder is also a rather wordless emotion. No one babbles "with wonder." Annie Dillard has given herself the job of rendering wonder with words, then letting wonder mature into an act of wisdom.

"Bear with me one last time," writes Dillard near the end of her year, near the end of her time with us. And she explains as best she can what this time of seeing, of noticing, of letting this small corner of the world seep into and shoot through her has meant. She ultimately says we cannot know even though she has tried.

> Ezekiel excoriates false prophets as those who have not yet "gone up into the gaps." The gaps are the thing. . . . The gaps are the cliffs in the rock where you cower to see the back parts of God. . . . Go up into the gaps; if you find them. They shift and vanish too. This is how you will spend this afternoon and tomorrow morning and tomorrow afternoon. Spend the afternoon. You can't take it with you.[5]

We can try to capture the enormity of what we experience even in a single day. But Dillard says "the world is wilder than all that."[6] Succeeding is not understanding or summation. It isn't neatness or completion or the period at the end of a sentence. Completion is the next sentence and the next one after that. Success is in the attempt at doing.

Annie Dillard had written her master's thesis on *Walden* and seemed okay with the comparisons between her book and that of transcendentalist writers like Thoreau and Ralph Waldo Emerson. She has not been okay with being called an "essayist" (fair enough; *Tinker Creek* had been serialized in several magazines before publication, but its narrative is too unbroken to be called a collection of essays) or a "nature writer" (also fair; if a year in nature is opportunity to explore larger themes of belonging, consciousness, and awe, instead of just plants, animals, and mountains, I take her mission at its word). "Nature writing" is probably the heading you'd find this book under if you assigned it in a classroom. *Tinker Creek* is not only a bestselling and prize-winning work of nonfiction; its release coincided with the birth of the modern environmental movement. The first Earth Day and the founding of the United Nations Environment Programme had been established only a few years before the book's publication. Edward Abbey's novel *The Monkey Wrench Gang* (the inspiration for the environmental advocacy group Earth First) was published the same year as *Tinker Creek*.

Like *Walden*, *Tinker Creek* benefits from multiple passes read through multiple sets of glasses. "Nature writing" works the first time around. Subsequent reads can be from the point of view of theology, memoir, and the early work of a distinguished author's career. But unlike *Walden*, whose language is precise, almost surgical, Annie Dillard's prose is more like acupressure—gentle, wavelike, and without clear beginnings and endings. You can drift off, even fall asleep, and then awaken not knowing quite where you are.

In the afterword of *Tinker Creek*, Dillard explains the beginning stages of putting the book together as "why not write some sort of nature book?—a theodicy? I fooled around with the idea and started filling out five-by-seven index cards with notes from years of reading." Indeed, Dillard's mind is so full and her prose winds its way so lightly through her thoughts that one must read alert while feeling relaxed. It's rewarding all over, but not always easy. Give yourself adequate breaks for water, stretching, and thinking, as well as time for questioning to free those thoughts.

This time, when I returned to *Tinker Creek*, it felt like Dillard's year there was an attempt at understanding, instead of conclusion, an attempt to understand how much we belong to the world and can hear its invisible rhythms, while realizing that we are just guests here. We still need to try to understand that, because without that sense of belonging, there isn't much to being alive. That attempt is heroic both in its size (the gaining of wisdom, experience, a sense of the world) and in its humility.

A pilgrim is someone who makes not just a journey but a journey with the intent of understanding, of wisdom, and of witness. A pilgrim by definition is also someone who does not stay. By calling her book *Pilgrim at Tinker Creek*, Annie Dillard was speaking both to herself and to us. To herself: "This will not be your final journey or the last story you will tell." To us: "Make your pilgrimage, see everything you can, try to understand. Then come back, write it down, then keep going."

45

HOW TO TELL A HERO STORY

*T*he *Things They Carried* came into my life exactly five weeks after my eighteenth birthday. It was my first week of college, and a neighbor in my dorm joked that watching the freshman class all move in weighted down by desk chairs and laundry hampers reminded him of *The Things They Carried*. I told him I didn't understand, and he told me *The Things They Carried* was the best book he'd ever read about the Vietnam War. I thanked him and didn't think of the book again for a decade. I figured when it came to Vietnam, I'd read and seen all I needed (Mark Baker's *Nam*, Wallace Terry's *Bloods*, Oliver Stone's *Platoon*, Stanley Kubrick's *Full Metal Jacket*, and Bill Couturié's documentary *Dear America: Letters Home from Vietnam*). I was a toddler when Saigon fell and lived with the war's aftermath in news and popular culture for the entire 1980s. The recent past was someone else's problem. Time to worry about today.

Actually, that's not what happened at all. I did find out about *The Things They Carried* from a neighbor in my freshman dorm. But I don't remember when or how. I don't remember how long after that I bought the book or read it. I never resented it for being about Vietnam.

I've recommended *The Things They Carried* countless times and have given it as birthday, graduation, holiday, and thank-you gifts. But I barely recall how we first met. So I told a story to make sense of a history that is lost to memory. In *Things They Carried*, author Tim O'Brien argues that "story-truth" does just as good a job as actual truth.[1] But he's a novelist. Being in favor of "story-truth" is in his job description.

I'm not a novelist and this book isn't fiction. Was the telling of that story understandable or dishonest? Did I do something artful or just lie? That's the difficult question and great reward at the heart of *Things They Carried*. It insists we ask ourselves what we're doing when we make up stories about events we don't remember. We can call it lying or sleaze, but we could just as easily call it human. If we did not organize, even force, memories into narrative, would there be history, fables, myths, even the instinct to write fiction? Would we remember or understand anything difficult at all if we could not organize it as a story?

Now try asking these questions about soldiers and combat as O'Brien does, and things get even harder. By definition, a "war story" contains an element of fiction, an understandable attempt to apply structure and meaning to something chaotic and terrifying. Then complicate that even more by adding the question of heroism. The issue of soldiers as heroes was at its most contentious during the Vietnam War. But the very act of creating heroes at all is an act of "story-truth." Great deeds can have only a finite number of witnesses, and *hero* seems a title aimed for eternity. We may call someone a hero for liberating a child from a burning building or for leading a nation to independence. But heroes are only heroes after the fact, after they've risked themselves in heroic pursuit, and, even then, after we've told their story. Heroes and their myths cannot be separated.

The Things They Carried is an interlocking set of short stories about an infantry platoon in the Vietnam War and has heroism somewhere at the back of its mind. The idea shows its face just a few times in the book: one grunt says in story 3, "If I could have one wish, anything, I'd wish for my dad to write me a letter and say it's ok if I don't win any medals."[2] But after I'd finished reading, the idea arrived like a late party guest and never left. Heroes need their stories told in order to exist. But perhaps the telling of a story itself is a heroic act, heroic not by its valor and sacrifice but by its humanness and frailty.

The Things They Carried comprises twenty-two stories. Six of those are as much about how a story is told as the narrative itself. The eponymous opening tale points to those priorities a little further into the collection. It organizes itself as a packing list of a combat soldier in Vietnam. "The things they carried were largely determined by necessity . . . pocket knifes, heat tabs, wristwatches, dog tags, mosquito repellent." Each paragraph opens this way—"They carried" or "He carried"—followed by an inventory. While the structure remains constant, meaning lifts upward until we realize that we are not just talking about the contents of a soldier's rucksack but also his mind and heart—a sense of responsibility, fear, and memories to tell of afterward. "They carried all they could bear, and then some, including a silent awe for the terrible power of the things they carried."[3]

About two-thirds through the book, O'Brien makes this confession:

I'm 43 years old, true, and I'm a writer now and a long time ago I walked through Quang Ngai province as a foot soldier. Almost everything else is invented.[4]

He hasn't lied to us. *The Things They Carried* is subtitled "A Work of Fiction." But O'Brien also has not been very clear about it. The book is dedicated not to his wife or children or his agent but to the fictional soldiers in his platoon. There is a soldier in the platoon named "Tim O'Brien." "How to Tell a True War Story" is the name of the book's seventh story. It includes this explanation:

In any war story, but especially a true one, it's difficult to separate what happened from what seemed to happen.

And then just a bit later:

A thing may happen and be a total lie. Another thing may not happen and be truer than the truth.[5]

We are in a different country here than even most fictional treatments of the Vietnam War, where authenticity and the truthfulness of the soldier experience are the first order of business. But Tim

O'Brien was nearly a half dozen books into his career as a writer and twenty years removed from the war when *Things They Carried* was published in 1990. O'Brien had served as an infantryman in 1968 and published a memoir of that experience called *If I Die in a Combat Zone* in 1975, as well as two acclaimed, more straightforward works of fiction—*Where Have You Gone, Charming Billy?* (1975) and *Going after Cacciato* (1979)—about soldiers and combat. *The Things They Carried* takes this platoon—based on his own, but largely imagined—and uses it to frame questions of why we tell stories and what this says about us as a species.

"My life is storytelling," O'Brien told the *New York Times* around the publication of *Things They Carried.* "I believe in stories, in their incredible power to keep people alive, to keep the living alive, and the dead."[6] Indeed the final story, "The Lives of the Dead," is both a vindication and an acknowledgment of the limits of O'Brien's methods. In it, he talks about his childhood girlfriend, Linda, who died in elementary school from a brain tumor. By telling the story of her short life, argues O'Brien, he can see her again, if only in his imagination. He can make her grow up, marry, age, or even just smile. He can imagine the soldiers who died in Vietnam with a life after the war. "In a story, which is a kind of dreaming, the dead sometimes smile and sit up and return to the world."[7]

"Dreaming" is the perfect word. O'Brien acknowledges at the story's end that we can't live in dreams; that we all wake up; are older, not younger; that present becomes past. The act of imagining, though, of telling stories, is our own comfort with that fact, an understanding that we, too, will die but that we needn't be helpless and terrified knowing that.

That may seem silly, an attempt to argue with time. Or it might be the basis of the thing beyond survival that we live for: to understand our own experience and learn from it. As human beings, we haven't found many better ways of doing that than fashioning our experiences into a story.

It's perhaps a bit more complicated when talking about war.

Though O'Brien has many readers and admirers who are also veterans, I would feel awkward gifting this book to one of them. *The Things They Carried* feels to me like a book written from the vantage point of many years away, when military service can be seen as memory, safely fiction rather than still-open wounds.

It's also a rather difficult time for the question of military service and heroism that haunts this book. Since the US involvement in Iraq and Afghanistan, it has been repeatedly argued that perhaps we have shifted too far the other way from Vietnam on this question—that we now valorize combat service thoughtlessly out of fear of seeming unpatriotic. Doing this, the argument goes, both ignores terrible realities—appallingly high incidents of rape within the military and domestic violence and suicide following combat service—and makes us a nation that shoots first and asks questions later because no one pins a medal on the suit lapel of a diplomat.

Things They Carried asks us quietly but without equivocation to see heroism differently. That we be courageous enough to tell our own stories, to imagine them if we can't remember them, to believe in the humanity of storytelling while acknowledging what it cannot do. Are we then still human—courageously, fragile humans who believe that dreams and imagination aren't children's toys but are among the few things that give us not only comfort but wisdom?

You can grab *Things They Carried* if you like great war fiction. Hell, grab it if you simply like colorful, immediate, blood-rushing-to-your-fingertips fiction. But I'd especially pick it up if your own imagination is a bit atrophied, your own story a bit stale, if you feel like an observer rather than the hero of your own life. Heroes all have stories told about them. It is not cheating to tell your own.

PART 10
THE FUTURE

46

BEWARE OF REVOLUTIONARIES WHO LOOK LIKE PIGS

In both his diary and letters to his agent, George Orwell spoke of his 1945 novel *Animal Farm* as an allegory of Stalinist Russia, at the time a World War II ally of his native England. At first glance, we can see why. Under its fur and feathers, Orwell's "fairy story" is the tale of a revolution gone terribly wrong, creating a society of fear and repression instead of the utopia fought for and promised.

This initially made me less inclined to give the book another go-round in adulthood, even though I wolfed it down about two dozen times as a teenager. Oppression is cheap and plentiful to a teenager, as relatable as loud music and fried food. To a grown man and basically happy person, not so much. And the fact that Orwell had a now-extinct political regime in mind makes *Animal Farm*'s continued relevance an even tougher sell. The horror of watching "four legs good, two legs bad" morph into "four legs good, two legs better" is still there. But unless the collapse of America arrives tomorrow (an entertaining thought, but c'mon), *Animal Farm* has what, exactly, to say to the reader of today? Not much, it seems, unless that reader smells the coming of fascism with every change in the political winds.

George Orwell was making a very specific political point with *Animal Farm*, as specific as those he made with his essays on Dickens or socialism or the shooting of elephants. But sixty years and a new century later, his little book also has a quieter, bigger warning: beware of what political scientists call "Year One" thinking; that great change, even revolution, means a clean slate. A new regime never means a completely new beginning, for even after the tyrants are gone, their statues toppled, and the streets alive with celebration, we are still capable of repeating our sins. We are still capable of the same greed, intolerance, and lust for power that we claimed to have banished.

We cannot overthrow our own humanity. Perhaps the unintended irony of *Animal Farm* is that revolution can change everything except what makes us human.

If you don't remember the story of *Animal Farm*, give yourself a half hour and a slow evening, and you'll have read six chapters without blinking. *Animal Farm* is a fast, brief book, told in the same clear, chilly style as Orwell's essays. It is a fable of the animals of Manor Farm in the English countryside. Fed up with poor treatment and backbreaking labor, they revolt and drive away their human overseers. The new animal regime, led by the pigs Snowball and Napoleon, establishes Seven Commandments of Animalism, each one underscoring how animals are different than humans but equal among each other. But a schism between Napoleon and Snowball leads to Snowball being chased from the farm in what appears to be a coup d'état. As the years pass, the pigs under Napoleon grow fat with privilege; the other animals are worked and starved. The Seven Commandments of Animalism are amended one at a time to benefit the leadership of the pigs until they are reduced to a single, devastating maxim.

ALL ANIMALS ARE EQUAL, BUT SOME ANIMALS ARE MORE EQUAL THAN OTHERS.[1]

And in a little over a hundred pages, the pigs who once led the overthrow of human tyrants have become human themselves.

George Orwell was not a man short of opinions, but those opinions hardly followed a pattern. He called himself "a democratic socialist" and was equally critical of left-wing intellectuals, whom he saw as sympathizing with the working class without really wanting to associate with it.[2] In his book *Why Orwell Matters*, Christopher Hitchens notes that the Right embraced Orwell for his assault on communism; the Left, for his hatred of imperialism and centralized power. Hitchens based his own praise on approach rather than ideology—independence of mind, fairness, and a willingness to take his own moral temperature and change his mind.[3]

Orwell was already respected as a literary critic and political journalist when he published *Animal Farm*. The book was an immediate bestseller, which also made him well known as a novelist. His next (and last) novel, *1984*, left him in the mind of high school students everywhere as a crusader against tyranny and a spyglass through which we spot the insidious creep of power. *1984* has left perhaps a larger footprint on our culture with such terms as *doublethink*, *Newspeak*, and *Big Brother* becoming part of everyday language. The same cannot be said of *Animal Farm*, which seems more of an inspirational jumping-off point than a directly quoted source. Pink Floyd called their 1977 album *Animals* in tribute to *Animal Farm* but conceived the record as an economic critique of the England of the 1970s. The Clash, contemporaries of the Sex Pistols, used artwork from the novel for a political broadside: the band's 1979 single "English Civil War," a rebuke of the far right making its presence known in British politics. A decade later, American band R.E.M. would use *Animal Farm* images for its song "Disturbance at the Heron House," which is about the absurdities of Ronald Reagan's America. In 2000, the hip-hop group Dead Prez released "Animal in Man," about how the last thing revolutionaries should bring to a revolution is trust in its leaders.

Animal Farm has inspired, entertained, and terrified—and will continue to do so, if only in the limited context of a battle. Novelist Julian Barnes has said that Orwell was at his best when "writing against" something.[4] I'd hate to think of the same restriction applied to a reading of Orwell's fiction, that *Animal Farm* is more than a fable only if we have an ax to grind and a heart full of anger.

As I write this essay in December of 2011, the Occupy movement demonstrations and encampments, armed with the slogan "We are the 99%," have become fixtures in cities around the world. Begun in anger at social and economic inequality (the slogan refers to everyone not balanced atop the apex of capitalism), the goals of the movement are many and difficult to quantify. Ask someone frustrated with the demonstrations who doesn't just hate protests on principle, and they'll probably say, "What do they want?" Their next gesture will be an exasperated shrug.

Compelling arguments have been made that the Occupy movement does not have to know its endgame right now. Or ever. I'm fine with the protesters not knowing. But this in-between period of the movement reveals a very hard truth: Revolution is sexy, telegenic, dangerous, and fun. It is also by definition brief when compared to the business of setting up and running the world to come. Running the society you get following a revolution is often unsexy, sluggish, fractured, and soul crushing. It's not the part anyone looks forward to when crowds are gathering on the streets.

George Orwell wrote *Animal Farm* as a critique of a revolution gone wrong. His version of that was centralized power, stifled dissent, and fear among citizens who had fought alongside each other just a short time before. But if the Arab Spring of 2011 and the US invasion of Iraq have shown us anything, it's that toppling a dictator is much easier than cleaning up the mess afterward. Implementing the changes you fought for is even harder.

I keep that front of mind when reading *Animal Farm*. Be careful when dreaming of revolution, especially if those dreams come true. Because what you do with your victory is an entirely separate and harder issue than how you won it in the first place.

I haven't plotted to overthrow anything since the tenth grade, and that was a student council election that hinged on the issue of whether we could hang heavy-metal posters on our locker doors. But I am terribly guilty of the kind of Year One, "everything will be better when" thinking Orwell captures so grimly in *Animal Farm*. Everything will be better when we run things, when I get that promotion, finish that assignment, get through the holidays, lose ten pounds. Even if it all happens, you are still you. You don't get to leave your own baggage behind, even when everything changes. And everything will change again, sooner than you think.

The mules, goats, chickens, and sheep of *Animal Farm* trust the pigs they placed in charge. Orwell labels that obedience their fatal mistake. Less loudly than in the past, but more relevant for our time, *Animal Farm* is an argument against assuming that change is total. We are still ourselves, even after we have achieved everything we want—still very human and more than a little bit animal. The challenge of change, says *Animal Farm,* is not how to bring it about but what we do once we have.

47

MEET THOMAS PYNCHON, YOUR DRIVING COMPANION

The title of Thomas Pynchon's *The Crying of Lot 49* refers to a stamp auction. "Crying" is what the auctioneer does to solicit bids, and "Lot 49" is the stamp collection that belongs to the protagonist's dead lover. You don't get these rather mundane details until just about the end of the book, which is exactly where they should be. If the title rolled itself out over several chapters with hints and clues, my head would have exploded. At 183 pages, *Lot 49* may be Thomas Pynchon's shortest novel (he called it "a short story, but with gland trouble"[1]), a frenetic fable that goes down quickly and crackles like a mouthful of Pop Rocks®. It also contains enough ideas, images, characters, and narrative pirouettes to make you feel like the novel will spill out onto the floor if you leave the book open too long. Quick reading it might be, but "quick" couldn't be further from "slight" or "disposable."

The Crying of Lot 49 (1966) is Pynchon's second novel and tells a quest story as old as the *Odyssey, The Wizard of Oz,* or *The Lord of the Rings.* There's a hero (in this case, a California housewife named Oedipa Maas) and a journey (Maas has been named executor of the estate of her mogul-like ex-lover. She needs to visit his range of investments to see that his wishes for them are carried out). However, the objective of said quest changes almost immediately as Oedipa begins seeing a mysterious glyph of a horn with two bells stacked inside each other everywhere, first in a ladies' room, then as a paper watermark, and soon, too many places to ignore. Like just about everything else in this novel, Pynchon has taken our age-old expectations of story-telling and hung them by their ankles.

What is this horn? It is the insignia of Trystero, a centuries-old organization that has built its own communication network in defiance of established systems like the postal service. And yet finding out what Trystero does isn't the goal; the novel makes very little of the insights about it. The point instead is who Oedipa runs into along the road, not monsters to slay or sages to learn from but rather a large group of roadside attractions: a therapist who interned at Buchenwald concentration camp; a boy band called the Paranoids; an assembly of deaf-mutes; a community theater troupe performing a "Jacobean revenge play"; a man named Winthrop Tremaine, a clothing salesman looking to release SS uniforms into the teenage market; and a twelve-step group looking for people who wish to swear off falling in love. Each may mark a step on Oedipa's trip, but in the blanched California of the mid-1960s, they are as lost and searching as she is. "They think they're getting somewhere, they think they're looking for someone," critic Louis Menand said of *Lot 49*'s menagerie. "They realize they're already where they want to be, the only place it makes any sense to be, which is on the road."[2]

I've made it sound like reading *Lot 49* is the narrative equivalent to being outnumbered in a snowball fight—which sounds like a lame attempt at a Pynchonian image, so let me apologize for that. What I'm trying to get at is the fear I had in picking up the book at all. I first heard about Pynchon in high school from a classmate who was reading *Lot 49* for the senior-year contemporary literature class I didn't take. As he endorsed "Pynchon," he deliberately bit off the *ch*, just as he had punched out the first *t* in "Dostoyevsky," his favorite novelist. Dostoyevsky couldn't write anything under five hundred pages, so far as I could tell, and it all sounded mind-numbingly grand and difficult and Russian. I was afraid Pynchon was just the stateside equivalent, too many characters, ideas, and plot twists, too little mercy for the slow-to-get-it like me. This friend could also breeze through a Thomas

Hardy novel in a weekend, whereas I took a month with *Tess of the d'Urbervilles* and gave up without finishing.

I couldn't imagine anything by "Pin-*ch*in" being a pleasurable read. Never mind the fact that every supercilious jerk in my college creative-writing department couldn't shut up about *Gravity's Rainbow*, Pynchon's eight-trillion-page third novel that *New York* magazine once called "perhaps the least-read must-read in American history."[3] The "Advice for Pynchon Newbies" section of the unofficial site ThomasPynchon.com devotes only a paragraph to *Lot 49* (what "some say [is the] most accessible novel") and then devotes the rest of the page to (you guessed it) *Gravity's Rainbow* and Pynchon's fifth novel, *Mason & Dixon*. *Mason & Dixon* weighs about as much as a baby hippo. "Difficult, schmifficult!" announces one contributor.[4] No thanks.

Lot 49, I am happy to say, is neither "difficult" nor "schmifficult." It is twitchy, breathless, random, and I think it is fair to call it insane. But you are not in the hands of a madman toying with your expectations for his own pleasures. Rather, Pynchon here seems to have two gears for this road trip: the novel's first, say, sixty pages are in overdrive. Pynchon talks a blue streak and tosses brilliant images out the window as the engine guns: California towns are "less an identifiable city than a grouping of concepts—census tracts, special purpose bond-issue districts, shopping nuclei." Wasted time is "a fat deckful of days."[5] After that, Pynchon shifts into cruise. Sentences lengthen, his voice changes to an easy shuffle. He's no longer in a hurry to create the novel's world at a blinding scatter. It's here. Anything could happen next. Ride with me.

Thomas Pynchon is often named with other giants of postmodern literature—John Barth, William Gaddis, Don DeLillo, and Robert Coover, to name a few. These guys (there seem to be very few women novelists who carry this flag) create worlds distorted by a deluge of images, symbols, and fragmented thoughts singed by the hot glow of communication and media. Their narrators are often untrustworthy, their plots nonlinear and difficult to explain. The feeling I get from many of them is a kind of quiet hostility toward the reader.

The message: "This is going to be difficult. I hope you are up to it. If you are not, the one at fault is you. Your pleasure is not my concern."

Not so with Pynchon, at least not here. *Lot 49* is wacky, often inscrutably so, but it is never aggressive or condescending. Its tone is sunny, even bemused. Pynchon seems to be revving himself up, high on the joy of storytelling and the storehouse of language available to him. The world of *Lot 49* is crazy; you don't know what's coming next and will not understand most of it. And that's good, Pynchon says. It's exciting to not know because that's the starter's pistol of possibility. Certainty is for squares.

It's just as easy to see *Lot 49* as asphalt-covered tragedy, a study in disconnectedness and the difficulty in ever really being understood. Characters seem to be talking past one other. Oedipa never accomplishes what she set out to, and, come book's end, we barely know what that was. It's fair to see her journey as a brilliant, nutty waste of time.

More than one person has cited Trystero's underground communication as a faint forerunner of the great possibilities of the Internet, the dispossessed being able to reach each other wherever they are. We could just as easily see it as pointing to the Internet's shortcomings—false connectedness, deadened sensitivity to real experience, half conversations and bits of thoughts in place of the real thing, quests uncompleted and overwhelmed by disorder. *Lot 49* can feel stocked full of all those too.

Ultimately it's up to us. I'm eager to read more Pynchon now. I like this idea that life is overwhelming and nuts and that I don't understand much of it. And that's not the scary end of youth but the beginning of something different, something exciting.

Thomas Pynchon doesn't do interviews or appearances or allow himself to be photographed, which you probably knew already. It's also the least interesting thing about him as a writer. Anne Tyler, Cormac McCarthy, Annie Dillard, and Harper Lee made the same choice, and it doesn't drive their readers into nearly the same tizzy. Pynchon seems to have been emerging from hiding in recent years and is having fun with the idea of being a mystery man of letters. He has published at increasing speed since the early 1990s, lobbied on behalf of writers Salman Rushdie and Ian McEwan, contributed an encomium to *The Daily Show*, and had his cartoon likeness show up three times on *The Simpsons* (in the first, he stood by the side of the road with a bag over his head, next to a blinking sign that said "Thomas Pynchon's House. Come on in!"[6]). In 1996, *New York* magazine ran an article called "Meet Your Neighbor, Thomas Pynchon," which described how Pynchon had been living for some time in Manhattan, goes by "Thomas" and not "Tom," does his own grocery shopping, and likes to see live music.[7] The editors, professors, and literary comrades who keep his privacy seem more invested in the myth of "Pynchon the Recluse" than he is. Pynchon may be in his mid-seventies, but he plans to continue writing books; his last novel, *Inherent Vice*, came out in 2009, so the need to explain his choices, unlike those of the silent and nonproductive J. D. Salinger, isn't really there.

And yet thanks to the sheer bounty of Pynchon's imagination, we want answers. We want to know why and how and where from and what do to with the heap of images and ideas that spills over the covers of his books. But I don't think answers are the point. *The Crying of Lot 49* is much more an uncertain future thanks to a wildly changing present, a quest whereby the journey, not the end, matters most. The end doesn't even exist. The only even vaguely stated goal is to understand that the journey might change at any minute and be ready for anything.

It's a rarely comforting place Pynchon has dropped us in, but it's also not cruel of him to do so. Instead, the Pynchon universe feels just like hitting a certain age when you no longer recognize what everyone is talking about, when you know much less than you once thought, and when you begin to understand that the world will go on dancing and exploding without you. Our first instinct is annoyance, maybe even fear ("This music is weird"; "Why do people dress this way?"; "What is everyone talking about?"). *Lot 49* says, "Stop it already. Feeling crazy is the point. If you're cut loose from expectation, think of how much there is to see, to do, to experience, to not yet know."

48

THE *REMAINS* OF TOMORROW

*T*he *Remains of the Day* is a novel set in the 1950s, written in flashback about the 1930s, and published in the 1980s by Kazuo Ishiguro, an author whose most ambitious work came in the 1990s. The story tells of butlers and domestics, English manor homes and presiding lords, "discretion" and "dignity" mentioned without irony, repressed emotions, and tight-lipped self-deception. It has provoked comparisons to the works of Edith Wharton and Henry James. *The Remains of the Day* was published in 1989, the year the Berlin Wall fell. Even then it probably felt about as contemporary as a lace curtain.

And yet I've read it three times, and with each go it feels a little more like a quiet lesson about one's future. Its characters may not see their future coming (no one really can), but to pretend it won't come at all ignores what makes us human—the mess of uncertainty, the indignity of pain and longing, and the unfiltered promise that change will come and that our humanity is measured by what we do with it. A life, this book says, is a measurement of days well spent, not a grasping at their remains vanishing behind us.

Remains is therefore that strange novel whose impact arrives via a trick of mirrors: a story so firmly one thing that it ends up teaching us the opposite. It passes no judgment; it sits there, literal and still as a portrait session, and then whispers its wisdom as if the author were standing just behind the reader's shoulder.

"You are not a servant. Your life is not orchestrated by rules invented before you were born. Given that, why have you obeyed them and made the same mistakes as these characters?"

That's me talking. Ishiguro stops short of calling his main characters' actions mistakes, but we can come to that conclusion ourselves. His narrator, Stevens (his first name, mentioned obliquely, is James), is a butler in the English manor house of Lord Darlington. The time is between the world wars. Stevens comes from a family line of butlers and as a young man is already serving supper and polishing silver alongside his father. Stevens was also so committed to the honor code of his profession—discretion, implacability, and not letting personal affairs interfere with the job—that he arrives on time to serve supper on the evening of his father's death.

This makes Stevens a very good butler and a very incomplete man. He turns the other way at Darlington's fascist loyalties and abrupt dismissal of two of his Jewish colleagues. Stevens is likely in love with Miss Kenton, another domestic at Darlington Hall, but he tells her nothing of his feelings. He even finds colleagues who "are simply going from post to post looking for romance" a "major irritation," below the absurd standards he and his profession have colluded in setting.[1]

Stevens tells his own story many years after the fact. He has gone on a road trip to visit Miss Kenton, now the married Mrs. Benn. It is the 1950s, and Stevens is butler to an American businessman. Darlington Hall and the place of butlers in British society are long gone. The story concludes with the meeting between the two former colleagues. I won't spoil the ending except to say that Stevens is not someone you'd want to hire as a life coach.

Ishiguro has set up *Remains* this way for two reasons. First, he wants us to see Stevens not as a victim of the circumstances he was born into but as a man with choices he has excised from his very being. Second, the bulk of the story exists in Stevens's memory, which he himself admits is faulty. Everyone's memory is faulty (where are your house keys right now?), but the deeper we read, the more we see that Stevens's polite apology for having a few senior moments is actually a distraction from his moral failings. He has deluded himself into thinking he has lived a noble life as a member of a noble profession. He has actually chosen a noble profession that leaves no room for him to be a real person. This choice demands that Stevens lie to himself in order to believe his life has not been wasted. He's too refined to do this openly. He has to then resort to what *New York Times* book critic Michiko Kakutani called "a doctrine of decorum that actually masks an appalling coldness and pragmatism."[2]

Ishiguro, an Englishman born in Japan, wrote *The Remains of the Day* in the closing years of Prime Minister Margaret Thatcher's administration. Prime Minister Thatcher desperately wanted to return England to the mythic glory of its nineteenth-century era of empire. Culturally, the decade she embodied opened with the film *Chariots of Fire*, which won the Best Picture Oscar® in 1981, revitalized the nation's dying film industry, and featured the story of two runners, one Jewish and one Scottish, returning honor to England after the horror of the First World War.[3]

Remains is set a decade or so later than *Chariots of Fire* and also has an England in transition as its setting. Only here its characters are studies in frailty, not triumph, of opportunities missed, of myths believed at the expense of self-respect and wisdom. Stevens and Miss Kenton are older and regretful, not young and looking forward. The iconic England of duty and service, the nation Margaret Thatcher dreamed of bringing back, has changed and left no place for them. However, Ishiguro's quiet critique of the decade is not one of pity but of sadness. If *Chariots of Fire* began the decade with outsiders who enter the house of England in triumph, *Remains* ends it with insiders quietly expelled from the manor by time and their lack of understanding of its passage.

It's worth asking why the tale of sad, silly James Stevens is now so moving. At the very least he's a butler, and do those even exist anymore? At worst, he has brought unhappiness upon himself. But the flaws Ishiguro gives Stevens are not about the character's occupation or shortcomings. Regardless of who we are and what we do, how many of us struggle each day, each hour, between what we must do out of obligation, and what we also must do to be true to who we are? How many of us are terrified of making mistakes, of presenting poorly and showing the messy imperfections that make us flawed, yes, but flawed like gemstones, the very things that make us ourselves?

In Stevens, Ishiguro might have given us a character who, through his choice of occupation, cannot be sloppy or frayed or human. But in this tiny, contained example, he's also shown us a person who has gotten himself stuck long after the job requires it, who has convinced himself that his destiny belongs entirely in the service of another. That can be a very fulfilling future if it works for you, but I think *Remains* is saying it's impossible: that fundamental to being human is the room to stumble into whom we are supposed to be.

The Remains of the Day was awarded Britain's highest literary honor, the Man Booker Prize and is on a half dozen lists compiled by British newspapers of the country's great twentieth-century novels. Ishiguro was thirty-five years old and had written only two other novels when this all happened. His next three novels were larger, wider efforts, a break from the trio of intimate character stories that *Remains* capped off. *The Remains of the Day* was also made into a 1993 film starring Anthony Hopkins and Emma Thompson, which is excellent and worth seeing.

Picking up a used paperback of *Remains* with its modest page count; historical setting; and elegant, calm prose means flirting with the temptation to read it over a long vacation weekend somewhere quiet and hilly. Resist that temptation. I have forgotten far too many great books simply because I read them while trying to escape from life for a while. *The Remains of the Day* requires time to simmer. Time to see what Mr. Stevens is up to and how even the remains he has left for himself are illusory, like disappearing wands of sunlight. Time to realize that, even though a slow meander through a short book might seem indulgent, you'll see how much more time in your future you have than you once thought. As long as you remember that it is yours.

49

FOUR DIFFERENT WAYS THAT
THINGS FALL APART

*T*hings Fall Apart is the debut novel by Nigerian author Chinua Achebe. Published in 1959, it is the first novel written in English by an African author to achieve worldwide acclaim and readership. *Things Fall Apart* is the story of three years in the life of Okonkwo, a village leader and wrestling champion in late-nineteenth-century Nigeria, just before the arrival of European missionaries. It has been translated into over fifty languages and is read in high schools throughout the world. *Time* magazine included *Things Fall Apart* on its 2005 list of the 100 Greatest Novels of the twentieth century.

Achebe structured *Things Fall Apart* as a Greek tragedy, telling of a hero whose strengths mask his shortcomings, which will ultimately lead to his undoing. He has also added the dimension of the world changing irrevocably just beyond the borders of Okonkwo's understanding. Within Okonkwo's world, Achebe deals with a great many things—ambition in conflict with family loyalty, tradition in a tug-of-war with change, an African story with Africans at center stage instead of serving as bystanders to European colonialism. But, surrounding it, like trees at the edge of a clearing, is the all-too-human fear of looking into an uncertain future, a fear that transcends race, nation, continent, even the old-fashioned definition of tragedy. Exactly how much can we blame someone for not accepting a future they can't do anything about?

The chaos of mind that results from those impossible circumstances is evident both from the swift, sad act of violence that concludes the novel and from the passage of poetry that opens it:

> Turning and turning in the widening gyre
> The falcon cannot hear the falconer;
> Things fall apart; the centre cannot hold;
> Mere anarchy is loosed upon the world, . . .[1]

These four lines are half of the opening stanza of William Butler Yeats's poem "The Second Coming," the source of Achebe's title. Composed of twenty-two lines in two stanzas, "The Second Coming" is one of Yeats's most beloved and widely read works. Written in 1919 and published the following year, the poem is commonly thought to be an interpretation of the savagery of World War I and the apocalyptic moment Europe had reached immediately following it. Earlier versions of the poem (several of which survive) are more specific, as though Yeats had national instead of continental or worldwide upheaval in mind. Literary critic Harold Bloom has submitted that the poem refers to the Russian Revolution of 1917.[2] Either way, it is quite clear that "The Second Coming" is about a moment in history when the past has been obliterated and the future is unknown but arriving any dark minute now. There is great fear in the land Yeats has created—fear borne not of the inescapability of change but of the uncertainty of exactly what that change will be. Okonkwo thinks he knows what the change will be, and he does something horrifying about it. Yeats does not—and ends his poem with this immortal image:

> And what rough beast, its hour come round at last,
> Slouches towards Bethlehem to be born?[3]

Yeats has reached back all the way to the birth of Jesus for much of the poem's visual power. The title and repetition of the phrase "The Second Coming," the references to "twenty centuries" and "Bethlehem" recall the Book of Revelation and the coming of the apocalypse. The apocalypse and the Second Coming of Christ represent, of course, another fulcrum where one age is ending and another is about to begin. But as any believer will tell you, "the future" of the Christian Second Coming is not uncertain at all. You just have to go through hell to get there. The "widening gyre" further complicates what kind of future we are to expect. A "widening gyre" is a spiral getting bigger and growing farther away from the center, never to return to its point of origin, what it once was and knew.

———

In 1968, a decade after the publication of *Things Fall Apart,* Joan Didion published *Slouching towards Bethlehem,* her first collection of nonfiction. The book contains twenty essays divided into three sections—"Life Styles in the Golden Land," "Personals," and "Seven Places of the Mind."[4] Didion's subject in sections 1 and 3 (the longest two sections) was California in the late 1960s, the state where she had been born and which had elbowed itself into the cultural spotlight, thanks to psychedelia, rock 'n' roll, and the Technicolor® happenings in San Francisco's Haight-Ashbury district. "The market was steady and the GNP was high," Didion wrote in the title essay. "It had been a spring of brave hopes and national promise. . . . At some point we had aborted ourselves and butchered the job."[5]

Didion had been an editor at *Vogue* magazine and published her first novel, *Run River* (1963), while on staff there. It was the publication of *Slouching towards Bethlehem* five years later that cemented Didion's reputation as one of her generation's great nonfiction storytellers (in league with Tom Wolfe, Hunter S. Thompson, Norman Mailer, and Gay Talese) and as someone who understood the grim horror of the social revolution of the 1960s. If the future foreseen by the missing children of Haight-Ashbury when Joan Didion showed up was communal, peaceful, and beyond hatred and war, what Didion saw it become was "a country of bankruptcy notices and public-auction announcements and commonplace reports of casual killings."[6]

Didion waited ten years before publishing another essay collection, *The White Album,* in 1979. *The White Album* takes its title from the colloquial name for the Beatles ninth album. The title essay (the entire first section of the book) is Didion's autobiographical look at the 1960s while living in Southern California. The fifth and concluding section is titled "On the Morning after the Sixties." *White Album* is a book self-conscious of the decade it is examining. It is a book looking back at something that is gone. Its predecessor, *Slouching towards Bethlehem*, is an attempt to understand a decade as it is happening.

The closing essay of *Bethlehem* is called "Goodbye to All That" and is Didion's account of moving back to California, of leaving the city that held her early adult life. It describes the realization that "at some point the golden rhythm was broken and I am not that young anymore."[7] We have just read an entire book on California, on the frightening, confusing changes happening there, and now Didion, the detached, stone-faced observer, concludes, not by leaving but by returning to it. "Goodbye to All That" seems to refer to both New York and a sense of being able to draw tangible conclusions. Didion knows only that the center does not hold. She has no idea where we will end up because of it. She does not even offer to find out. The opening of "Goodbye to All That" tells as much: "It is easy to see the beginnings of things, and harder to see the ends."[8]

Things Fall Apart is the fourth studio album by the Philadelphia hip-hop band The Roots. Released in February of 1999, it is considered the group's breakthrough effort, their first certified platinum record that also won the band its first of four Grammy® Awards. Named after Achebe's novel, *Things Fall Apart* is now considered a seminal record both of the period in hip-hop music and in the career story of The Roots themselves, the point of no return at which a musician no longer belongs to individual fans but to the culture at large.

Things Fall Apart was also the first Roots album to be named after a work of literature, a convention they would return to on their sixth album, *The Tipping Point* (after Malcolm Gladwell's book of the same name), and their eighth, *Rising Down* (after William T. Vollmann's seven-volume study of violence *Rising Up and Rising Down*). As of this writing, The Roots have released thirteen albums, were named one of the world's greatest live bands by *Rolling Stone* magazine, are the house band on the television show *Late Night with Jimmy Fallon*, and are considered likely contenders for induction into the Rock and Roll Hall of Fame.

Things Fall Apart begins with a vocal collage of an argument taken from the Spike Lee film *Mo' Better Blues*. Two musicians are having a backstage disagreement, bemoaning the fact that they see few black people at their concerts:

> *Musician 1:* If we had to depend on black people to eat, we would starve to death. . . . You on the bandstand. . . . What do you see? You see Japanese, you see . . . you see West Germans, You see Slobovic, you know, anything, except our people, man . . .
> *Musician 2:* Everything, everything you just said is bullshit. . . . If you played the shit that they liked, then the people would come. Simple as that.

At that moment, The Roots insert a third voice into the collage. It says:

> Inevitably, hip-hop records are treated as though they are disposable. They are not maximized as product, not to mention as art.[9]

The remainder of *Things Fall Apart* is a rebuke to that statement. In the late 1990s, hip-hop music experienced both an explosion in popularity and a narrowing of the form's acceptable styles. Acts that sold millions of records specialized in songs aimed at the dance floor, whose lyrics glorified money, sex, and violence. Their masterminds were behind-the-scenes producers with encyclopedic memories of sound samples. The Roots were a live band who played in concert venues, high school nerds who trafficked in sounds taken from jazz, soul, and gospel—music of eras before they were born.

When the band recorded *Things Fall Apart* in New York City

between 1997 and 1999, the present did not seem to belong to musicians like them. But the future, they concluded, might. At the same time they were recording *Things Fall Apart*, the band contributed to albums by friends and musical collaborators. Each of those projects—Erykah Badu's *Mama's Gun*, Common's *Like Water for Chocolate*, and D'Angelo's *Voodoo*—drew from similar, less fashionable influences, just as The Roots had done. Each, along with *Things Fall Apart*, is now considered both a classic of the period and a seminal album in the respective artist's career.

The Root's *Things Fall Apart* was recorded amid an alienating present with an uncertain future coming into view. The album submits that that future will be of our own making.

———

I've sketched out only the barest bones of the story behind the phrase "things fall apart"—its origin, direct descendant, and stepchild. The phrase also makes an appearance in Stephen King's *The Stand*, a Joni Mitchell song, and an iteration of the Batman comic-book series. But I had something specific in mind with my few examples. In two books, one poem, and a hip-hop record, each artist has used the phrase as an illustration of the present crumbling before us and a future not yet known. What kind of unknown and how we react to it are at the core of each text. Chinua Achebe seems to think that an unwillingness to accept the coming future is a death of the spirit. Joan Didion says we have to close the door on the past to open up the window to the future and that one can't exist in the presence of the other. Yeats was terrified of what came next. The Roots argue that what comes next is largely up to us. All paths are understandable; humans are the only animal cognizant of something called "a future" and of our role, if any, in shaping it.

50

A LETTER

Dear Old Sport,

As I write this in the early fall of 2011, the world has reaffixed its attention on *The Great Gatsby*. A new film version (the seventh) began shooting in Australia last week and will come out next Christmas, starring Leonardo DiCaprio as Gatsby and Carey Mulligan as Daisy Buchanan. The acclaimed New York theater group Elevator Repair Service just completed a run of *Gatz*, an eight-hour, thirteen-actor production in which the novel is read word for word. A Wisconsin orchestra has created *The Gatsby Suites*, and a recently published spin-off novel continues the story from the point of view of Daisy's daughter Pamela. I've also been distracted from writing sooner by the *Great Gatsby* video game, where your weapon is Nick Carraway's fedora flung like a boomerang at oncoming enemies.

I think we both know this is not a "comeback," old sport. *Gatsby* is too indelible for that. Although considered a commercial disappointment when published in 1925, the book found its footing upon rerelease after World War II and has been with us since. It's among the most assigned books in American high schools (where I'm sure you first laid eyes on its odd blue cover featuring a green light and a woman crying a single tear), and it's a leading contender for the elusive standing of The Great American Novel.[1] F. Scott Fitzgerald made a paltry $8,000 on *Gatsby* during his lifetime. The book now regularly generates $500,000 a year for his heirs.

We may have never stopped caring about Gatsby, Nick, Daisy, and Tom, but the world seems to be sharing our passion these days, and

I'm not quite sure why. In an article last month, the BBC speculated that the worldwide financial crisis may have something to do with it.[2] Perhaps single-minded ambition ends in the tragic rebuke, not the fulfillment, of the American Dream as it was for Lehman Brothers and Jay Gatsby. Perhaps you can work hard and still not get everything you want, as millions of foreclosed homeowners will attest. The actual house on which Fitzgerald modeled Gatsby's was demolished this past spring after lying neglected and forgotten for too long.

But let us not forget, old sport, that we were not in that kind of crisis when Fitzgerald imagined Gatsby. America was dancing and drinking its way through the Jazz Age, a ten-year victory lap after emerging as the world's most prosperous nation after the First World War. F. Scott Fitzgerald was famous, handsome, married to the love of his life, and living in Paris. We've seen the pictures: Zelda and Scott embodied the era that *The Great Gatsby* launched. We cannot separate the sparkling elegance of Gatsby's parties from the life his creator was living.

Dear friend, I was not fortunate enough to read *The Great Gatsby* as a young person. It was never assigned to me in high school, and I only remember "Gatsby" as the name of a tavern where my family once had a meal in Boston. I had heard of the book as a slim ode to 1920s glamour that ended tragically. I was unprepared for just how tragic that ending would be, and how sad it would make me until I read *Gatsby* as an adult.

I decided to pick up the book after I turned on the radio one weekday evening several months ago and heard Fitzgerald's final passage read aloud:

> Gatsby believed in the green light, the orgastic future that year by year recedes before us. It eluded us then, but that's no matter— tomorrow we will run faster, stretch out our arms farther. . . . And then one fine morning—
> So we beat on, boats against the current, borne back ceaselessly into the past.[3]

I began to cry the moment the actress stopped speaking. F. Scott Fitzgerald was all of twenty-eight when he wrote this and had the world at his feet. Why did he feel such sorrow? Who would end the great literary achievement of their lives, of the century even, by asking: Can we define our struggles as a past we cannot alter or outrun? Are we doomed to be battling the current forever, or is the real tragedy that we never learn, as Gatsby did not, to anchor the boat, exit the river, and accept what has come before rather than row against it?

We have been searching for eighty-six years for what Mr. Fitzgerald "meant" by those last paragraphs. Biographies tell us how he must have felt at the time. He was nearly a decade into alcoholism, a young father whose wife was having an affair. His last major work, the play *The Vegetable*, had been a failure. It is not wild psychoanalysis to see how, having become famous just four years before, he now felt exhausted, beaten, like his moment had already passed him by. Even before his thirtieth birthday.

He would die at age forty-two, believing himself a failure, an imposter who wrote himself as Nick Carraway but ended up like Jay Gatsby, never regaining what he had lost. He would never return to his birthplace of Minnesota. Regard for his books lay dormant for another fifteen years. That painful last line of *The Great Gatsby*, about all we must leave behind and will never get back, is the inscription on his gravestone.

I do realize, old sport, that my coming to Gatsby after most contemporary readers has no doubt altered my view of it. Had I picked it up as a young person or been assigned to read it in school, what would I have seen? A portrait of 1920s America, a character study of an elusive man, or a dissection of the American Dream? All of them, I'm guessing. And maybe Gatsby's last pages would not have hit me so hard if I, as a grown man, did not feel the current of time beneath me.

But perhaps I am lucky for it. *Gatsby* feels very much about what Robert Penn Warren called "the awful responsibility of time."[4] The world carries on without our permission. Our past will have some bearing on who we are. Our happiness to some great degree will be based on our humility before that fact. Let us not forget, old sport, that *The Great Gatsby* is written in flashback about a man and a time that is gone, even though the novel gave birth to the era itself. We are subject to the current even if we declare ourselves lords of the river.

I don't know about you, my friend, but that realization would be enough to keep me from ever reading *Gatsby* again. The adult world throws enough pain and cruelty our way. *Gatsby* is light on event, heavy on mood and setting (another reason I think it would have been lost on me in adolescence). How it feels is more important than what happens. Are the sadness and loss F. Scott Fitzgerald had in mind feelings I wish to have in mind?

It would seem so. I have gone back to *Gatsby* several times since, each time remembering a detail or a gesture I had missed, each time thinking I am ready for the final passages and being wrong. I don't think Mr. Fitzgerald meant for us to put down his novel feeling like dreams were pointless and our future was always a taunting green light in the distance. I wonder if he meant us to see the future as something we must try to be ready for, even though we cannot fully be ready; that we cannot be someone we aren't, but that there, in the very unpredictability of the future, lies opportunity for newness, for growth, for the second acts he didn't believe in but still got. He and Jay Gatsby were saved by the "one bright morning" that came years after they were both gone.

Good night, old sport. I await your reply.

With love,

Kevin

NOTES

PART 1. YOUTH AND GROWING UP

1. The Midlife Crisis of *Huckleberry Finn*

1. Clifton Fadiman and John S. Major, *The New Lifetime Reading Plan* (New York: Harper Perennial, 1999), p. 211.
2. Ibid.

2. *Candide* Says Relax. Then Get to Work.

1. Voltaire, *Candide* (New York: Penguin Classics, 1947), p. 20.
2. Ibid.
3. Ibid., p. 144.

3. *A Separate Peace* and the Dream of Best Friends Forever

1. John Knowles, *A Separate Peace* (New York: Scribner, 2003), p. 204.

4. Owners of Our Lonely Hearts

1. Dana Gioia, "The Heart Is a Lonely Hunter," Big Read, National Endowment for the Arts, 2009, http://www.neabigread.org/books/lonelyhunter/radioshow.php (accessed September 1, 2011).
2. Carson McCullers, *The Heart Is a Lonely Hunter* (Boston: Mariner Books, 2004), p. 6.
3. Richard Wright, "Inner Landscape," *New Republic*, no. 103 (August 1940): 195.
4. Lev Grossman and Richard Lacayo, "All-TIME 100 Novels," *Time*, October 16, 2005, http://entertainment.time.com/2005/10/16/all-time-100-novels/ (accessed October 13, 2012).

5. Virginia Spencer Carr, *Understanding Carson McCullers* (Columbia: University of South Carolina Press, 2005), p. 124.

6. "Carson McCullers," Penguin Classics, http://www.penguinclassics.co.uk/nf/Author/AuthorPage/0,,1000021816,00.html (accessed June 15, 2012).

5. How the Uncaged Bird Sings

1. Maya Angelou, *A Song Flung Up to Heaven* (New York: Bantam, 2003), p. 224.

2. George Plimpton, "Maya Angelou, The Act of Fiction," *Paris Review*, Fall 1990.

3. "Nathaniel Hawthorne Quotes," goodreads, http://www.goodreads.com/quotes/2597-easy-reading-is-damn-hard-writing (accessed October 26, 2012).

4. Maya Angelou, *I Know Why the Caged Bird Sings* (New York: Bantam, 1983), p. 6.

5. Paul Laurence Dunbar, "Sympathy," PotW.org, http://www.potw.org/archive/potw219.html (accessed June 10, 2012).

6. Angelou, *Caged Bird*, p. 304.

7. Hilton Als, "Songbird: Maya Angelou Takes Another Look at Herself," *New Yorker*, August 5, 2002, http://www.newyorker.com/archive/2002/08/05/020805crbo_books (accessed June 10, 2012).

8. Francine Prose, "I Know Why the Caged Bird Cannot Read," *Harper's Magazine*, Scribd., September 1999, p. 92, http://www.scribd.com/somethingthereof/d/38552954-I-Know-Why-the-Caged-Bird-Cannot-Read (accessed June 10, 2012).

9. John McWhorter, "Saint Maya," *New Republic*, May 20, 2002, http://www.tnr.com/article/saint-maya (accessed June 10, 2012).

10. Ian Buruma, "The Joys and Perils of Victimhood," *New York Review of Books*, April 8, 1999, http://www.nybooks.com/articles/archives/1999/apr/08/the-joys-and-perils-of-victimhood/?pagination=false (accessed June 10, 2012).

11. Maya Angelou, interview by Larry King, *Larry King Live*, CNN, November 4, 2008.

PART 2. IDENTITY

6. Real Indians Play Rock 'n' Roll

1. Sherman Alexie, *Reservation Blues* (New York: Warner Books, 1995), p. 59.

2. Ibid., p. 159.

7. *The Autobiography of Malcolm X*: Yours and Mine

1. David Remnick, "This American Life: The Making and Remaking of Malcolm X," *New Yorker*, April 25, 2011, http://www.newyorker.com/arts/critics/books/2011/04/25/110425crbo_books_remnick (accessed May 2, 2012).

2. Malcolm X as told to Alex Haley, *The Autobiography of Malcolm X* (New York: Ballantine Books, 1973), p. 375.

3. Darryl Pinckney, "The Two Conversions of Malcolm X," *New York Review of Books*, September 29, 2011, http://www.nybooks.com/articles/archives/2011/sep/29/two-conversions-malcolm-x/?pagination=false (accessed May 1, 2012).

4. Haley, *Malcolm X*, p. 380.

5. Obituary, *New York Times*, February 22, 1965.

6. Kurt Anderson, "American Icons: The Autobiography of Malcolm X," *Studio 360*, podcast audio, August 26, 2011, http://www.studio360.org/2011/aug/26/ (accessed May 1, 2012).

7. Remnick, "This American Life."

8. Haley, *Malcolm X*, p. 382.

8. Edith Wharton: *"Innocence* Is for Wimps"

1. Edith Wharton, *The Age of Innocence* (Oxford: Oxford World Classics, 2008).

2. *The Age of Innocence*, directed by Martin Scorsese, streaming video, 1993 (Culver City, CA: Columbia Home Video, 1994).

3. Elaine Sciolino, "Edith Wharton Always Had Paris," *New York Times*, October 8, 2009.

4. Jonathan Franzen, "A Rooting Interest: Edith Wharton and the Problem of Sympathy," *New Yorker*, February 13, 2012, http://www.newyorker.com/reporting/2012/02/13/120213fa_fact_franzen (accessed February 15, 2012).

5. Dana Gioia, "The Age of Innocence Audio Guide," Big Read, National Endowment for the Arts, 2009, http://www.neabigread.org/books/ageofinnocence/radioshow.php (accessed February 10, 2012).

6. Ibid.

9. The Us Yet to Come

1. Margaret Atwood, *Surfacing* (London, ON: Bloomsbury, 1970), p. 3.

2. Ibid., p. 20.

3. Ibid., p. 280.

10. Am I a Man or an Android?

1. Lev Grossman and Richard Lacayo, "All-TIME 100 Novels," *Time*, October 16, 2005, http://entertainment.time.com/2005/10/16/all-time-100-novels (accessed May 6, 2012).

2. "VALIS,"   goodreads,   http://www.goodreads.com/book/show/216377 .VALIS (accessed October 26, 2012).

3. Judith B. Kerman, *Retrofitting* Blade Runner*: Issues in Ridley Scott's* Blade Runner *and Phillip K. Dick's* Do Androids Dream of Electric Sheep? (Madison, WI: Popular Press, 1990).

4. Philip K. Dick, *Do Androids Dream of Electric Sheep?* (New York: Del Rey, 1996), p. 179.

5. *Blade Runner,* directed by Ridley Scott, DVD, 1982 (Burbank, CA: Warner Home Video, 1997).

6. Paul Williams, "The True Stories of Philip K. Dick," *Rolling Stone*, November 6, 1975, p. 93. http://www.philipkdick.com/media_files/PKD%20Rolling%20 Stone%20article.pdf (accessed May 5, 2012).

PART 3. THE INNER AND THE OUTER WORLD

11. If This *Library* Is Paradise . . .

1. My version came from the American publication *Labyrinths: Selected Stories and Other Writings* (New York: New Directions, 1988), pp. 51–59.

2. Ibid., p. 59.

3. Ibid., p. 52.

4. Ibid.

5. Ibid., p. 56.

6. James Gleick, *The Information: A History, A Theory, A Flood* (New York: Pantheon Books, 2011), p. 373.

12. Staying Out of the *Bell Jar*

1. Al Alvarez, "A Poet and Her Myths," *New York Review of Books*, September 28, 1999, http://www.nybooks.com/articles/archives/1989/sep/28/a-poet-and-her -myths/ (accessed January 30, 2012).

2. Emily Gould, "*The Bell Jar* at 40," *Poetry Foundation*, http://www.poetry foundation.org/article/242402 (accessed January 30, 2012).

3. Sylvia Plath, *The Bell Jar* (New York: Harper Perennial Modern Classics, 2006), p. 265.

4. David Rieff, "Swimming in a Sea of Death," interview by Terry Gross, *Fresh Air*, NPR, January 10, 2008, http://www.npr.org/templates/story/story .php?storyId=17989334 (accessed June 15, 2012).

5. Jack Kerouac, *On the Road* (New York: Penguin Classics, 2002), p. 5.

13. You May Find Yourself Trapped in Alexander Portnoy's Head . . .

1. Philip Roth, *Portnoy's Complaint* (New York: Vintage, 1994), p. 75.

2. Ibid., p. 3.

3. Roger Ebert, "Portnoy's Complaint," *Chicago Sun-Times*, July 7, 1972, http://rogerebert.suntimes.com/apps/pbcs.dll/article?AID=/19720707/REVIEWS/207070301/1023 (accessed October 16, 2012).

14. *Cannery Row*: Where Everybody Knows Your Name

1. John Steinbeck, *Cannery Row* (New York: Penguin Classics, 1994), p. 5.

2. "Arthur Miller on John Steinbeck," PEN American Center, http://www.pen .org/viewmedia.php/prmMID/95/prmID/514 (accessed April 2, 2012).

3. Thomas R. Edwards, "The Innocent," *New York Review of Books*, February 16, 1984, http://www.nybooks.com/articles/archives/1984/feb/16/the-innocent/ (accessed April 4, 2012).

4. Ibid.

5. Roger Sale, "Stubborn Steinbeck," *New York Review of Books*, March 20, 1980, http://www.nybooks.com/articles/archives/1980/mar/20/stubborn-steinbeck/ (accessed April 3, 2012).

15. My Favorite Book of Them All

1. Mike Weiss, "Randy Shilts Was Gutsy, Brash and Unforgettable. He Died 10 Years Ago, Fighting for the Rights of Gays in American Society," *San Francisco Chronicle*, February 17, 2004, http://www.sfgate.com/cgi-bin/article.cgi?f=/c/a/2004/02/17/DDGGH50UAU1.DTL&ao=all#ixzz1yS0wXYY8 (accessed June 21, 2012).

PART 4. LOVE AND PAIN

16. *Pride and Prejudice*: Jane Austen for the Clumsier Sex

1. Clifton Fadiman and John S. Major, *The New Lifetime Reading Plan* (New York: Harper Perennial, 1999), p. 152.
2. Ibid.
3. "Mr. Darcy Voted Dream Date," BBC News, June 2, 2003, http://news.bbc.co.uk/2/hi/entertainment/2955396.stm (accessed October 16, 2012).
4. "Top 100," Big Read, BBC, http://www.bbc.co.uk/arts/bigread/top100.shtml (accessed June 16, 2012).

17. Marriage Counseling from Henrik Ibsen

1. Christopher Innes, ed., *A Sourcebook on Naturalist Theatre* (London and New York: Routledge, 2000), pp. 79–81.
2. Henrik Ibsen, *Four Great Plays* (New York: Bantam Classics, 1984), p. 65.
3. Lawrence S. Cunningham and John J. Reich, *Culture & Values, Volume II: A Survey of the Humanities with Readings* (Cengage Learning, 2009), p. 492, http://books.google.com/books?id=KiW8xOi0FvYC&pg=PA492#v=onepage&q&f=false (accessed June 15, 2012).
4. Elizabeth Hardwick, "A Doll's House," *New York Review of Books*, March 11, 1971.
5. Ibid.
6. Ibid.
7. Ibsen, *Four Great Plays*, p. 3.
8. Ibid., p. 63.

18. *Eyes* on Love

1. Dana Gioia, "Their Eyes Were Watching God," Big Read, National Endowment for the Arts, 2009, http://www.neabigread.org/books/theireyes/ (accessed June 3, 2012).
2. Zora Neale Hurston, *Their Eyes Were Watching God* (New York: Harper Perennial, 1990), p. 7.
3. Alice Walker, "In Search of Zora Neale Hurston," *Ms.*, March 1975.
4. Lev Grossman and Richard Lacayo, "All-TIME 100 Novels," *Time*, October

16, 2005, http://entertainment.time.com/2005/10/16/all-time-100-novels/#how -we-picked-the-list (accessed June 2, 2012).

   5. Hurston, *Their Eyes Were Watching God*, p. 184.

   6. Ibid., p. 90.

   7. Jeff Klinkenberg, "Telling Zora Neale Hurston's Story Took Time," *Tampa Bay Times*, March 30, 2008.

   8. Richard Wright, "Between Laughter and Tears," review of *Their Eyes Were Watching God*, *New Masses*, October 5, 1937, pp. 22–23, http://people.virginia .edu/~sfr/enam358/wrightrev.html (accessed June 15, 2012).

   9. Henry Louis Gates, afterword to *Their Eyes Were Watching God*, by Hurston, p. 195.

   10. Gioia, "Their Eyes Were Watching God."

19. I've Been Young and Afraid, Joyce Carol Oates. Thank You for Asking.

   1. Joyce Carol Oates, *Where Are You Going, Where Have You Been? Selected Early Stories* (New York: Ontario Review Press, 1993), p. 136.

   2. Ibid.

   3. Don Moser, "The Pied Piper of Tucson," in *True Crime: An American Anthology*, ed. Harold Schechter (Des Moines, IA: Library of America, 2008).

   4. B. Ruby Rich, *Chick Flicks: Theories and Memories of the Feminist Film Movement* (Durham, NC: Duke University Press Books, 1998), p. 337.

   5. Oates, *Where Are You Going*, p. 120.

20. *The Scarlet Letter*: I Don't Like It Either

   1. Jonathan Franzen, "Mr. Difficult," *New Yorker*, September 30, 2002, http:// www.newyorker.com/archive/2002/09/30/020930fa_fact_franzen (accessed April 30, 2012).

   2. Ibid.

PART 5. WORKING

21. *Bartleby* in the Breakroom

   1. Herman Melville, *Billy Budd and Other Tales* (New York: Signet Classics, 1961), p. 126.

2. Ibid., p. 140.

3. Ibid.

4. Sven Birkerts, "The Mother of Possibility," *Lapham's Quarterly* 4, no. 2 (Spring 2011): 177.

22. The Work/Life Balance of Sherlock Holmes

1. Sir Arthur Conan Doyle, *The Hound of the Baskervilles* (New York: Scholastic Book Services, 1964).

2. Cecil Adams, "Did Sherlock Holmes Really Exist?" Straight Dope, April 8, 2003, http://www.straightdope.com/columns/read/2088/did-sherlock-holmes-really-exist (accessed January 26, 2012).

3. Doyle, *Hound of the Baskervilles*, p. 10.

4. Lynn Neary, "The Enduring Popularity of Sherlock Holmes," NPR Books, December 19, 2011, http://www.npr.org/2011/12/19/143954262/the-enduring-popularity-of-sherlock-holmes (accessed June 22, 2012).

23. Working at Relaxing with David Foster Wallace

1. David Foster Wallace, interview by Charlie Rose, *Charlie Rose*, PBS, March 27, 1997.

2. David Foster Wallace, *A Supposedly Fun Thing I'll Never Do Again: Essays and Other Arguments* (New York: Little, Brown, 1997).

3. Daniel B. Roberts, "Consider David Foster Wallace, Journalist," Salon, February 20, 2012, http://www.salon.com/2012/02/20/consider_david_foster_wallace_journalist/ (accessed February 27, 2012).

4. David Foster Wallace, "Shipping Out," *Harper's*, January 1996, http://harpers.org/media/pdf/dfw/HarpersMagazine-1996-01-0007859.pdf (accessed March 1, 2012).

5. David Foster Wallace, interview by Laura Miller, Salon, March 9, 1996, http://www.salon.com/1996/03/09/wallace_5/ (accessed March 1, 2012).

6. Wallace, *Supposedly Fun Thing*, p. 293.

7. Ibid., p. 305.

8. Ibid., p. 312.

9. Richard Rayner, "Book Review: 'The Pale King' by David Foster Wallace," *Los Angeles Times*, April 15, 2011, http://articles.latimes.com/2011/apr/15/entertainment/la-et-book-20110415 (accessed October 16, 2012).

10. Wallace, *Supposedly Fun Thing*, pp. 272, 278, 297.

11. Ibid., pp. 21–83.

24. At the Office with *"Master Harold"* . . . *and the Boys*

1. Frank Rich, "'Master Harold.' Fugard's Drama on the Origin of Hate," *New York Times*, May 5, 1982, http://theater.nytimes.com/mem/theater/treview .html?_r=1&res=9504E6DC1738F936A35756C0A964948260 (accessed May 1, 2012).

2. Athol Fugard, *"Master Harold" . . . and the Boys* (New York: Penguin, 1984), p. 53.

3. Ibid.

4. Ibid., p. 13.

5. Lloyd Richards, "Athol Fugard, The Art of Theater No. 8," *Paris Review*, no. 111 (1989), http://www.theparisreview.org/interviews/2416/the-art-of-theater-no -8-athol-fugard (accessed October 16, 2012).

25. Burning Books: One Crappy Job

1. Dana Gioia, "Fahrenheit 451," Big Read, National Endowment for the Arts, http://www.neabigread.org/books/fahrenheit451/ (accessed October 18, 2012).

2. Jill Stewart, "The Writer—Ray Bradbury," *LA Weekly*, April 23, 2009, http:// www.laweekly.com/content/printVersion/529859/ (accessed September 1, 2011).

3. Ray Bradbury, *Fahrenheit 451* (New York: Ballantine Books, 1991), pp. 60–61.

4. Neil Postman, *Amusing Ourselves to Death: Public Discourse in the Age of Show Business* (New York: Penguin, 2008).

5. Bradbury, *Fahrenheit 451*, p. 171.

6. "Fahrenheit 451 Becomes E-Book despite Author's Feelings," Technology, *BBC News*, November 30, 2011, http://www.bbc.com/news/technology-15968500 (accessed June 22, 2012).

PART 6. FAMILY

26. Why *To Kill a Mockingbird* Makes a Great Father's Day Gift

1. *Hey, Boo: Harper Lee and 'To Kill a Mockingbird,'* directed by Mary McDonagh Murphy, DVD, 2010 (New York: First Run Features, 2011).

2. Harper Lee, *To Kill a Mockingbird* (New York: Warner Books, 1982), pp. 214, 273.

3. Ibid., p. 281.

4. "AFI's 100 Heroes & Villains," AFI.com, http://www.afi.com/100years/handv.aspx (accessed June 22, 2003).

5. *Hey Boo.*

6. Lee, *Mockingbird*, p. 279.

7. *To Kill a Mockingbird*, directed by Richard Mulligan (Universal International Pictures, 1962).

8. Lee, *Mockingbird*, p. 221.

9. Ibid., p. 95.

27. The Ambivalent Family of Toni Morrison

1. Hilton Als, "Ghosts in the House," *New Yorker*, October 27, 2003, http://www.newyorker.com/archive/2003/10/27/031027fa_fact_als (accessed October 26, 2012).

2. Adam Begley, *The Salon.com Reader's Guide to Contemporary Authors*, ed. Laura Miller (New York: Penguin-Putnam, 2000), p. 271.

3. "The Nobel Prize in Literature 1993," press release, Nobelprize.org, October 7, 1993, http://www.nobelprize.org/nobel_prizes/literature/laureates/1993/press.html (accessed June 24, 2012).

4. Elissa Schappell, "Toni Morrison, The Art of Fiction," *Paris Review*, no. 128 (Fall 1993).

5. D. G. Myers, "MLA Rankings of American Writers," *Commentary*, March 26, 2012, http://www.commentarymagazine.com/2012/03/26/mla-rankings/ (accessed October 21, 2012).

6. Toni Morrison, *Sula* (New York: Plume, 1982), p. 8.

7. Barbara Smith, "Toward a Black Feminist Criticism," *Women's Studies International Quarterly* 2, no. 2 (1979): 189.

8. Als, "Ghosts in the House," p. 66.

9. Schappell, "Toni Morrison."

10. Toni Morrison, Nobel lecture, Nobelprize.org, June 24, 2012, http://www.nobelprize.org/nobel_prizes/literature/laureates/1993/morrison-lecture.html (accessed October 21, 2012).

11. Ibid.

12. Ibid.

28. Of Wontons, Mah-jongg, and Time

1. Amy Tan, *The Joy Luck Club* (New York: Penguin, 2006).

2. Michael Dorris, "Mothers and Daughters," *Chicago Tribune*, March 12, 1989.

3. Frank Chin, "Come All Ye Asian American Writers of the Real and the Fake," in *Aiiieeeee! An Anthology of Asian-American Writers*, ed. Lawson Inada (New York: Plume, 1997).

4. "Insane Clown Poppy," *The Simpsons*, episode 251, directed by Bob Anderson; original airdate November 12, 2000.

29. A Family of Giant Insects

1. Zadie Smith, "The Limited Circle Is Pure," *New Republic*, November 3, 2003.

2. Franz Kafka, *Metamorphosis and Other Stories* (London: Penguin Books, 2007).

3. Vladimir Nabokov, *Lectures on Literature*, ed. Fredson Bowers (New York: Harcourt Brace Jovanovich, 1980), pp. 251–85.

4. Smith, "Limited Circle."

5. Walter Benjamin, quoted in Zadie Smith, "F. Kafka. Everyman," *New York Review of Books*, July 17, 2008, http://www.nybooks.com/articles/archives/2008/jul/17/f-kafka-everyman/?pagination=false (accessed June 23, 2012).

30. *Maus*: A Comic Book about Fathers, Sons, and Genocide

1. Art Spiegelman, *Maus: A Survivor's Tale* (New York: Pantheon Books, 1993).

2. Peter Murphy, "Art Spiegelman's Ghosts," *Irish Times*, November 5, 2011, http://www.irishtimes.com/newspaper/weekend/2011/1105/1224307062733.html (accessed June 22, 2012).

3. Harvey Pekar, "Maus and Other Topics," *Comics Journal* 113:54–57.

4. Adam Gopnik, "Comics and Catastrophe," *New Republic*, June 22, 1987.

5. Marjane Satrapi, "The 2005 TIME 100," WebCite, April 18, 2005, http://www.webcitation.org/5wQIfXO4j (accessed October 21, 2012).

PART 7. IDEAS AND LEARNING

31. The Renaissance Nerds of *The Phantom Tollbooth*

1. Adam Gopnik, "Broken Kingdom: Fifty Years of 'The Phantom Tollbooth,'" *New Yorker*, October 17, 2011, http://www.newyorker.com/reporting/2011/10/17/111017fa_fact_gopnik?currentPage=all (accessed October 23, 2012).

2. Norton Juster, *The Phantom Tollbooth* (New York: Alfred A. Knopf, 1989), p. 9.

3. Paul Barman, "Norton Juster," *A.V. Club*, June 15, 2011, http://www
.avclub.com/articles/norton-juster,57562/?utm_medium=promobar&utm_campaign
=recirculation (accessed October 23, 2012).

4. Juster, *Phantom Tollbooth*, p. 256.

32. Camping It Up with Susan Sontag

1. Susan Sontag, *Against Interpretation and Other Essays* (New York: Picador, 2001), p. 276.

2. Margalit Fox, "Susan Sontag, Social Critic with Verve, Dies at 71," *New York Times*, December 28, 2004, http://www.nytimes.com/2004/12/28/books/28cnd
-sont.html?pagewanted=print&position (accessed October 23, 2012).

3. Daniel Stern, "*The Benefactor* by Susan Sontag," *New York Times*, September 8, 1963.

4. Fox, "Susan Sontag, Social Critic."

5. Sontag, *Against Interpretation*, p. 286.

6. Ibid., pp. 290–91.

7. Fox, "Susan Sontag, Social Critic."

8. Craig Seligman, "Sontag & Kael," *New York Times*, May 30, 2004, http://www
.nytimes.com/2004/05/30/books/chapters/0530-1st-seligman.html?pagewanted=2
(accessed October 30, 2012).

9. Sontag, *Against Interpretation*, p. 14.

33. "The Work of Art in the Age of Mechanical Reproduction" by Walter Benjamin, Notes by Kevin Smokler

1. Susan Sontag, "The Last Intellectual," *New York Review of Books*, October 12, 1978, http://www.nybooks.com/articles/archives/1978/oct/12/the-last-intellectual/
?pagination=false (accessed October 24, 2012).

2. For all Benjamin quotations in this chapter, I referred to this version of the essay: Walter Benjamin, "The Work of Art in the Age of Mechanical Reproduction," Marxists Internet Archive, http://www.marxists.org/reference/subject/philosophy/
works/ge/benjamin.htm (accessed October 24, 2012).

34. Hello, I'm William Shakespeare

1. Clifton Fadiman and John S. Major, *The New Lifetime Reading Plan* (New York: Harper Perennial, 1999).

35. *Understanding* Marshall McLuhan

1. "Marshall Mcluhan Full lecture: The medium is the message—1977 part 1 v 3," YouTube video, 14:23, from ABC TV, Monday Conference, posted by "mywebcow tube." http://www.youtube.com/watch?v=ImaH51F4HBw&feature=player_embedded (accessed October 24, 2012).

2. Gary Wolf, "The Wisdom of Saint Marshall, the Holy Fool," *Wired*, January 1996, http://www.wired.com/wired/archive/4.01/saint.marshal.html (accessed October 24, 2012).

3. Marshall McLuhan, *Understanding Media* (Cambridge, MA: MIT Press, 1994), p. 204.

4. Lewis Lapham, introduction to McLuhan, *Understanding Media*, p. xi.

5. Wolf, "Wisdom of Saint Marshall."

6. McLuhan, *Understanding Media*, p. 199.

7. "Essay: The Playboy Interview: Marshall McLuhan," from "The Playboy Interview: Marshall McLuhan," *Playboy*, March 1969, Next Nature, http://www.next nature.net/2009/12/the-playboy-interview-marshall-mcluhan/ (accessed October 24, 2012).

8. Brooke Gladstone, *The Influencing Machine* (New York: W. W. Norton, 2011), p. 192.

PART 8. VIOLENCE AND LOSS

36. Holden Caulfield, That Little Brat

1. Customer reviews for *The Catcher in the Rye*, Amazon, http://www.amazon .com/The-Catcher-Rye-J-Salinger/product-reviews/0316769177/ref=cm_cr_dp_qt_hist _one?ie=UTF8&showViewpoints=0&filterBy=addOneStar (accessed October 24, 2012).

2. Thomas Beller, "Holden's New York," *New York Times*, July 22, 2001.

3. Aidan Doyle, "When Books Kill," Salon, December 15, 2003, http://www .salon.com/2003/12/15/books_kill/singleton/ (accessed October 24, 2012).

4. Ibid.

5. *Six Degrees of Separation*, directed by Fred Schepisi, DVD, 1993 (Culver City, CA: MGM Home Video, 1994).

6. Kenneth Slawenski, "Holden Caulfield's Goddam War," *Vanity Fair*, February 2011, http://www.vanityfair.com/culture/features/2011/02/salinger-201102?printable =true (accessed October 24, 2012).

7. Ibid.

8. J. D. Salinger, *The Catcher in the Rye* (New York: Back Bay Books, 2001), p. 257.

9. Adam Gopnik, "Postscript: J. D. Salinger," *New Yorker*, February 8, 2010, http://www.newyorker.com/talk/2010/02/08/100208ta_talk_gopnik (accessed October 24, 2012).

10. Louis Menand, "Holden at Fifty: 'The Catcher in the Rye' and What It Spawned," *New Yorker*, October 1, 2001, http://www.newyorker.com/archive/2001/10/01/011001fa_FACT3?currentPage=all (accessed October 24, 2012).

37. Albert Camus, the Unsexy *Stranger*

1. Adam Gopnik, "Facing History: Why We Love Camus," *New Yorker*, April 9, 2012, http://www.newyorker.com/arts/critics/atlarge/2012/04/09/120409crat_at large_gopnik (accessed October 24, 2012).

2. Susan Sontag, "The Ideal Husband," *New York Review of Books*, September 26, 1963, http://www.nybooks.com/articles/archives/1963/sep/26/the-ideal -husband/ (accessed October 24, 2012).

3. Albert Camus, *The Stranger* (New York: Vintage Paperback, 1988), p. 109.

4. Ibid., p. 8.

5. Ibid., p. 59.

6. Ibid., p. 121.

38. Shirley Jackson's Rituals of Violence

1. Shirley Jackson, *The Lottery and Other Stories* (New York: Farrar, Straus and Giroux, 2000), p. 302.

2. Ibid., pp. 292–97.

39. The Stone-Faced Trip of *Slaughterhouse-Five*

1. Kurt Vonnegut, *Slaughterhouse-Five* (New York: Dell Paperback, 1974), pp. 19, 22.

2. Ibid., p. 23.

3. Dinitia Smith, "Kurt Vonnegut, Novelist Who Caught the Imagination of His Age, Is Dead at 84," *New York Times*, April 12, 2007, http://www.nytimes .com/2007/04/12/books/12vonnegut.html?_r=1&pagewanted=all (accessed October 24, 2012).

4. Vonnegut, *Slaughterhouse-Five*, pp. 101–107.

40. An Act of Violence, a Book of Forgiveness

1. George Garrett, "Bastard Out of Carolina by Dorothy Allison," *New York Times,* July 5, 1992.

2. Dorothy Allison, *Bastard Out of Carolina* (New York: Plume, 2012), p. 307.

3. Simon Wiesenthal, *The Sunflower: On the Possibilities and Limits of Forgiveness* (New York: Shocken, 1998).

4. Desmond Tutu, *No Future without Forgiveness* (New York: Image, 2000).

PART 9. WE THE HERO

41. The Shameless Case of Walt Whitman

1. Walt Whitman, *Song of Myself and Other Poems* (Berkeley, CA: Counterpoint, 2010).

2. John Updike, "Walt Whitman: Ego and Art," *New York Review of Books,* February 9, 1978, http://www.nybooks.com/articles/archives/1978/feb/09/walt -whitman-ego-and-art/?pagination=false (accessed October 25, 2012).

42. Emily Dickinson's Lessons for Success

1. Christopher Benfey, "The Mystery of Emily Dickinson," *New York Review of Books,* April 8, 1999, http://www.nybooks.com/articles/archives/1999/apr/08/the -mystery-of-emily-dickinson/?pagination=false (accessed October 25, 2012).

2. Ibid.

3. John Barr, "The Poetry of Emily Dickinson Audio Guide, Big Read, National Endowment for the Arts, http://www.neabigread.org/books/dickinson/radioshow .php (accessed October 25, 2012).

4. Ibid.

5. Elaine Showalter, *A Jury of Her Peers: American Women Writers from Anne Bradstreet to Annie Proulx* (New York: Alfred A. Knopf, 2009), p. 152.

6. Joyce Carol Oates, "Ardor in Amherst," *New York Review of Books,* April 8, 2010, http://www.nybooks.com/articles/archives/2010/apr/08/ardor-in-amherst/ (accessed October 25, 2012).

7. Benfey, "Mystery of Emily Dickinson."

8. Clifton Fadiman and John S. Major, *The New Lifetime Reading Plan* (New York: Harper Perennial, 1999), p. 206.

9. Each of these Dickinson poems is available in print and audio at the Academy of American Poets website, http://www.poets.org.

10. Barr, "Poetry of Emily Dickinson."

11. Ibid.

12. Fadiman and Major, *New Lifetime Reading Plan*, p. 207.

13. *Spider-Man 2*, directed by Sam Raimi, DVD, 2005 (Culver City, CA: Sony Home Video, 2004).

14. "Hope is the thing with feathers," Poets.org, Academy of American Poets, http://www.poets.org/viewmedia.php/prmMID/19729 (accessed October 25, 2012).

43. Little Heroes and *Locust*

1. Nathanael West, *Miss Lonelyhearts & The Day of the Locust* (New York: New Directions, 1962), p. 60.

2. Ibid., p. 62.

3. Elizabeth Hardwick, "Funny as a Crutch," *New York Review of Books*, November 6, 2003, http://www.nybooks.com/articles/archives/2003/nov/06/funny-as-a-crutch/?pagination=false (accessed October 25, 2012).

4. Roger Ebert, "Batman Returns," *Chicago Sun-Times*, June 19, 1992, http://rogerebert.suntimes.com/apps/pbcs.dll/article?AID=/19920619/REVIEWS/206190301/1023 (accessed October 25, 2012).

5. Jonathan Lethem, *The Ecstasy of Influence: Nonfictions Etc.* (New York: Doubleday, 2011), p. 391.

6. Ibid.

7. Virginia Heffernan, "True West," *Boston Phoenix*, August 1997, http://www.bostonphoenix.com/archive/books/97/08/07/NATHANIEL_WEST.html (accessed October 25, 2012).

8. West, *Miss Lonelyhearts*, p. 61.

9. Elizabeth Hardwick, "Funny as a Crutch."

44. Visit *Tinker Creek*. Then Keep Going.

1. "100 Best Nonfiction," Modern Library, http://www.modernlibrary.com/top-100/100-best-nonfiction/ (accessed October 25, 2012).

2. Annie Dillard—Official Website, http://anniedillard.com/ (accessed October 25, 2012).

3. Annie Dillard, *Pilgrim at Tinker Creek* (New York: Harper Perennial Modern Classics, 2007), p. 11.

4. Ibid., p. 267.

5. Ibid., p. 268.

6. Ibid.

45. How to Tell a Hero Story

1. Tim O'Brien, *The Things They Carried* (New York: Broadway Books, 1998), p. 180.

2. Ibid., p. 36.

3. Ibid., pp. 2, 7.

4. Ibid., p. 179.

5. Ibid., pp. 71, 80.

6. D. J. R. Bruckner, "A Storyteller for the War That Won't End," *New York Times*, April 3, 1990, http://www.nytimes.com/books/98/09/20/specials/obrien-story teller.html (accessed October 25, 2012).

7. O'Brien, *Things They Carried*, p. 225.

PART 10. THE FUTURE

46. Beware of Revolutionaries Who Look Like Pigs

1. George Orwell, *Animal Farm: Centennial Edition* (New York: Plume, 2003), p. 118.

2. Julian Barnes, "Such, Such Was Eric Blair," *New York Review of Books*, March 12, 2009, http://www.nybooks.com/articles/archives/2009/mar/12/such-such -was-eric-blair/?pagination=false (accessed October 25, 2012).

3. David Brooks, "Orwell and Us," review of Christopher Hitchens, *Why Orwell Matters* (New York: Basic Books, 2002), in *Weekly Standard*, September 23, 2002, http:// www.weeklystandard.com/Content/Public/Articles/000/000/001/653xorlj.asp ?nopager=1 (accessed October 25, 2012).

4. Barnes, "Such, Such Was Eric Blair."

47. Meet Thomas Pynchon, Your Driving Companion

1. Mel Gussow, "Pynchon's Letters Nudge His Mask," *New York Times*, March 4, 1998, http://www.nytimes.com/1998/03/04/books/pynchon-s-letters-nudge-his -mask.html?pagewanted=all&src=pm (accessed October 25, 2012).

2. Louis Menand, "Entropology," *New York Review of Books*, June 12, 1997, http://www.nybooks.com/articles/archives/1997/jun/12/entropology/ (accessed October 25, 2012).

3. Nancy Jo Sales, "Meet Your Neighbor, Thomas Pynchon," *New York*, November 11, 1996, http://nymag.com/arts/books/features/48268/ (accessed October 25, 2012).

4. "Advice for Pynchon Newbies," ThomasPynchon.com, http://www.thomas pynchon.com/newbies.html (accessed October 25, 2012).

5. Thomas Pynchon, *The Crying of Lot 49* (New York: Harper Perennial, 2006), pp. 2, 13.

6. "Diatribe of a Mad Housewife," *The Simpsons*, episode 323, directed by Mark Kirk; original airdate January 25, 2004.

7. Sales, "Meet Your Neighbor."

48. The *Remains* of Tomorrow

1. Kazuo Ishiguro, *The Remains of the Day* (New York: Vintage, 1989), p. 51.

2. Michiko Kakutani, "An Era Revealed in a Perfect Butler's Imperfections," *New York Times*, September 22, 1989.

3. Roger Ebert, "Chariots of Fire," *Chicago Sun-Times*, January 1, 1981, http://rogerebert.suntimes.com/apps/pbcs.dll/article?AID=/19810101/REVIEWS/101010313/1023 (accessed October 25, 2012).

49. Four Different Ways That *Things Fall Apart*

1. Chinua Achebe, *Things Fall Apart* (New York: Anchor Books, 1994).

2. Harold Bloom, *Yeats* (New York: Oxford University Press, 1972), p. 318.

3. "The Second Coming," Poets.org, Academy of American Poets, http://www.poets.org/viewmedia.php/prmMID/15527 (accessed October 25, 2012).

4. Joan Didion, *Slouching towards Bethlehem* (New York: Farrar, Straus and Giroux, 2008).

5. Ibid., p. 84.

6. Ibid.

7. Ibid., p. 238.

8. Ibid., p. 225.

9. The Roots, *Things Fall Apart*, Geffen Records, 1999.

50. A Letter

1. F. Scott Fitzgerald, *The Great Gatsby* (New York: Scribner Classics, 1986).

2. Tom Geoghegan, "The Great Gatsby: What It Says to Modern America," *BBC News*, August 9, 2011, http://www.bbc.co.uk/news/world-us-canada-14238693 (accessed October 25, 2012).

3. Fitzgerald, *Great Gatsby*, p. 182.

4. Robert Penn Warren, *All the King's Men* (New York: Bantam, 1963), p. 438.